REINHOLD NIEBUHR (1892–1971)
A CENTENARY APPRAISAL

McGill Studies in Religion
McGill University

Edited by
Arvind Sharma

Volume 3

REINHOLD NIEBUHR (1892–1971)

A Centenary Appraisal

edited by
Gary A. Gaudin and Douglas John Hall

REINHOLD NIEBUHR (1892–1971)

A Centenary Appraisal

edited by
Gary A. Gaudin
Douglas John Hall

Scholars Press
Atlanta, Georgia

REINHOLD NIEBUHR (1892–1971)
A Centenary Appraisal

edited by
Gary A. Gaudin
Douglas John Hall

cover design by Ian Culley

Library of Congress Cataloging-in-Publication Data
Reinhold Niebuhr (1892–1971) : a centenary appraisal / edited by Gary
    A. Gaudin, Douglas John Hall.
        p.   cm. — (McGill studies in religion ; v. 3)
    Chiefly papers presented at the Reinhold Niebuhr Centenary
Symposium, McGill University, Sept. 1992.
    Includes bibliographical references.
    ISBN 0-7885-0042-2 (alk. paper)
    1. Niebuhr, Reinhold, 1892–1971—Congresses. 2. Theology—
History—20th Century—Congresses. I. Gaudin, Gary A. II. Hall,
Douglas John, 1928–   . III. Reinhold Niebuhr Centenary Symposium
(1992 : McGill University) IV. Series.
BX4827.N5R42   1994
230'.092—dc20   94-34072
                                                 CIP

Printed in the United States of America
on acid-free paper

To

Ursula M. Niebuhr

*...the faith and vision of Reinhold Niebuhr are not dated. We are all aware of the changes in his thought but one can always find continuities. Do we not see continuities between the sermons in **Beyond Tragedy** and so much that is said in **The Irony of American History** and that superb chapter in Volume II of **The Nature and Destiny of Man** entitled "The Kingdom of God and the Struggle for Justice"? As we relate his faith and wisdom to our decisions, we should take as an example what June Bingham called in the title of her first biography of Niebuhr, "Courage to Change." We must not connect Niebuhr with a Neo-Orthodoxy or a Neo-Conservatism, which is now the more likely error.*

The biblically inspired faith of Niebuhr was for him and can be for us a source of grace, judgement, love and hope with no essential order of those gifts of faith. His wisdom included Christian Realism and it is not dated in our time if it is combined with his confidence in the intermediate ethical and spiritual gains that are possible for persons and within human history.

From John Coleman Bennett's greetings to the Niebuhr Symposium at McGill University, September 1992

CONTENTS

PREFACE

Gary A. Gaudin

Under the general rubric *Reinhold Niebuhr (1892-1971)*, the Faculty of Religious Studies of McGill University in Montréal hosted two carefully co-ordinated events between September 26th and 29th, 1992. *The Reinhold Niebuhr Centenary Symposium* and the annual *Birks Lectures* were both dedicated to the thought of one of this century's most influential Christian theologians, whose contributions to the intellectual and pastoral life of the church, to social relations and public policy were such that the anniversary of his birth could not go unacknowledged — also in Canada, where his heritage is strong and his emphases are sustained in the work of many educators, a number of whom who have contributed to this present volume.

The *Symposium* brought together Niebuhr scholars from Germany, the United States and Canada in an examination of Niebuhr's thought and its pertinence to contemporary religious and political life. The papers which were presented were then revised by their authors in the light of the comments made by official respondents and subsequent plenary discussion. It is the revised form of each essay which is included in this collection.

As will be evident, the perspectives brought to this study are varied. That is as it should be: Niebuhr's interests were many, and the insights he offered are too important for confinement to a single point of view. While these papers retain much of their aural qualities, two elements integral to the success of the *Symposium* could not be represented in this collection. The first is the sense of lively discussion and exchange initiated by carefully prepared responses to each paper, and which carried over into mealtime (and other) conversations. The second element was equally impossible to capture: the engaging contributions of Mr. Christopher Niebuhr throughout the sessions, but particularly during an evening "Table Talk" gathering. We are profoundly grateful that Mr. Niebuhr was able to participate in the event, and to offer clarifications and insights into his father's life and thought that could have come from no other source.

Immediately following the *Symposium,* three *Birks Lectures* were delivered by the current Reinhold Niebuhr Professor of Social Ethics at Union Theological Seminary in New York City, Larry L. Rasmussen. First established in 1950 through the generosity of the late William M. Birks, the Birks lecturers have included Northrup Frye, Jürgen Moltmann, and Krister Stendahl. Under the general title "Reinhold Niebuhr: Ethics and Power," Professor Rasmussen developed a closely reasoned critical appreciation of the fundamental relationship between these central categories in Niebuhr's thought. These lectures are presented here in a revised form.

Each of these addresses represents original scholarship appearing in print for the first time. There are two exceptions. The essay by Dietz Lange has since appeared in German. And the essay of Douglas John Hall, initiator of the *Symposium*, appeared first in a collection of essays given at King's College in London, England, and published both in Britain and the United States. It is included (with permission) in order to represent a perspective on Niebuhr otherwise not elaborated in the present collection.

A great many people helped to make this event the stimulating intellectual occasion it was. Particular thanks are due to the Social Sciences and Humanities Research Council of Canada and to the Faculty of Religious Studies of McGill for funding the *Symposium*. To the Dean, Professor Donna R. Runnalls, and the Staff of the Faculty of Religious Studies we owe a debt of gratitude. Particular mention should be made of the extensive display of Niebuhr materials assembled by the Faculty's Librarian, Ms. Norma Johnson.

INTRODUCTION

Douglas John Hall

The following paragraphs are taken from Reinhold Niebuhr's "Intellectual Autobiography"[1] — the closest he ever came to permitting himself to undertake a direct and sustained statement about his own spiritual-intellectual pilgrimage, though some passages from the recently published letters of the Niebuhrs offer valuable clues to Professor Niebuhr's internal development:[2]

> The Christian faith asserts about God that He is a person and that He has taken historical action to overcome the variance between man and God: "God was in Christ reconciling the world unto himself." Both propositions are absurd from a strictly ontological standpoint....The whole of modern theology in its various aspects is involved in the effort to reduce the absurdity of the idea of God involved in history and taking action in historic terms. This is done by reducing the message of the Bible to eternal principles of ethics or of ontology. Thus Harnack characteristically defines the "essence of Christianity" as the affirmation of the transcendent value of the individual (a proposition which Christianity does not affirm but takes for granted) and the brotherhood of man in love (whereas Biblical faith derives the injunction that we love one another from the original historical affirmation that God, in Christ, loved us). In the desperate effort of the modern Christian to make his faith acceptable to the intellectual scruples of modern men, he reduces it to ontological absurdities or to ethical truisms. These also become absurd when, for instance, the love commandment is interpreted as a simple possibility by modern Christian moralism.
>
> We are confronted with the fact, in other words, that man evidently is a historical creature and that any reduction of religion to ontological and non-

1

historical proportions obviously denies or obscures some element or dimension of his complex nature. On the other hand, a religion of history and revelation in history is not acceptable to the "wise and prudent" of our generation. To judge from Christ's observation, it has not been acceptable to the wise of any generation. In this situation it would be foolish to predict some easy return to the faith by this generation even if the alternative faiths of modern secular liberalism and Marxism have proved to be erroneous and involved in incredible utopian illusions which are either dangerous or pathetic; while the only other alternative which seems available to the "wise and prudent" is a form of mysticism which annuls the meaning of history and runs counter to modern man's creative involvement in historical problems.

While Christian apologists cannot hope for too much success, it has become progressively clearer in my mind, since I wrote my several books, what line the apologetic venture of the Christian Church should take. I hope to follow out this line in the years of activity still allotted to me. We must make it clear that the concepts of both personality and history are ontologically ambiguous. Personality, whether God's or man's, is defined only in dramatic and historic encounter. Though these dramatic and historical media of personality are not inherently "irrational," they are not subject to the ordinary "scientific" tests of rational intelligibility. Nothing in history follows as it does in nature or reason, "in a necessary manner." The personality is bound by historical destiny rather than by natural or ontological necessity. The revelation of "God in Christ," for instance, is a force of destiny for the community of faith which has been gathered by that revelation: the Christian Church. The Church does not exist to propound eternal ethical truths, though it significantly regards the "love of Christ" as normative for human existence. But the truth in Christ cannot be speculatively established. It is established only as men encounter God, individually and collectively, after the pattern set by Christ's mediation. The creative consequences of such encounters, the humility and charity of true repentance, the absence of pride and pretension, must be the proofs that there has been an encounter with the only true God and not on the one hand with an idol of our own imagination who is invented to establish some interest of ours; and not on the other hand with a vast ocean of fullness and nothingness which condemns our individuality and particularity in a judgment in which the whole of history is also annulled. The encounter between God and man, as the encounters between men in history, must be by faith and love and not by the discovery of some common essence of reason or nature underlying individuals and particulars.

There is no way in which, in introducing this collection of papers from McGill's Niebuhr *Symposium*, I can improve upon these words from Dr. Niebuhr's own hand. The more one studies Niebuhr's writings themselves (and may I add, the *less* one is tempted to read him through the lenses of the little orthodoxies of the right and the left who use and abuse his work), the more one realizes not only the profundity of his account of the faith and of our context but also the remarkable way in which his thought and his life are all of a piece. Such exposure to Niebuhr's own work, if it were sufficiently sustained, would dispel once and for all the insidious and still-repeated charge of "the stricter sects of theologians" (RN) that he was not, after all, a theologian, did not have a Christology, a doctrine of the church, an epistemology, and all of those other things reputedly necessary to the complete theological angler! Like Luther, he was not, to be sure, a *systematic* theologian. But if anyone can read, mark and inwardly digest the words that I have just quoted — and literally millions of others like them — and not sense a theology, including a christology, an ecclesiology and an epistemology, then I, for one, shall want to examine that person catechetically with a view to dullness of imagination, the greatest heresy!

The truth is that Reinhold Niebuhr was a theologian of the most classical Protestant ilk. He *lived* 'the Protestant principle' that Paul Tillich talked about, and, as one who was a reputed "Barthian" during the seven years he studied under Niebuhr, I venture to assert (as did the late Ellen Flessemann van Leer) that Reinhold Niebuhr and Karl Barth had much more in common than is frequently thought by those who follow in their train. In Ursula Niebuhr's recently published correspondence, while Reinhold shares with his wife certain misgivings about Barth's near-biblicism,[3] "otherworldliness"[4] and patriarchalism,[5] he seems far less inclined to criticize Barth than are many who interpret their relation; and at least one occasion in the letters he notes that what Barth and he have in common is their existential, post-liberal exposure to the thought of the sixteenth century Reformers and to the Scriptures.[6]

While Niebuhr wished to be a *public* theologian; while he was at work within a socio-historical context very different from that of Karl Barth; and while, like Brunner and in the Augustinian tradition, he certainly intended to seek for *Anknüpfungspunkten* [points of contact] between the gospel and ordinary human experience, his basic theological disposition belonged to the same fundamental ethos as that of Barth. More than Niebuhr's longtime colleague, Paul Tillich, both of these other giants of the immediate Protestant past had their feet solidly planted in . . . *the Bible*. The *sola scriptura* was not merely a principle for them — the so-called 'formal principle' of the Reformation; it was the meditative core of their lives. To use George Lindbeck's laudable image,[7] the Bible was the "lens" through which they looked upon their world, and for that reason neither of them, (and I would say this especially of Niebuhr) was willing to *reduce* their world to abstractions and predictabilities. They were always (to use Barth's expression) ever newly astonished by events, "like a child in a forest, or on Christmas eve."[8]

In fact, the *beginning* of the passage that I have quoted above, where Niebuhr sets the tone for his critique of modern theology as being "involved in the effort to reduce the absurdity of the idea of God involved in history," makes just that point:

> Though I have meditated on these issues for some time, I have only recently come to realize fully why the dramatic-historical account of the Bible (about which an earlier generation of modern theologians have been unduly apologetic) should give a truer view of both the nobility and the misery of man than all the wisdom of scientists and philosophers. The fact is that the human self can only be understood in a dramatic-historical environment. Any effort to co-ordinate man to some coherence, whether of nature or of reason, will falsify the facts; because the self's freedom, including both its creative and destructive capacities, precludes such coordination.[9]

It is perhaps precisely this refusal of Reinhold Niebuhr's to develop a theological "system," this fear that the abstractions that are almost necessary to the theological enterprise will give the lie to reality, this revulsion against what he called "the menace of finality,"[10] that not only kept him faithful to the historical-narrative approach of the scriptures of Israel but also insured that there would be no distinguishable Niebuhrian-school. So far as I am aware — though I may be mistaken because I am notoriously disinterested in these matters — there is no such thing as Niebuhr Society, international or otherwise. There is a Barth Society, and a Tillich Society and a Bonhoeffer Society. They meet regularly, not only on centenary occasions, and I once had described for me a meeting of the European Barth Society in which at least seventy percent of those in attendance were (like the Master) smoking pipes and wearing berets.

It is not surprising, then, that what comes across in the papers collected in this volume is not adulation but gratitude. These are statements of Christian thinkers, most of them Niebuhr's own students, who are grateful for the manner in which a splendid teacher and modest human being has exemplified for them what it means to be passionately involved with the world that God so loved and loves. They are grateful for the intellectual acumen and personal courage that he demonstrated, from which they have derived some of the courage that they, in turn, need to encounter and interpret the always-new and sometimes unnerving turnings of this same beloved world. These writers do not believe that Reinhold Niebuhr delivered the Truth; for they learned, in part from him, that Truth is not possessable. Niebuhr was so faithful to the livingness of God and of Creation that he feared to kill them both with absolutes.

Yet, unlike some who learned too well (and not well enough!) his lesson about history's "ambiguities," Niebuhr's abhorrence of finalities did not immobilize him. Perhaps more than any other figure in the history of Christendom, he gave himself to almost-daily commentary on the unfolding of events. (And of course he did not stop at *commentary*!) As Friedrich Hufendiek has suggested in his essay, it is necessary to read not only the great tomes of Niebuhr but the thousands of little and larger articles in which he entered a running discourse on his world, without being debilitated by the academic's phobia that he might in the process sometimes contradict himself!

Reinhold Niebuhr belongs to the ages now. He did not, could not, anticipate all the things that would occur with the onrush of the decades. I suppose it is an attestation to his greatness (a word he would greatly despise in this context) that many people today appear to believe that he should have understood everything that would transpire after him. Reading some of his most recent critics one has the impression that Niebuhr's great sin was that he was confined to time and was mortal. He *did*, in fact, anticipate *much* that would happen — and it would be interesting now, for instance, to go back over his long dialogue and struggle with Marxism in the light of what has in fact taken place during the past few years. But as for himself, he was too conscious of the mystery of existence to think that he held some eternal key to it.

In his last letter to me, written at the height of the death-of-God episode, he remarked: "...the death of God theologians are a source of confusion, and one wonders whether they ever really studied the long history of western thought. They seem to have no idea of either mystery or history and of how important it is for the Christian faith to make meaning out of history by appealing to the sovereignty of a mysterious Creator and Redeemer. We seem to be in for a rather flat culture, if this is the best that our younger theologians can produce."[11]

Mystery and meaning: two of Niebuhr's key words. We are all of us thrust into the mystery of the world's unfolding, including the unfolding of our own lives, and so far as we have the courage to try to understand what we believe, we are bound to search for whatever meaning we can discern in that mystery, the mystery *in* history, not above it.

Niebuhr never gave up that search — the quintessential human search, according to his friend Abraham Heschel — and he never gave up, either, believing that "the tradition of Jerusalem" (George P. Grant) provided the richest source of contemplation and wisdom for human beings engaged in that search. For the others who write in these pages, let me then express our common thanks: In an age of religious simplism, when easy religious answers abound to difficult human questions, we are thankful that we have been exposed, personally or through his writings, to one for whom Judeo-Christian faith was deep, nuanced, and *profound* in its simplicity. In an age when the perennial ideological taint and temptation of theology is strong, and when ideology is frequently given forth as if it *were* theology, we are thankful for one who understood (and I quote from the above) that "There is a dimension of human existence which makes all purely rationalistic interpretations inadequate." In an age and a culture which has moved visibly, and with a brilliant display of humanity's penchant for extremes, from a promethean to a sisyphean image of the human, we are thankful for an analyst of human existence who, though he concentrated — as he had to! — on the hamartiological polarity of pride, was fully conscious of the opposite pole of sloth, and would certainly understand, had he lived into the 1990s, that his *apologia* now must be addressed, not to Henry Ford but to Willy Loman. Low Man!

It would quite wrong to construe this gratitude of ours as any sort of obeisance. Reinhold Niebuhr was sometimes critical of Calvin — though more often (and characteristically) of Calvin*ism*. But he understood intuitively and well the dictum of that Reformer: *soli Deo gloria.*

NOTES

1.   Charles W. Kegley and Robert W. Bretall, *Reinhold Niebuhr: His Religious, Social, and Political Thought* (New York: The MacMillan Company, 1956): 1 ff.

2.   Ursula M. Niebuhr, *Remembering Reinhold Niebuhr: Letters of Reinhold and Ursula M. Niebuhr* (N.Y.: HarperSanFrancisco, 1991).

3.   ibid., 238.

4.   ibid., 258.

5.   ibid., 262.

6.   ibid., 239.

7.   *The Nature of Doctrine: Religion and Theology in a Postliberal Age* (Philadelphia: Westminster Press, 1984): 119.

8.   *Church Dogmatics*, III/3: 243.

9.   op. cit., 11.

10.   Ursula M. Niebuhr, op. cit., 398.

11.   The letter is dated Nov. 21, 1966.

THE THOUGHT OF REINHOLD NIEBUHR
AND THE TWILIGHT OF LIBERAL MODERNITY
IN CANADA

Terence R. Anderson

Reinhold Niebuhr's place in the history of Christian social ethics and American social thought is secure. But times have changed. The many social issues he addressed have now, of course, a quite different configuration, and new ones have arisen. Since Niebuhr, a whole generation of Christian ethicists and theologians have come and almost gone. The development in the discipline of Christian ethics in that time has been enormous. Does Niebuhr's thought still have relevance for it? Why do I still teach Niebuhr and draw so much on his thought in the enterprise of Christian ethics?

Niebuhr's interpretation of the Christian faith, I believe, has enduring insights for a Christian social ethic. These become apparent in fresh ways in the emerging conditions in Canada appropriately designated as the "twilight of liberal modernity." By "modernity" I mean broadly the worldview and cultural concomitant of the technologically induced industrialization most characteristic of the western world since the seventeenth century.[1] Stephen Toulmin describes this worldview as a "cosmopolis," a particular understanding of the cosmos marked by the assumptions of Newtonian science combined with a particular view of the political order characterized by the nation state.[2]

By "liberal" (another notoriously ambiguous term), I mean the set of beliefs regarding the value, freedom, and rights of autonomous individuals and the related political theories regarding limited government. Two world wars, the

7

Great Depression, and the Holocaust produced a crisis for liberal modernity especially in Europe and to a lesser extent in the United States. Protestant 'neo-orthodoxy' in Europe was in part a response to this crisis. This period was also the occasion for Reinhold Niebuhr's critical assessment of and major corrective to liberalism, both its political theory and some of the assumptions of modernity reflected in secular and religious liberalism. He did this first with the help of Marxism, then with his own developing theology. He used that theology also to identify fault lines in the Marxist socialist version of modernity that were beginning to show in Eastern Europe and the Soviet Union.

All these predicaments and challenges, however, were experienced less acutely in Canada. Here the basic confidence that modernity (in either its liberal or socialist forms) is the inevitable path of the future was only slightly shaken. Thus Niebuhr's social thought did not have the same widespread impact in Canada. In any case, by the late 1950s and early 1960s full-blown trust in modernity had returned. As Barth put it, "the nineteenth century came back."[3]

Recently, however, new challenges to the worldview and assumptions of liberal modernity have been appearing. Fundamental changes are occurring such as the internationalization of capital, the growth of transnational organizations, the collapse of command economies and the entire Soviet empire, and the worldwide political renaissance of "peoples." The alarming deterioration of the globe's natural environment is another. In "high culture" there is the move in the sciences away from mechanistic paradigms to more ecological ones; a rebellion against the hegemony over all aspects of life by instrumental reason[4] with its focus on maximum efficiency; an epistemological and moral relativism replacing the Enlightenment confidence that reason provides a universal ground of meaning and morality.

Are such changes simply trajectories of convictions, values, and patterns of behaviour that characterize particular aspects of modernity? Or are we entering a new period with a distinctive worldview, a "post-modern" era, as a growing number of thoughtful people claim? Without tracing the details of this discussion, I note the convergence of opinion from a variety of disciplines that "there has been a sea-change in cultural as well as in political-economic practices since around 1972."[5]

Taken together, they appear to constitute a shift away from the fundamental worldview and ethos of the modern epoch. The discussion about modernity and postmodernity is itself significant for it manifests the erosion of one of the distinctive features of modernity, namely, the complete confidence that it represents the inevitable and desirable path of the future for the entire globe. Of equal significance is the fact that those who perceive the decline of modernity attribute it not to some external force but to fundamental flaws in the western seventeenth and eighteenth century Enlightenment roots. Hence, I speak of the "twilight" of modernity.

Not surprisingly, there are various assessments of this phenomenon. Are the changes symptoms of a decaying modernity or foretastes of the emerging new post-modern age? Albert Borgmann speaks of *Crossing the Postmodern Divide*, whereas Charles Taylor speaks more cautiously of *The Malaise of Modernity*. Is this perceived shift to be celebrated as beneficial or lamented and resisted as a disaster? Should we seek to shore up the defenses of modernity, hasten its demise, reform and revitalize it, or recall it to its true identity and vision from which it has deviated? The answers, of course, are bound up with an understanding of the meaning of life, of the good society, the kind of social analysis employed, and moral criteria for setting and assessing economic and political goals for the future.

This is where the wisdom and insight of Niebuhr is needed. His way of bringing the Christian gospel, faith and theology to bear upon such matters, his resulting insights into the weaknesses and strengths of modernity in both its liberal and Marxist-Leninist forms have fresh pertinence. I am *not* claiming that Niebuhr anticipated these problems *nor* that his thought is sufficient for dealing with them. Rather, the questions to focus on are how does the Christian gospel address us in the twilight of modernity? How are we to live faithful to Christ both in our personal behaviour and in the way we seek to organize and govern our collective lives? Then we may ask, in what ways does Niebuhr's particular appropriation of the Christian faith and his interpretation of its guidance assist us in developing a Christian social ethic for dealing with these questions? I will sketch three of the several ways in which I think Niebuhr's thought contributes important building blocks for a sound Christian social ethic for these times, the twilight of modernity.

THE BASE FOR CHRISTIAN SOCIAL ETHICS

The first is Niebuhr's belief that the *basis* for the moral life and Christian ethics is trust in "a mystery of grace...beyond the conscious designs and contrivances of men." This faith is not a special kind of religious experience but rather "a total attitude toward the mystery of God and life, which includes commitment, love, and hope."[6] Niebuhr, then, did not ground Christian ethics in a purportedly universal rational order or even a common human quest.

Not many years ago such a basis seemed, in the cultures of modernity, quaint, parochial and irrelevant. I remember how difficult it was coming from the ethos of Union Theological Seminary, where this approach of Niebuhr's to Christian ethics prevailed, to a western Canadian university where liberal rationalism and logical positivism dominated the field of philosophical ethics. But the "house of intellect" is changing. Rapidly disappearing is belief in a universal reason as the ground for a morality common to all humanity. The Enlightenment enterprise to find such a ground is a failure, announces Alasdair MacIntyre.[7]

"Ambivalence of viewpoint is the prevailing sentiment: *nothing* is accorded a privileged status and *everything* is relativized," writes Nathan Scott. In this climate, assertions of belief, rooted in a particular tradition, are now the mode of knowledge within which everyone must operate: "For, amidst the radical pluralism that distinguishes the contemporary intellectual scene, the time when 'Truth' ('and in the singular') prevailed seems very remote indeed, and any attempt at reviving that former age is greeted with a suspicion that does not trouble to conceal its resolute hostility."[8]

Thus a basis for ethics, let alone Christian ethics, that is unabashedly grounded in a particular tradition is appropriately modest. In the twilight of modernity, it may be accorded more respectability if not credibility. Response to divine grace as the basis of the moral life and Christian ethics is hardly Niebuhr's distinctive idea of course! It is the way he spells out this basis that provides us, I think, with a sound approach on which to build. First, Niebuhr combines this "sure foundation" with his theology of human finitude and sin in such a way as to expose the relativity of all human moral wisdom and accomplishments. He was a powerful critic of any claim to possess truth absolutely:

> The fatal error of rationalism is its failure to recognize that reason is universal only in purely formal terms. Logic and mathematics may be universal; but no judgment which fills logical forms with material content is universal. A rationalism which does not recognize this fact invariably mistakes its particular judgments for genuinely universal judgments, failing to see how it has insinuated its partial and finite perspective into its supposedly universal standards.[9]

The rediscovery of the relativity of human endeavours by post-modern and deconstructionist thought hardly comes, therefore, as a startling surprise to those acquainted with Niebuhr.

Second, the mystery of grace is a base, a place to stand. Niebuhr's comment of nearly fifty years ago on the crisis of liberal modernity speaks directly to the current situation: "We do not maintain that the period of disillusionment in which we now find ourselves will necessarily restore the Christian faith. It has merely re-established its relevance. There is always the alternative of despair, the 'sorrow of the world' to the creative despair which induces a new faith."[10]

Niebuhr spoke about a validation of the Gospel in such circumstances: "Negatively the Gospel must and can be validated by exploring the limits of historic forms of wisdom and virtue. Positively it is validated when the truth of faith is correlated with all truths which may be known by scientific and philosophical disciplines and proves itself a resource for coordinating them into a deeper and wider system of coherence."[11]

All our comprehensions of the truth may be partial and distorted by sin, but nonetheless there is a truth to be known in the gospel of Jesus Christ. This is a truth for the whole of humankind, not simply for one belief group. Niebuhr was at home with and even promoted a sense of *relativity* but he did not subscribe to the *relativism* emerging in our time — that there is no truth to be known.

Third, the particular faith basis for Christian social ethics did not lead Niebuhr to retreat to the community that acknowledges it. He moved from this basis into vigorous public discourse. With the growing pluralism of values, traditions and even underlying worldviews in western societies and the collapse of Enlightenment claims for universal reason, what common grounds and language is there for public moral discourse? Some Christian ethicists like Stanley Hauerwas have responded by urging Christians to put their own house in order and recover their distinctive narrative tradition. Out of this, a community of virtuous character will grow. This can be a powerful witness to the way of the Gospel as an alternative to the confusing babble of the culture which no longer has an over-arching sense of meaning and ground for truth.

Niebuhr's approach to ethics offers an alternative to this in a time of relativism. I think his way of carrying on public conversation from the basis of particular faith tradition is instructive. He sought to make a case in public for a Christian perspective on social justice, not in terms of the criteria of some supposedly universal reason, but on the grounds that it illuminates life and its problems as we currently experience it. Further, it provides a ground for creative action in response. This kind of conversation, then, does not depend upon the recovery of some commonly accepted foundation for moral truth. Nor are we able to make sense only to our own communities. Rather, we converse with others about how to understand and deal with the complexities of the issues and struggles before us, and how the truth claims of the Gospel illuminate and bear on these.

It is worth listing the ways that Niebuhr did *not* bring the Christian gospel into conversation with the culture. He did not (except at a very early stage) seek to trim his theology of sin and redemption to fit the plausibility structures of the time and thus gain a hearing. Nor did he attempt to synthesize Christian concerns with a particular ideology. He did not use the faith as a private add-on to the wisdom of the culture, or as a merely personal ground out of which to struggle for social justice, or as a way of providing religious sanction to the culture's norms and practices. Rather Niebuhr sought to show how the "foolishness of the gospel," or more precisely a theology growing out of it, could interpret and illuminate social systems, structures, and conditions. He provided a theological understanding of society and events that challenged the conventional wisdom and its underlying thought forms in both appreciative and critical ways. This is a lead we should follow. Niebuhr's later reflection that he might have used different and less alienating language is only a strategic qualification, not a backing away from this kind of public theological discourse.

Fourth, this basis for Christian ethics, trust in the mysterious grace of God, facilitates in another way both public discourse and dialogue with those of other traditions. Personal identity and worth are secured by the mercy of God in Christ. Insofar as we rely on this grace, we can be more open to other worldviews and beliefs and their criticisms without our fundamental identity being threatened. Of course, that grace moves us to seek a new life of love and justice. This plunges us into the contentions and struggles between humans over the truth and the right. The differences between people with their various beliefs and behaviour are therefore important and to be taken seriously and respected. But remembering that all humans, including Christians, remain God's beloved children only by God's mercy and that finally salvation is dependent on God's grace, these differences between humans are seen to be of only relative, not absolute, significance.

A Cherokee practitioner of his traditional "Night Hawk" religion explained what he looked for in seeking a non-native, Christian dialogue partner. He wanted such a partner to explore religious matters which he regarded as essential to the survival of his people. This person must be someone who "knows who he is," he said, one who is not "anxiously searching for an identity." Such a person will not be blown away by hard questions and criticisms nor one who simply agrees in order to be "in with Indians." A Christian ethic based in the mystery of God's grace in the fashion Niebuhr developed is a resource for such an undertaking.

THE CORE OF CHRISTIAN SOCIAL ETHICS

Niebuhr's conviction that love and justice are the *core* of Christian ethics is another important building block for a contemporary Christian social ethic. It is especially relevant in a time of changing economics and the collapse of older ideologies. There is little doubt that from the very beginning of his career, Reinhold Niebuhr saw love of neighbour which entails the pursuit of justice as the very heart of Christian ethics. His first public address to an interdenominational audience was based on Matthew 10:39, and Niebuhr followed the thrust of liberal Christianity by proclaiming that the solution to the problem of life, both personal and social is love and self-sacrifice.[12] This theme receives much more sophisticated treatment in *Nature and Destiny of Man* (*NDM*), but it is present throughout Niebuhr's work.[13] God's love revealed in the cross of Christ was for Niebuhr the proper ground and model for neighbour love rather than God's love revealed in creation and covenant. There are few aspects of Niebuhr's ethics that have engendered more controversy than his interpretation of the norm of neighbour love in terms of self-giving.[14]

These discussions have yielded, I think, both clarification as to what Niebuhr meant and helpful suggestions for modification. Thus, by self-giving or self-sacrifice setting aside the self's interests for the sake of the other, Niebuhr did not mean (as the word seems to connote to some) the denial of self-worth or loss of a centered self. Nor did he minimize the importance of mutual love. Self-giving love makes the true communion of mutual love possible. But even with clarifications and elaborations, Niebuhr's emphasis on self-giving in contrast to a focus on proper self-love and mutuality continues to be controversial. The debate is part of a wider ongoing discussion regarding the vexing question of whether *agape* is a quite different kind of love (marked by self-giving) from *eros* or the "human loves" (marked by drawing unto the self that which is loved), or simply a redirecting of human loves from pursuit of false values to seeking the true good.

The continuing significance of these matters, and thus of Niebuhr's insights concerning them, is illustrated by Charles Taylor's argument in *The Malaise of Modernity*. Taylor agrees with the widespread criticism that liberal modern societies are currently characterized by the atomism of separated selves pursuing their own self-interest and preoccupied with their own individual rights, with a subsequent decline of community, public virtues and public life. But unlike a number of other social critics (including those influenced by Niebuhr), Taylor does not locate the problem in preoccupation with self-fulfilment. Nor does he think the answer lies in greater regard for others, love as self-giving. Rather he claims that self-fulfilment is a legitimate moral ideal, better identified as *authenticity*. What is needed is restoration of this ideal to its true meaning and a repudiation of "debased and deviant forms" of it. The problem is not in seeking self-fulfilment but rather failure to understand what truly constitutes such fulfilment. Clearly, the debate about self-love and self-giving is still with us.

But regardless of the disputes about Niebuhr's precise formulation of the norms of neighbour love and justice, I believe that his interpretation of the radical open-ended quality of both remains valid. A sound Christian social ethic will continue to make them its core. In emphasizing the suffering love of Jesus Christ who poured himself out for others, Niebuhr continues the perfectionist thrust found in the New Testament and some strands of the tradition. The "impossible possibility" is not the happiest phrase for expressing this. However, I think the underlying insight is valid, namely, that "while love is never *fully* embodied in any human motive or human action, it remains relevant as a standard for both motive and action. It is relevant because we are judged by it and because, if in humility before God we avoid the pretensions which most seriously distort our life, we are *able to approximate* such love."[15]

Love of neighbour always entails seeking of justice, but the open-ended demands of love impart a similar open-ended quality to the pursuit of justice. Any achievement of justice always falls short of the demands of love, and so we are called to yet ever higher levels of justice. The test for justice is the treatment accorded to and condition of the least powerful, the *anawim*, the oppressed, the prisoner, the blind, the "bowed down." Justice has to do with meeting the concrete needs of such persons and restoring them to their proper place of power and dignity in the community. For Niebuhr, then, the open-ended quality of justice means that it can never be entirely encapsulated by any set of standards let alone any particular program or social practice. Further, the pervasiveness of sin and finitude make it impossible for humans to arrive at any objective and unbiased set of criteria. Principles and resulting calculations over what a just outcome would look like are adequate to the extent that the poor and the dispossessed are empowered to have a more equal voice in shaping them. Love judges all actual systems and structures of justice: "Each new level of fulfilment also contains elements which stand in contradiction to perfect love. There are therefore obligations to realize justice in indeterminate degrees; but none of the realizations can assure the serenity of perfect fulfilment." As John Bennett says, "Niebuhr's criticism of inequalities — racial and economic — never ceased."[16]

Niebuhr does use equality as a guiding principle for justice. Equality includes impartiality in the determination of needs and rights. It also sets the burden of proof upon any who would defend an unequal distribution, though this may indeed be appropriate for those with special needs or having to perform special functions for society. But equality as he employs it is useful partly because it reflects to some degree the open-ended quality of both love and justice: "Equality as a pinnacle of the ideal of justice implicitly points towards love as the final norm of justice, for equal justice is the approximation of brotherhood under the conditions of sin."[17]

This quality of open-ended demand that characterizes love and justice as Niebuhr interprets them, has at least two implications that are important for a responsible Christian social ethic in the twilight of modernity. First, it provides an ongoing call and focus for Christian social ethics even in these times of uncertainty about social vision. The collapse of command economies and Marxist-Leninist ideology together with the rising forms of a post-modern economy labelled "postindustrial, electronic, service, information, or computer economy"[18] render most older social analyses and agenda suspect or plainly untenable. What should be the church's social task now, asks a disillusioned and troubled Czech Christian? The confusion is heightened for those who have tasted the cultural pluralism and relativism described earlier. A veteran woman activist states her bewilderment about a new social agenda. Who decides it and how? For those whose view of social justice allowed it to be virtually equated with one of these visions and programs, one temptation is despair. Another is defiant clinging to old slogans, programs and strategies in the mistaken notion that they so embody justice that to abandon them would be to desert justice itself. The result is a dangerous kind of strategic fundamentalism. An alternative, exhibited by Daniel Bell, is the celebration of the emerging new economic order with its technical experts and service and information industries as a classless and ideology free era.[19]

A Christian social ethic, however, that learns from Niebuhr to make its core a love and justice understood in the open-ended way we have described, will find there are no conditions that warrant complacency. Neither are there any circumstances that should divert attention from seeking greater justice for the least advantaged. Programs, strategies for justice, even social movements may come and go. At their best, they only partially embody the concerns of love and justice. The calling and direction remain clear regardless of the obsolescence and demise of such vehicles. The motivating force of love and justice for the neighbour and their guidance for action is thus not restricted to any particular set of social conditions nor tied to the fate of any particular cause. The same can be said regarding ideologies. This is a second implication of Niebuhr's view of love and justice as open-ended in demand and placed at the core of a Christian social ethic. It affects how we regard ideology. The term "ideology" is used in various ways. It is sometimes used to refer to any belief system, worldview or collection of opinions and doctrines. In this sense of the term everyone has an ideology, whether consciously held or only implicitly assumed. Another use more common in political matters is an idea system which relates one's beliefs and ethics to political goals and strategies. Ideologies of this kind "demand a hardening of commitment." They are an amalgam of "information, ideas, purposes, and emotional tones."[20] Ideologies serve as a kind of packaged fighting creed that gives us clear direction and provides ready responses to a variety of issues that confront us. Niebuhr actively espoused ideologies of this second kind — democratic socialism and later in his life a pragmatic, welfare liberalism. How he related the Christian faith, including love of neighbour and justice, to such political ideologies is once again instructive.

His approach to ideologies in both uses so far described is connected to a third use of the term. This use designates the *function* of ideas and belief systems. Niebuhr followed Marx's analysis that idea systems, whether of the broader kind or more restricted "political ideologies," function as masks which hide the vested interests of privileged groups behind lofty sounding rationales. They operate, without the intention or awareness of their believers, to distort reality, to stereotype persons, to justify or obscure particular interests or power realities. As we observed earlier, for Niebuhr finitude and sin affect all human theories, attitudes, ideals and political creeds: "Knowledge of the truth is thus invariably tainted with an 'ideological' taint of interest, which makes our apprehension of truth something less than knowledge of *the* truth and reduces it to *our* truth."[21]

One of Niebuhr's earliest most persistent criticisms of Marxism is its failure to see its own "ideology" in this masking function sense. The proletarian class, the ruling oligarchy of that class, and the socialist elite are blinded to some degree by their own particular situation: "The pathos of Marxian spirituality is that it sees the qualified and determined character of all types of spirituality except its own."[22] On the basis of his theology of human nature, Niebuhr perceived an even more extensive masking function of ideologies than Marx had discerned. Besides cloaking the interests of a group, they also cloak an uneasy conscience and "obscure the deep tension between the individual conscience and the moral realities of man's collective life...a reminder to individual man of the moral ambiguity of all human virtue."[23]

No one has been more consistent than Niebuhr in exposing the taint of self-interest and the contingent character of all rational endeavours and ethical claims, whether of social science, theology, philosophy, religious and secular systems, or various forms of nationalism. He does not attempt to exempt even any remnant of prophetic Christianity. Just as spiritual pride is the most subtle and in many ways the most dangerous form of sin, religious ideology is the ultimate type of ideology: "Historic religions, which crown the structure of historic cultures, thus become the most brutal weapons in the conflict between the cultures."[24] Niebuhr's recognition of this persistent "ideological" (masking) function together with his conviction regarding the open-ended demands of love and justice, led him to make only very modest claims for any political ideology or cause. It prevented him, for example, from ever identifying the work of the Kingdom, or the embodiment of social justice, or even or the social agenda of the Christian faith with the socialism or later the mixed economy that he espoused.[25]

The relationship of the Christian faith to a particular social movement and ideology he viewed in ethical and pragmatic terms rather than religious ones. Socialism, for instance, was not seen as the social embodiment of the Christian faith as it was for his colleague Harry F. Ward or the religious philosopher, John Macmurray. Nor did Niebuhr make the more modest claim that socialism is the imperfect manifestation of God's judgment and renewal as did Paul Tillich. Rather, Niebuhr regarded socialism simply as the next step in achieving social justice. Christian allegiance to a particular movement and ideology is provisional and not ultimate. It is subject to change as historical conditions alter or new empirical evidence about its efficacy in achieving higher social justice emerges.

Such an "instrumental" view of ideologies — they are useful to love and justice but always subject to these higher standards — is important for a Christian social ethic in the twilight of modernity. We live in an era when ancient political ideologies have become uncouth. They no longer address new social conditions or they have become overwhelmed by their dark side including their masking function. This is less traumatic if the ideology has been understood as the next step toward greater social justice than if it had become part of the religious centre of one's life. Rather than embittered and immobilizing despair, one may move on to fashion a more appropriate political ideology for advancing love and justice in these conditions and times.

In addition, this more modest claim for political ideologies helps Christian ethics with its important task of mitigating the inevitable dark side of all ideologies. It assists in the endeavor of checking the tendency of political ideologies to become closed and rigid, unable to respond to new realities and changing conditions. Uncritical religious or moral legitimation of an ideology heightens these problems. But even making the support provisional cannot eliminate the masking function of an ideology either in the sense of it cloaking the interests of a group or hiding an uneasy conscience. There is no ground on which one can stand and be entirely free of these masking functions, claimed

Niebuhr. Christian ethics can, no more than any other undertaking, find "non-ideological" (non-masking) truth. Rather, it must seek to find in its grounding in God's grace a perspective from which the ideological taint in all claims of truth, including its own, may be acknowledged and accepted without cynicism.

The core of a Christian social ethic, then, should be love of neighbour and justice rather than some social ideal or movement or social analysis or program or the aspirations of a class or group onto which messianic qualities and expectations are loaded. Some of these may have a useful place in a social ethic, but the test of any policy and practice should be its actual effect on the least advantaged, the *anawim*. Is that effect such that justice in harmony with love of neighbour is advanced?

THE CONTROLLING CENTRE OF CHRISTIAN SOCIAL ETHICS

Reinhold Niebuhr's explicit use of theological convictions and doctrines as the *controlling centre* of his social ethic is another aspect of his thought that should be carried forward and developed. Niebuhr made use of theological convictions as a base point for ethical reflection to a greater extent than many other Christian ethicists who rely more either on norms and standards or moral character and virtues. In John Bennett's words, "Niebuhr's social ethics are immediately controlled by his theology. This is especially true of his doctrine of man and of his understanding of justification by faith."[26]

Niebuhr used these to expose and critique the often hidden presuppositions of modern thought, both liberal and Marxist, which informed their analysis and practice. He developed a theological understanding of society and its events instead of relying only on secular understandings to inform his own analysis. In the ethos of the twilight of modernity, many of the basic presuppositions of modernity, both liberal or Marxist, are under question. Both Niebuhr's approach, then, as well as some of his particular theological insights have fresh relevance for this context. We need to note that Niebuhr was never very explicit about exactly how beliefs regarding reality (who are we, where are we, what is wrong with the world and what is the remedy), relate to beliefs about what we ought to do. Readers are often puzzled as to how he could reach political conclusions from theological convictions. Modern philosophy has insisted that statements about reality are of quite a different kind than those about what we ought to do. It is surely correct in observing that there is no logical, necessary connection between the two types of belief. A particular understanding of what *is* does not yield by itself a directive as to what *ought* to be done. One cannot read off a specific political policy or action solely from a particular set of basic convictions regarding God, Christ, and human beings. Yet as Niebuhr kept insisting, there is some kind of connection between the two. Oliver O'Donovan suggests that our understanding of reality is action-evoking even though not action-prescribing.[27]

In turn, actions bear witness to a certain understanding of reality even though those same actions do not necessarily require such convictions. Our basic convictions, including theological ones, do influence and evoke certain behaviour and understandings of what is the right, the good and the fitting, but they do not do so in a simple or direct way. I think that theological convictions help guide behaviour by shaping moral character, by determining the interpretation of particular moral norms, and by affecting our analysis of what is happening in any given social context or situation. Niebuhr's theology controlled his ethics in these ways even though he did not make this clear.

I shall illustrate the continuing pertinence both of making theological convictions the controlling centre of a Christian ethic and of some of Niebuhr's own particular theological insights regarding human nature by showing their connection to the current communitarian-liberal debate. Obviously, I can only sketch that complex debate here. The heart of the communitarian challenge is that liberalism in all its variations is informed by an inadequate, individualistic understanding of the self and a deficient view of community.[28] One type of critique claims that this inadequacy has helped to create increasingly atomistic conditions in liberal societies and thus a paucity of community. Individuals have become so preoccupied with their own aims, needs and rights that there is little concern for public life and the good of the community as a whole. Another type of communitarian critique identifies the problem differently. It is not that liberal societies lack community but rather the kind of community they exhibit and depend upon is not acknowledged by liberal theory. Most strands of liberal theory reject the idea of a community with a shared understanding of a common good. Instead they espouse a "framework" for communities and individuals each of which is free to define and pursue their own conceptions of the good, subject to the constraint that they respect the liberty of other individuals and communities to do so as well. But this understanding of community entails its own notion of a common good, namely, that individuals should be allowed to define the good for themselves. Further, argue the Communitarians, such a view of the good is morally deficient.[29]

Embedded in this debate are a number of key convictions about human beings. Different understandings of "shared relations" is one example of this. In liberal thought relations are characteristically viewed as "contingent," that is, "a relationship between two or more antecedently defined separate selves which, however much it may affect their attitudes and behaviour, does not penetrate the identity of the separate selves." Communitarians, on the other hand, typically apprehend relations as "essentially" shared ones: "When two selves essentially share a relation, the identity of each self is partially or wholly constituted by the relation."[30]

Another conviction regarding human beings has to do with different understandings of collectivities. A collectivity may be described as a group of individuals with a distinct existence and identity of its own that seeks benefits for the group as such and not simply for its members. Michael McDonald, a Canadian philosopher, distinguishes between two types of collectivity. In one type, persons "identify with the group." They *choose* to become a citizen of a state, or play with a particular team, or join a particular association. This voluntarily chosen collectivity is the type that liberals espouse. In the second type of collectivity, members *recognize* a significant existing commonality with others and *acknowledge* a group to which they belong. Families, ethnic communities, peoples or nations are examples of this type.[31]

The liberal tradition in all its variants has difficulty with this type because the very essence of liberalism is choice. Communitarians, on the other hand, believe that collectivities of this second type are necessary for a good life and society. The matter of self identity — who am I? — underlies these differences. Are we primarily individuals and only secondarily members of community? Or are we social creatures who discover our identity in relationship? Classical liberalism, with its strong individualism, would say 'yes' to the first question and 'no' to the second. C.B. McPherson summarizes this view as follows: "What makes a man human is freedom from dependence on the will of others....Freedom from dependence on others means freedom from any relation with others except those relations which the individual enters voluntarily with the view to his own interest....The individual is essentially the proprietor of his own person for which he owes nothing to society."[32]

A very different understanding of "who we are" is exhibited, e.g., by the Papago people, an aboriginal nation on the border of Mexico and southern Arizona. The question we frequently ask young people in our liberal, modern cultures — "What are you going to be when you grow up?" — makes little sense to the Papago young people. The question is puzzling to them because they already "are," so to speak. As members of the Papago people surrounded by relations, they have a strong identity. They do not find it necessary to go out and "find themselves" or create an identity by becoming independent of all relationships as required in liberal cultures. Being a strong self does not mean being a separate self but rather one that is secure in enduring relations. Freedom is not escaping from relations and traditions with their binding limits but rather being able to live in right relations.

Enough has been said about the debate between liberals and Communitarians to indicate the wisdom of Niebuhr's claim that a doctrine of human nature is operative in very significant ways in political theory and policy. Theological understandings of human nature clearly bear on the issues that are the subject of this debate. Does Niebuhr's own theology of human nature provide insight on these matters? Niebuhr saw the relation of the individual to the community as a complex one. On the one hand, the self especially in infancy is dependent both physically and spiritually upon the community for socialization and formation. Even in adulthood, "though he may reach a height of uniqueness which seems to transcend his social history completely," the individual's achievements "grow into, as well as out of, the community and find their final meaning in the community."[33]

The individual "looks up at the community as the fulfilment of his life and the sustainer of his existence."[34] On the other hand, the individual's essential freedom, the capacity to stand outside one's self, as it were, enables the individual to look "down" on the community and see its limits, especially its moral shortcomings. As a First Nation's elder put it about his own kinship society, "It is a wonderful place to grow up in, to have and raise children and to live when you are old. But for young people it is boring and frustrating. Further, it has great difficulty with strangers." In Niebuhr's words, "The community will always remain both the fulfilment and the frustration of the individual."[35]

The kind of community Niebuhr was referring to at least in these passages is the kind that Communitarians speak about. It entails essential relations and is the type of collectivity which is discovered rather than chosen. Among the factors needed to preserve or strengthen community, Niebuhr observed, are

> ...traditional, historical, organic and natural forces of communal cohesion such as common language, ethnic kinship, geographic factors, experiences, and common perils. All of these factors operate below the level of conscious decision and bind men together in ways which are not explicitly coercive on the one hand but are on the other hand not the contractual relations of the business community. They create large areas of habitual rather than voluntary association, but their cohesive force is implicit rather than explicit, and covert rather than overt.[36]

Such communities are as primordial as the individual. Niebuhr was critical, therefore, of liberal social contract theories which claim that societies and their governments can be formed by pure artifact: "The success of voluntarism was of course accompanied by confident rationalism. It was thought that men would only have to exercise their reason to conceive of more just social and political integration."[37] The belief of liberals is that older, more organic forms of community based on tradition and religion would eventually be dissolved by the visions of a more astute intelligence.

Like present day Communitarians, Niebuhr pointed out the dependency of liberal societies upon their own form of community ties and relationships. Even the United States, which came closer than any other nation to birth by "contract," presupposed a previous union based on a sense of community fashioned out of a common struggle against the common foe. Observed Niebuhr, "even the wisest statecraft cannot create social tissue. It can cut, sew and redesign social fabric to a limited degree. But the social fabric upon which it works must be 'given.'"[38]

The practical ramifications of these convictions about human nature are manifold. The meaning of justice and freedom, individual rights and collective rights, understandings of the common good, analysis of the nation state, etc., are all affected. For example, the difficulty that liberalism has with more "organic" forms of community like kinship groups and peoplehood has strongly impacted both First Nations and the Quebecois. This is why many Canadians have difficulty understanding, let alone accepting, either. Such non-chosen collectivities are expected to disappear as antiquated "tribalisms" to be replaced by freely chosen collectivities. If they are not disappearing, they should. The pressures to assimilate into liberal individualism have been enormous. Welfare liberalism, however, has come to recognize the importance of groups of this non-chosen type.[39]

True respect for individual persons entails recognition of the culture, language and community in which the individual's identity is rooted. Further, it is acknowledged that "becoming an autonomous person requires a social context in which one acquires an identity not just as an individual but as a member of a community. Language and culture are central to the formation of an autonomous identity."[40] But Michael McDonald warns of a new more subtle danger in this: welfare liberals will only support non-chosen type of groups which they judge to be producing the kind of individuated selves of which they approve. The assimilation pressures become more devious.

The failure of classical liberal theory to take seriously non-chosen organic forms of community, like kinship and peoplehood, has led to some serious mistakes in social analysis with resulting political errors. Mistakes were made in assessing the Viet Nam situation as primarily an ideological conflict: policy makers failed to grasp the strength and relevance of peoplehood in that situation. Over twenty years ago Zbigniew Brzenzinski predicted that the "nationality problem" would become as politically important in the Soviet Union as the racial issue was in the United States. A few years later another expert on the Soviet warned of an explosion if the persisting strength of the sense of peoplehood amongst various republics was not taken seriously.[41] These observations were virtually ignored at the time. We are witnessing their truth today.

If Niebuhr and others are correct that human nature requires communities for identity formation and fulfilment, then we should look to the practice of liberal societies to see how our economic system and political policies enhance or undermine them. There is concern that the erosion of this kind of collectivity in liberal societies fosters increasingly individuated persons who do not have a strong self-identity. Such persons are vulnerable to manipulation by media and mass movements that proffer an identity. Ironically, this is precisely what liberal individualism has been concerned to avoid.

On the other hand, Niebuhr's insight into the essential freedom of human individuals that enables them to transcend any given community indicates that a good society will need to make provision for the exercise of such freedom: "The individual cannot be a true self in isolation. Nor can he live within the confines of the community which 'nature' establishes in the minimal cohesion of family and herd. His freedom transcends these limits of nature, and therefore makes larger and larger social units both possible and necessary."[42] It is not only the individual that benefits from such freedom, however. Society "is as much the beneficiary of freedom as the individual. In a free society new forces may enter into competition with the old and gradually establish themselves. In a traditional or tyrannical form of social organization new forces are either suppressed, or they establish themselves at the price of social convulsion and of people."[43]

Further, "whenever communities throttle the individual's uneasiness and insist that the collective sense of the good is absolute, they sink as does modern totalitarianism, into a consistent brutality."[44] Political theory, therefore, based on a sound view of human nature will recognize the need both to work with non-chosen forms of collectivity and essential relationships, but also provide space for individual freedom and chosen forms of relationship that may widen the scope of community and improve its understanding of both liberty and justice. It is this combination that should inform any new constitution for Canada.

But Niebuhr's understanding of human nature probed deeper. His analysis of sin reveals its distorting power both in groups and individuals. With groups, it is displayed in narrow nationalisms, ethnic idolatry and racial intolerance. With individuals, it shows up in self-seeking at the expense of others and the well-being of the community. Such a theology of sin, therefore, should help us avoid the illusion that either restoring and strengthening the "given" type of collectivities or replacing them with free autonomous individuals and voluntary collectivities will cure the malaise of modernity. Rather, this theology of sin presses us to ask not simply whether we should have more communitarian society, but what form of communitarian society? We are moved to inquire not only about what individual freedom and rights we should foster, but how to do this in a way that does not generate the kind of individual who undermines the survival of those same rights.[45]

A Christian social ethic should continue Niebuhr's practice of making theological convictions its controlling centre. They not only provide the grounding for norms and virtues and shape the way they are interpreted, but such convictions also illuminate social analysis. An ethic so controlled means that it will not simply choose one social analysis and legitimate it nor simply adapt itself to fit some contemporary political theory. Instead, it will investigate and challenge underlying assumptions of all of these in a way that may well point to new understandings and practices.

CONCLUSION

I have proposed that Reinhold Niebuhr's interpretation of the Christian faith proffers three enduring "building blocks" for a Christian social ethic. These have special pertinence, I think, for a Christian social ethic in Canada in the twilight of modernity. The building blocks are first, the mystery of God's grace as the *basis* for a Christian social ethic. Such a base provides a ground for entering public discourse about social issues. It provides a secure identity that engenders both firm commitments and at the same time respectful engagement with those of other persuasions. The second building block is open-ended love of neighbour and justice as the *core* of a Christian social ethic. This calls us in all circumstances to struggle with the least advantaged for ever higher expressions of more equal justice and mutual care. It helps us to keep ideologies subservient to that task and under critical scrutiny of the gospel. The third building block is basic theological convictions rooted in Scripture as the *controlling centre* of a Christian social ethic. Theology informs the interpretation of norms, shapes character, and illuminates social analysis. It constructively challenges the worldview and taken-for-granted assumptions of the culture.

Niebuhr is well known, of course, for his realistic appraisals of all the obstacles to achieving higher forms of justice. But throughout his thought and life runs a persistent hope. This is, I suggest in conclusion, yet another key element for a Christian social ethic. Such an ethic should be marked by a steady *disposition* of hopefulness whose object is the *shalom* of the Kingdom, whose ground is God's grace and not some form of progress or new order or messianic group. Partial realizations of this hope are possible in this life. Such possibilities beckon us to work and struggle for them. But such achievements are always only fragmentary fufillments of Christian hope, each marred by new forms of sinful distortion. Full realization will be accomplished only by God and in God's own time:

> Nothing worth doing can be achieved in our life time; therefore we must be saved by hope. Nothing which is true or beautiful or good makes complete sense in any immediate context of history; therefore we must be saved by faith. Nothing we do, however virtuous, can be accomplished alone; therefore we are saved by love. No virtuous act is quite as virtuous from the stand point of our friend or foe as it is from our standpoint. Therefore we must be saved by the final form of love which is forgiveness.[46]

NOTES

1. "Modern" is a notoriously ambiguous term with disputed meanings and various uses in different disciplines of study, from architecture to literature, science, and theology. The use of the term here is drawn from Peter Berger, Brigitta Berger and Hansfried Kellner, *The Homeless Mind* (New York: Random House, 1973).

2. Stephen Toulmin, *Cosmopolis: The Hidden Agenda of Modernity* (New York: Free Press, 1990).

3. Cited in Hendrikus Berkhof, *Two Hundred Years of Theology* (Grand Rapids: Eerdmans, 1989): 209.

4. "...the kind of rationality we draw on when we calculate the most economical application of means to a given end." Charles Taylor, *The Malaise of Modernity* (Concord, ON: House of Anansi Press, 1991): 5.

5. David Harvey, *The Condition of Postmodernity* (Oxford: Blackwell, 1989): vii.

6. Richard Fox, *Reinhold Niebuhr: A Biography* (New York: Pantheon, 1985): 296.

7. Alasdair MacIntyre, *After Virtue* (Notre Dame: University of Notre Dame Press, 1981).

8. Nathan A. Scott, "The House of Intellect in an Age of Carnival," *Journal of the American Academy of Religion* 55 (1987): 7.

9. Reinhold Niebuhr, *Beyond Tragedy* (New York: Scribners, 1937): 236f.

10. Reinhold Niebuhr, *The Nature and Destiny of Man* (*NDM*) (New York: Scribner's,

1953): II: 206f.

11.   Reinhold Niebuhr, *Faith and History* (New York: Scribner's, 1949): 152.

12.   Fox, 23.

13.   See especially volume II, chapter 9. This virtually replaces Niebuhr's earlier exposition in *An Interpretation of Christian Ethics (ICE)* (N.Y.: Scribner's, 1965). He does some late nuancing in *Man's Nature and His Communities*.

14.   See, for example, Daniel D. Williams, "Niebuhr and Liberalism," in Charles W. Kegley, ed., *Reinhold Niebuhr* (New York: Pilgrim Press, 1984): 284; Gene Outka, *Agape* (New Haven: Yale University Press, 1972): 24 ff.; J. Plaskow, *Sex, Sin and Grace: Women's Experience and the Theologies of R. Niebuhr and P. Tillich* (Washington, DC: University Press of America, 1990); B.H. Andolsen, "Agape in Feminist Ethics," *Journal of Religious Ethics* 9 (1981): 69–83; and B. Harrison, "The Power of Anger in the Work of Love," *Union Seminary Quarterly Review* 36 (1981): 41–57.

15.   John C. Bennett, "Reinhold Niebuhr's Social Ethics," in Kegley, 107. Italics added.

16.   Kegley, 141.

17.   *NDM* II: 254.

18.   Albert Borgmann, *Crossing the Postmodern Divide* (Chicago: University of Chicago Press, 1992): 60.

19.   Daniel Bell, *The End of Ideology* (New York: Macmillan, 1965).

20.   ibid., 333.

21.   *NDM* II: 214.

22.   *ICE*, 124.

23.   John A. Hutchison, ed., *Christian Faith and Social Action* (New York: Scribner's, 1953): 236.

24.   *ICE*, 117.

25.   This was in contrast to some of his friends and colleagues like John Macmurray, Harry F. Ward and others who proposed a kind of Christian Marxist synthesis.

26.   Kegley, 102.

27.   Oliver O'Donovan, "How Can Theology be Moral?" *Journal of Religious Ethics* (Fall 1989): 81f.

28.   Patrick Neal and David Paris, "Liberalism and the Communitarian Critique: A Guide for the Perplexed," *Canadian Journal of Political Science* 23 (1990): 419. See also, Charles H. Reynolds and Ralph V. Norman, eds., *Community in America: The Challenge of Habits of the Heart* (Berkeley: Univ. of California, 1988); and the double issue (1/2) of *Soundings* 59 (1986).

29.   ibid., 424.

30.   ibid., 425ff.

31.   Michael McDonald, "Indian Status: Colonialism or Sexism?" *The Canadian Community Law Journal* (1986): 36ff.

32.   C.B. MacPherson, *The Political Theory of Possessive Individualism* (London: Oxford University Press, 1962): 263.

33.   Reinhold Niebuhr, *The Children of Light and the Children of Darkness* (*CLCD*) (New York: Scribner's, 1941): 50.

34.   Reinhold Niebuhr, *The Self and the Dramas of History* (*SDH*) (New York: Scribner's, 1955): 35.

35.   ibid., 36.

36.   Reinhold Niebuhr, "Coercion, Self-Interest, and Love," in Kenneth E. Boulding, *The Organizational Revolution* (New York: Harper, 1953): 240f.

37.   *SDH*, 165.

38.   Reinhold Niebuhr, *Christian Realism and Political Problems* (New York: Scribner's 1953): 26.

39.   See, e.g., Will Kymlicka, "Liberal Individualism and Liberal Neutrality," *Ethics* 99 (1989): 903.

40.   Michael McDonald, "Should Communities Have Rights? Reflections on Liberal Individualism," *Canadian Journal of Law and Jurisprudence* 4 (1991): 235.

41.   Teresa Rakawske-Harmston, "Ethnicity in the Soviet Union," *Annals of the American Academy of Political and Social Science* 433 (1977): 73f.

42.   *CLCD*, 4.

43.   ibid., 5.

44.   *SDH*, 35.

45.   David Hollenbach, S.J., "The Common Good Revisited," *Theological Studies* 50 (1989): 70; and Douglas Sturm, *Community and Alienation* (Notre Dame, Indiana: University of Notre Dame Press, 1988) are two contemporary efforts to combine these concerns of individual rights and the common good.

46.   Reinhold Niebuhr, *Irony of American History* (New York: Scribner's, 1952): 63.

GERMANY, A DIFFICULT FATHERLAND
Reinhold Niebuhr's German Background

Friedrich Hufendiek

Reinhold Niebuhr was one of the rare figures in the history of Christian theology who was able to bridge the considerable gap between Germanic and Anglo-Saxon religious and political experience. In this paper, I shall locate the primary reason for this unique contribution quite explicitly in the person of his father, Gustav, who left for America from my home city of Bielefeld, Westphalia, in 1881, and who himself seems to have been a rather remarkable and 'original' sort of person. First, however, in order to show that the bridge Reinhold Niebuhr created carried *two-way* traffic, I shall describe something of the impact of his thought on recent German political and social history, as it is manifested in the biographies of some of my country's most progressive political and literary personalities.

NIEBUHR'S INFLUENCE IN POST-WAR GERMAN POLITICAL LIFE

There was a time in my life when I had no difficulties in identifying myself with "the difficult Fatherland." It was in the beginning of the 1970s, when Willy Brandt was Chancellor of the Federal Republic of Germany and Gustav Heinemann its President. The names of these politicians were symbols of freedom and democracy, and of personal integrity in the realm of power and politics. Brandt had been in Norwegian exile during the Nazi period, as a member of the resistance movement. On a visit to Poland in the 1970s he went to a monument in the city of Warsaw, built on the site of the former Jewish ghetto, and fell on his knees in front of all the assembled diplomats. It was a remarkable symbol of reconciliation after the period of the Cold War.

Heinemann had been active in the German *Bekennende Kirche* [Confessing Church]. As a member of the German church council he was responsible, together with other outstanding members of the council, for the text and publication of the *Stuttgarter Schuldbekenntnis*. The "difficult Fatherland" could be proud to have as its President a famous lawyer, the former Minister of Justice, who did more for humanizing the German system of law than anyone previously. The University of Bonn conferred upon him the honourary degree of Doctor of Divinity in December, 1967.

On that occasion, Heinemann delivered a lecture on the subject, "The Constitutional State as a Theological Problem: A Basic Concern for German Protestants."[1] At the end of the lecture, President Heinemann summarized his thoughts on the constitutional state by referring to Reinhold Niebuhr's well-known dictum: "Man's capacity for justice makes democracy possible, but man's inclination to injustice makes democracy necessary." The whole lecture is written in the Niebuhrian spirit. Since it shows that there has been a basic change in the "difficult Fatherland," I would like to refer to it.

President Heinemann pointed out that there has been, as is well known, a close historical link between *Thron und Altar* in the German church — the ideology of a God-given status of government — implying an obvious lack of participation in public affairs on the part of mature citizens. Looking back critically into our history, we recognize the existence of a four-hundred-year-old anti-democratic tradition, especially in the Lutheran territories. Politics in the German perspective has meant "thinking from above," *from* the posture of the authorities *to* that of the subjects, the *Untertanen*. Obedience has been a key word in this arrangement. The Bible was used to reinforce it.

Heinemann pointed to the weakness of the Weimar Constitution. There were no checks against the prospect that, during times of conflict and crisis, the laws of the land could be altered to suit the whims of government. The constitution did not define values and aims; in fact, it has been compared to a bus without any travel plans — it might move off in any direction, depending on its occupants! If the Nazis or the Communists attracted the largest number of travellers, they could change the constitution to suit their own aims, or declare it null and void. The important lack of limits could encourage criminals to use the instrument of the state to give people the impression of legality.

The new constitution is obviously different. The unchangeable basis of the Federal Republic is the dignity of the human being — *"Die Würde des Menschen ist unantastbar.*" The new constitution protects the freedom of the citizen, and the state is safe from the enemies of democracy. Thus Heinemann held up the constitution as a rare opportunity for change in German history. He called passionately for citizen-participation, especially on the part of Christians, in order to ensure the democratic process. In his doctoral lecture at Bonn, he summarized his own position by quoting Niebuhr's *The Children of Light and the Children of Darkness*. The lesson of the famous North American teacher had been heard and understood in the land of his forebears: commitment to democracy is necessary because human beings are sinners, tempted by power.

In addition to Heinemann, it was Chancellor Brandt who made it possible for me to identify with my difficult Fatherland, despite its problems. Born in the Hanseatic city of Lübeck (also the home of Thomas Mann), Brandt, the intelligent journalist and emigrant, who had come back from Norwegian exile, became the mediator between East and West. The Nobel Peace Prize that he received was a symbol of the new Germany that he represented.

It should be recalled that this same Willy Brandt was offered the Reinhold Niebuhr Award in September, 1972. The choice of Brandt was due to "the affinity between Niebuhr's theological ethics and his [Brandt's] political endeavour." The eulogy of the Committee points to Brandt's symbolization of a new mood and direction in Germany. It described him as "the brave rebel against Nazism, the indomitable mayor of the besieged city,...a steadfast champion of the Europeanization of Germany." He is called "the bold Pathfinder in the reconciliation of Europe...carrying forward the spirit of that American friend of the other Germany, Reinhold Niebuhr."[2]

What did Brandt know of Reinhold Niebuhr? The German Chancellor had read some of Tillich's writings: but did he read Niebuhr? The speech that he delivered in Bonn in September of 1972 certainly shows more than a close relationship to Niebuhr's thought. He acknowledged with deep gratitude that the award recognized the affinity between his own political endeavours and the theological ethics of the American thinker: "Niebuhr never ceased to fight arbitrariness and strove to place power in the service of justice," he said. He referred to the analytical writings on the East/West conflict and expressed the view that Niebuhr contributed important principles to guide the churches in their reflections on this difficult subject, especially his 'Christian Realism.' He compared Niebuhr's influence to the German church's memorandum on the eastern territories, the so called *Ostdenkschrift*, which in 1965 became the most important political memorandum of the Protestant Church in post-War Germany. The key sentence of Brandt's address reads: "Wherever the representatives of modern social policy and democratic socialism reflect on the moral foundations of their principles, their thoughts are bound to turn to Reinhold Niebuhr."[3]

When Willy Brandt delivered his first speech to the United Nations as Chancellor of the Federal Republic in September, 1972, he too referred to Niebuhr's dictum — though in a somewhat different formulation: "Man's capacity for reason made the United Nations possible. Man's inclination to irrationality makes the United Nations necessary."[4] In reading this address, one receives a lecture in 'Christian Realism,' noting in particular the "balance of power" concept. The necessity of checks and balances and of world justice as the presupposition of world peace is presented. And one is not surprised when Brandt confesses, "Such thoughts are bound to Reinhold Niebuhr."[5]

Brandt admired the lucid style in which Niebuhr analyzes the problems of the day, giving encouragement to some and inducing reflection in others. In fact, for the German Chancellor Niebuhr's thought seemed fascinating because it was permeated by hope, yet did not indulge in utopianism. "He," said Brandt, "is the master of us all."[6]

In sum, both Heinemann and Brandt, representatives of a new Germany seeking to overcome its problematic past, were able to draw upon this American Christian thinker, whose father had left the "difficult Fatherland," and had initiated his son in some of the lessons that were to be learned from that past. Reinhold Niebuhr learned from his father and, later, from his own experience of the old country some of the most important negative aspects, especially, of his political thought: naive glorification of the state, the dire consequences of personal detachment in religious and academic circles, etc. He was moved after the War to remark that "Germans cannot be trusted for some decades to come."[7] Today, one hopes that enough decades have elapsed that trust may be legitimate. If that is so, the careers of politicians like Brandt and Heinemann have helped to bring it to pass.

"EDUCATING FRITZ"

The movement of Germany towards a more Niebuhrian type of democracy is confirmed by another, more recent event. In 1990, a remarkable Symposium of the Goethe Institute took place in Los Angeles, in co-operation with the University of California. The event was written up in *Die Zeit* under the caption: "Educating Fritz: The Development of Germany from 1945 to the Present, Mirrored in German-American Relations."[8]

The final address in the Symposium was given by Marion, Gräfin Dönhoff, the grand old lady of German journalism. There is no question, Dönhoff avers, that the U.S.A. became the primary model of modern German society in the post-War situation: the open society, tolerance, free discourse, and never-failing optimism and trust in the future — such ideals were greatly admired. Countess Dönhoff recalls that her first visit to America after the collapse of the Third Reich seemed to her a veritable revelation. She felt gratitude and admiration. Soon, Germans were accepted by Americans as partners, and Americans looked to Germany as a kind of "little America" — reliable and economically efficient.

The first generation of post-War German students to go to America were fascinated and inspired by the moral claims of American politics. For the first time in their lives, they were introduced to the great political writers of the 18th Century, including the founding fathers of the U.S.A. They discovered modern writers. And they listened to Robert Hutchins, Paul Tillich, and Reinhold Niebuhr. They returned to Germany full of excitement and expectant with regard to the future. Forty years later, Gräfin Dönhoff notes, it is a different matter. Managers, scientists, and technicians have replaced political and theological students. A new generation of young Germans appear on these shores who know nothing of basic survival, care-packages, and the Marshall Plan; they are interested in business, communications, and technological innovation.

But Dönhoff, in her address, remembers the earlier students. Amongst them was Golo Mann, a famous son of a famous father — Thomas. Golo Mann published a study in 1955 entitled, *"Vom Geist Amerikas: Eine Einführung in amerikanisches Denken und Handeln."*[9] It is a work that gives concrete evidence of his sympathetic and profound understanding of Reinhold Niebuhr. The Americans, he writes, "would be poorer had they not had Reinhold Niebuhr in their midst. You cannot think of America without him. He is an integral part of the image, and he carries the philosophic burden of America's history, of *Zeitkritik* and national self-criticism."

Golo Mann understood the paradox in Niebuhr's anthropology, with its revitalization of the doctrine of sin to struggle against the naivities of liberalism. He analyzed *The Irony of American History*, the experience of ambiguities in all human encounters and achievements, the undercurrent of tragedy in the professedly optimistic society. Niebuhr, Mann felt, liberates humanity from illusions about its own state. But this liberation has kindness in it; it is carried out with *caritas*, in the knowledge that all human achievements are imperfect.[10]

Like Golo Mann and others, I was myself one of the German students who learned about America — and Germany! — from Reinhold Niebuhr. I will never forget the remark of Hans Heinrich Wolf, professor at Bethel Seminary in Bielefeld, after his return from a visit to the United States: "If you want a key to open the door of American theology," he said, "you should study Reinhold and Richard Niebuhr. One is the more prophetic, the other the more academic voice. Listen to both!" The remark was the immediate reason for my decision to study theology at Union Theological Seminary in the mid-1950s. "Educating Fritz" meant, quite literally for me, listening to Reinhold Niebuhr, whose horizon, though American, was inclusive of my "difficult Fatherland."

GUSTAV NIEBUHR: LINK BETWEEN OLD AND NEW

The German roots of Reinhold Niebuhr lie close to my own. The ancestral home is found in the province (*Fürstentum*, or Princedom) of Lippe-Detmold, near the city of Bielefeld and the famous city of the Anabaptists, Münster, Westphalia. A mistake in Niebuhr biographies needs to be corrected. Many writers assume that Reinhold Niebuhr stems from a famous family of German historians.[11] Niebuhr's ancestors were not scholars but farmers. The home of Reinhold's father, Gustav, was a large farm — really, a small manorial estate — in Hardissen near Lage and Lemgo. The estate is still held in the Niebuhr family; its present owner is Klaus Niebuhr, Reinhold's first cousin once removed. Interestingly enough, the parents of Reinhold Niebuhr's mother, Lydia, stem from the nearby county of Tecklenburg.[12]

The little principality of Lippe-Detmold is a traditionally Reformed territory of northern Germany. (Incidentally, Reinhold committed a minor geographical error in his 1962 article on Germany, when he wrote that "The beautiful HOF [farm-estate] in the little principality of Lippe-Detmold, *on the Dutch border...*"[13] In fact, the Dutch border and the Niebuhr farm are separated by about two-hundred kilometers, a not inconsiderable distance in European terms!) In German newspapers one occasionally finds remarks insinuating that the "Regierungsbezirk Ostwestfalen-Lippe" [the present political designation of the region] is "far behind the times." Reinhold Niebuhr told me when I met him in New York in 1955, that his father spoke and read "lower German."

Gustav had received, however, a rather sound education. He had attended the Engelbert-Kampfer-Gymnasium in Lemgo, a small town with Hanseatic traditions, in the neighbourhood of Hardissen. When Gustav left Germany in 1881, he was eighteen years of age and one year short of passing his 'Arbitur,' the final examination and certificate of the German Gymnasium. What did Gustav learn in the province, on the 'Hof,' in the beautiful old Hanseatic town with its then four thousand inhabitants? Of course Hebrew, Greek, Latin, English, and French. The Germans call it "*Klassische Erziehung.*" It proved a solid academic foundation for his later studies in the U.S.A.

Predictably perhaps, there was also a strong-willed father, Friedrich, in the foreground of Gustav's life, a man who dominated the family and the farm like a king. Gustav — as we read in an insightful article on Germany by Reinhold Niebuhr — was inspired to take his momentous decision to emigrate to America on account of his unhappiness with his father and his schoolboy's admiration for one of the father's of American democracy, Abraham Lincoln, who continued to fascinate Gustav throughout his life.[14]

One has to keep the context in mind: it was the time of *Thron und Altar* politics, of monarchy, of Bismarck. Democratic movements and labour parties had been suppressed. Local historical research in Lippe-Detmold, especially in Lemgo, shows that major struggles were taking place in schools, churches, and society at large, between liberals and reactionaries, revivalists and orthodox Christians. Indeed, in this principality a strong democratic movement survived in spite of Bismarck and the "Reich." The name of Lincoln in the biography of Gustav Niebuhr, the patriarch of a great American family, indicates the presence of a democratic spirit at work in this tiny German kingdom. Lemgo was in fact called the centre (*Hauptherd*) of democratic revolution in the country. The German roots of Reinhold Niebuhr should not be analysed only with benefit of ecclesiastical spectacles, therefore. For we see there also the beginnings of the political spirit that matured in Gustav Niebuhr, later the Pastor of Lincoln, Illinois, whose son Reinhold found him "the most interesting man in town."[15]

Gustav Niebuhr did not sever altogether his connections with the fatherland. As Pastor, he studied carefully the achievements of the Inner Mission Movement in Germany. He visited Bethel, a hospital-centre founded by Pastor Friedrich von Bodelschwingh especially for epileptic persons, as well as Kaiserwerth in the Rhineland, centre of the deaconess movement. He also visited the "Rauhe Haus" in Hamburg, a foundation of the famous Johann Hinrich Wichern, with schools and homes for orphans, a kindergarten, hospitals and asylums. These *Innere Mission* projects were largely based on private initiative, rather than being institutions of the official church or the state. The strength of the Inner Mission Movement was its spirit of revivalism, which impelled Christians to take up social causes of this nature. At the same time, the weakness of this German movement was a rather cloying association with reactionary powers, including the monarchy. The Social Democrats referred to the "Rauhe Haus" in Hamburg as a *"Brutanstalt kirchlicher und staatlicher Reaktion."* A certain distrust and distancing from these projects prevailed, therefore, in liberal circles.

Gustav Niebuhr adopted the best elements of the German Inner Mission Movement for his own remarkable foundations in the United States. In the field of Christian care of persons afflicted with epilepsy, he was a pioneer in America. The reactionary and monarchistic associations with which the Movement was inhibited in the old world were, through Gustav Niebuhr's influence, replaced by the spirit of Lincoln.

In fact, the father of Reinhold Niebuhr is one of the best examples one could find of a creative transition between the Germany of that period and the "New World." He contrasts markedly with those German immigrants, of whom there were many in Illinois, who wanted to create a "little Germany" in the midst of the United States of America. This nationalistic trend reveals itself in the fact that Reinhold Niebuhr's first language in his home country was German and not English. Even in High School he still had difficulty with English, such was the power of old world tradition.

But Gustav was another breed. He represents "the courage to change" — a theme fondly traced in the work of his son. Though he learned from "the difficult Fatherland," he translated the good that he found there into the new world context of freedom and responsibility. It was as a human being in whom the two cultures met that Reinhold Niebuhr perceived this first and perhaps most formative teacher —

> Young Reinhold was utterly fascinated by his father. He was thrilled by his sermons, awestruck by his steady stream of high synod officials, who passed through the house....He repeatedly stressed in later recollections that he made up his mind to be a minister [because of his father's impact on his life]. His father's vocation was more interesting, as he explained to an inquiring stranger in 1957, than that of any one else in Lincoln.[16]

Even at the end of his life, Reinhold Niebuhr asked himself whether his work would be acceptable in his father's judgement. A remarkable question!

The story of Gustav Niebuhr is evidence of how deeply rooted was the son in the soil of the *Vaterland,* and how well-versed in its best as well as its worst traditions. After World War II, many Germans were willing to read Reinhold Niebuhr, or listen to him. The "difficult Fatherland" was prepared, in its *kairos-*situation, to study the books of a prophet who, from afar, nevertheless knew something of its soul. Wolfgang Schweitzer, one of the publishers and interpreters of Reinhold Niebuhr's books in Germany, wrote in his foreword to *Pious and Secular America* (1962): "Protestant Christians in Germany have to get to know Niebuhr."[17] This statement still remains true.

NOTES

1.   G.W. Heinemann, "Glaubensfreiheit Bürgerfreiheit Reden und Aufsätze zu Kirche-Staat-Gesellschaft 1945-1975," ed. D. Koch.

2.   From the text of proceedings on the occasion of the award, as contained in a telegram sent by Brandt to Ursula Niebuhr, dated September 27, 1973: 4ff.

3.   ibid.

4.   *Frankfurter Rundschau* (September 27, 1973): 52.

5.   ibid.

6.   ibid.

7.   ibid.

8.   #49 (November 30, 1990): 52.

9.   1955, second edition.

10.   ibid.

11.   See Dietz Lange, *Christlicher Glaube und soziale Probleme: Eine Darstellung der Theologie Reinhold Niebuhrs* (1964): 13. See also William G. Chrystal, *A Father's Mantle: The Legacy of Gustav Niebuhr* (NY: Pilgrim Press, 1982).

12.   In his study of Gustav Niebuhr, Chrystal writes that Reinhold's maternal grandfather, the pastor, Edward Jacob Hosto, was born in Westerkappeln/Westphalia. I did not find any corroboration of this in the church registrations of birth and baptism in either Westerkappeln or Tecklenburg. I also discovered that no one in the town remembers the name, Hosto. Since Westerkappeln is also the home-town of the Niemöller family (the famous pastor and World War I submarine commander, Martin Niemöller is buried there) it can be assumed that the names, Niemöller and Niebuhr have been confused.
    Jacob Hosto and his wife, Clara Kemphafer, deserve special study themselves. Lydia Hosto, their daughter and Reinhold's mother, was one of twelve children. She recalled her father as a good teacher, who taught her to play the organ as well as rudimentary astronomy. He was "a thinker and biblical scholar, who lived his old-fashioned biblical faith," as one of his friends explained, "grieved by the shallowness of present-day theology" (Chrystal, 28).

13.   "Germany," in *Worldview* (June, 1973): 14.

14.   ibid.

15.   Richard W. Fox, *Reinhold Niebuhr* (New York: Pantheon Books, 1985): 11.

16.   ibid.

17.   *Reinhold Niebuhr: Frömmigkeit und Säkularisation* (1962): 5.

REINHOLD NIEBUHR AND JUDAISM

Alan T. Davies

In a late essay, Reinhold Niebuhr spoke of his "long love affair with the Jewish people" — an affair that began in Detroit during his early pastorate in that city when he enlisted local Jewish allies in his struggle for social justice in the fiefdom of the powerful industrialist Henry Ford.[1] Ford, an American folk-hero, drew Niebuhr's wrath because of his proud moral pretensions, and their underlying practical contradictions.[2] The latter's love affair was kindled by a prominent Detroit Jew, Fred M. Butzel, who, according to Niebuhr's biographer Richard Fox, was the first Jew that the young theologian knew intimately.[3] Because of his personal admiration for Butzel's "magnanimity and social shrewdness,"[4] Niebuhr attached these qualities to the Jewish spirit and the Jewish religion for the rest of his life: "The more I make contact with the Jews the more I am impressed with the superior sensitiveness of the Jewish conscience in social problems."[5] Other Jews, such as Justice Louis D. Brandeis, a man who, in Niebuhr's eyes, personified the "Hebraic-prophetic passion for social justice,"[6] confirmed this judgment.

The Jewish capacity for civic virtue became one reason for Niebuhr's later opposition to Christian proselytism. Society, he believed, would be impoverished if it lacked a Jewish presence because Judaism is concerned not so much with individual as with social salvation.[7] Christianity, on the other hand, especially Protestant Christianity, tends to concern itself with individual salvation, and, as a result, has developed a blind eye throughout most of its history with respect to social problems. In his great essay "The Relations of Christians and Jews in Western Civilization" (in my opinion, the most brilliant short statement on this

39

subject ever written by anyone), Niebuhr suggested two sources for Jewish superiority in the social sphere: a spiritual bond with the prophets of classical Israel, and a perennial minority status in the gentile nations.[8] Religious tradition and historical experience combine to give the Jews a creative edge in the struggle for a more humane social order. As a social prophet himself in modern America, Niebuhr depended too much for his own ideas on the great prophets of ancient Israel, whom he constantly cited (especially in his sermons) not to recognize the vitality of their religious legacy in their natural descendants. His appreciation of the Jewish capacity for civic virtue was also assisted by the Social Gospel movement in the American Protestant churches, but the fathers of the Social Gospel themselves owed no small debt to the prophetic tradition.[9] Because the prophets are easily forgotten by Christians — the Social Gospel was a rare exception — and because the church has become accustomed to its majority status in the West, this Jewish contribution is indispensable. Paul Tillich, incidentally, concurred.[10]

Although Niebuhr was well versed in the Hebrew prophets, he was less familiar with rabbinic Judaism, not to mention Jewish mysticism, despite the scholarship of George Foot Moore and Travers Herford.[11] Hence, he was prey to classic misapprehensions about the Pharisees, whom he saw as exemplars of "Hebraic legalism" in conflict with the "prophetic-messianic" religion of Jesus: a familiar dichotomy.[12] As David Seljak has noted, the "gentle chiding" of Abraham Heschel and other Jewish friends persuaded Niebuhr that Jewish thought was more complex than he realized; the ancient sages were also sensitive to the sins of the righteous and the paradoxical aspects of reality.[13] The Talmud, according to Heschel, regards human nature paradoxically — "the greater the man, the greater his evil inclination" — and the Zohar describes the universe in terms of tension, contrast and contradiction.[14] Heschel was correct, and Niebuhr, though still convinced that Christianity measured better the "inner contradictions of the human spirit," took pains to warn Christians not to claim moral superiority on this account, and not to deny the presence of grace in Judaism as well as Christianity.[15] Indeed, he declared, if the two religions are judged by their moral fruits, "the Jewish faith does not fall short, particularly in collective moral achievement."[16] Not the Old Testament prophets only, but also the creative elements in rabbinic theology and practice as nourished and expounded throughout the centuries, are responsible for the Jewish superiority in civic virtue. The religion of law is also a religion of grace.

Niebuhr's praise of Judaism and its "prophetic-dramatic-historical genius" was stimulated by two great modern Jewish thinkers, Franz Rosenzweig and Martin Buber, whom he admired especially.[17] Both Rosenzweig and Buber, in

Niebuhr's view, grasped the divine-human drama more profoundly than most Christian theologians. Rosenzweig drew a distinction between Judaism and Christianity by comparing the two religions to the fire and the rays of the same star — the "star of redemption" — which both separates and unites them.[18] As a native of Germany, moreover, he witnessed the struggle in the soul of the German nation between the Christian and the pagan, or the "man of the cross" and Siegfried, that reached its terrible climax after his own premature death (1929) in the Third Reich.[19] Niebuhr appreciated Rosenzweig's high estimate of Christianity as essentially Hebraic in its faith, criticizing only the notion that nothing divides the two religions except fire and rays.[20] His classification of Rosenzweig among the Hebrew prophets no doubt arose from the latter's protest against idolatry in the modern world: against the "blond and blue-eyed, or dark and small-boned, or brown and dark-eyed" Siegfrieds of the age who never wearied in their attempt to subvert the Jewishness of Jesus by inviting the Christian messiah to join the pantheon of pagan gods.[21] As an American fearful of the excesses of American superpatriotism, and the idolatrous corruption of American Christianity by a collective egotism in which America is cast as "the darling of divine providence,"[22] Niebuhr shared the same sensitivity to the dangerous 'isms' of modernity — particularly nationalism, racism and antisemitism.

Buber's 'I-Thou' philosophy, now out of vogue, was immensely influential in the post-World War II era, affecting both Christians and Jews: indeed, few escaped its shadow.[23] In the case of Niebuhr, the central theme of his book *The Self and the Dramas of History* (that the "self" rather than the "mind" constitutes the divine image in humanity, and that the self is a self in dialogue with itself, with other selves and with God) is obviously Buberian, a fact which the author acknowledged.[24] History is a drama, not a science, because the self is an actor and dialogue entails action, as the two great faiths of Judaism and Christianity founded on Israel's dialogue with God never cease to testify. The dialogical character of history, according to Niebuhr, makes prophecy possible, and prophecy makes the dream of justice possible, and the dream of justice is the gift of Jews and Christians alike — Jews, when they transcend "legalism" and Christians when they transcend "obscurantism" — to the world.[25] Buber was an anti-legalistic Jew, and this attribute appealed to Niebuhr, who remained convinced that classical Judaism can never eradicate entirely its legalistic components, despite its profundity. Why, otherwise, would "genuinely religious" Jews such as Buber have religious and moral problems?[26] Why, otherwise, would the latter inveigh against the "safe and secure ones" who hide behind the "defense-works of the law" for the sake of a spurious spiritual security?[27] Better the "holy insecurity" of those who dare to gaze into "God's abyss"![28] No Christian, declared Niebuhr, can fail to notice Buber's embarrassment. Interestingly, Tillich also drew the conclusion that Buber's anti-legalism — "the commandments are like stars" — only confirms the difficulties posed by the law (*Halakhah*) for conscientious Jews.[29]

In his tribute following Buber's death (in 1965), Niebuhr wrote that the Jewish philosopher had managed to cast light on every human problem except one: the "moral nature of all human collectivities of race, class and nation."[30] Despite his great book on the ancient prophets (*The Prophetic Faith*), and despite his own prophetic spirit, the modern existentialist could not transcend the innate limitations of existentialism in the social and political realm, i.e., the realm of 'I-It' rather than 'I-Thou.' Because the philosophy of existence concerns itself with subjectivity, no version of this distinctive twentieth-century mode of thought, whether Jewish, Christian or secular, is directly relevant to the moral ambiguities of race, class and nation, although every existentialist analysis is indirectly relevant, insofar as basic questions of what it means to be human are involved. Hence Buber's intensely idealistic form of Zionism, premised on Jewish authenticity and spirituality rather than political nationalism, ignored the harsh reality of Jewish-Arab animosity in the Middle East, and the inescapable power politics imposed by the struggle of two peoples over the same territory. "Political choices," according to Niebuhr, "are always more limited than our moral and religious ideas find convenient."[31]

Buber did not understand this truism, and, as a result, his dream of a bi-national state with the Arabs — a state ultimately dependent on an 'I-Thou' relationship between Arabs and Jews — was destined to fail. In fact, his faith in a spiritual Zion rooted in the earth and moulded in the heavens,[32] a Zion without tragedy, made Buber himself in the end almost a tragic figure, when the Israel in which he lived was forced repeatedly to draw the sword in order not to perish by the sword. This irony confirmed Niebuhr's reservations about Buber's social existentialism, and its uselessness in the face of non-existential moral dilemmas arising from collectivities as collectivities rather than as inter-personal thous. Although the Protestant theologian regarded the birth of the Jewish state in 1948 as a "thrilling" event and as "a kind of penance of the world for the awful atrocities committed against the Jews,"[33] he also believed that the "Jewish return into history" (as Emil Fackenheim later described it[34]) exacted a moral price that Judaism was ill-prepared to pay. Power always corrupts, and political states, as impersonal concentrations of power, are poor bearers of noble religious ideals, partly because they cannot avoid the pitfalls of injustice and partly because they breed self-righteous illusions in the form of national myths and ideologies. To return into history is to abandon innocence, and neither Christian America nor Jewish Israel are as pure as American Christians and Zionist Jews generally pretend. Niebuhr was pro-Israel and sympathetic to Zionism, but never a Christian Zionist, i.e., a champion of the special theological and biblical status of the state of Israel and the view that sees the Jews as the 'hinge of history.' His view that Judaism, "so impressively universal in the diaspora, so fruitful in leavening Western civilization," is not "morally safe" when embodied in a nation-state,[35] has not been refuted by the history of the Middle East since his death. The current tensions between "Jewish ethics" and "Israeli power" would not have surprised him, nor the intractable geopolitical issues surrounding the Palestinian question. Were he alive today, I suspect that he would appeal to the civic virtue of the Jews in order to argue on behalf of the Palestinians, while recognizing the impossibility of a perfect solution.

If Niebuhr disapproved of Buber's social existentialism, he approved of his definition of the creative tension between Judaism and Christianity, which he cited often: "Now to the Christian, the Jew is the incomprehensibly obdurate man, who declines to see what has happened; and to the Jew, the Christian is the incomprehensibly daring man, who affirms in an unredeemed world that its redemption has been accomplished."[36] Niebuhr's Christology, which is more biblical than classical, or more Hebraic than Hellenic, fitted into this mould.[37] The Niebuhrian Christ is a Jewish "prophetic-dramatic-historical" figure in whose life, death and resurrection the mysterious drama of human existence finds its final clarification and resolution. Both expected and unexpected, the crucified messiah is a paradox, and as a paradox sheds light on the paradoxical and sinful elements in life itself, which cause us both to yearn for the good and to crucify the good when we encounter it. Such a messiah makes religious (rather than rational) sense, and must be construed in the language of faith rather than the language of reason. Since the "divine *agape*, which stoops to conquer" and the "human *agape*, which rises above history in a sacrifical act" meet paradoxically in Jesus of Nazareth,[38] Christianity makes its daring and paradoxical claim in an apparently unredeemed world that its redemption has been accomplished. Not Greek speculation (or, by extension, Western philosophy) but Hebraic faith is the basis of Christian faith, which, according to Niebuhr (although not Buber[39]), rests on the legacy of the Hebrew prophets.

However defined, the Christ of Christian faith remains a stumbling-block for the Jews, as Paul declared in I Corinthians 1:23–24. Here, the two religions divide, but their division, in Niebuhr's mature view, does not justify Christian attempts to persuade Jews to abandon Judaism in favour of Christianity, a long standing obsession of the church. For one thing, the synagogue has access to

God in its own right, making Judaism approximately equal to Christianity in spite of its ambiguous character as part-nation and part-church. Jews, therefore, can be saved as Jews, regardless of the Johannine warning that to deny the Son is to deny the Father (I John 2:23) and regardless of traditional theology, ancient, mediaeval and modern. This apparent attack on Christian universalism drew the wrath of more conservative Christians, such as the Anglican bishop Stephen Neill.[40] However, Tillich agreed with Niebuhr,[41] and a significant body of Christian opinion has adopted this position. Incidentally, Reinhold credited his brother Richard with being the first Protestant theologian to state unequivocally that Christian missions to the Jews should be forsaken.[42] Because of its strong sense of biblical authority, Protestantism has been more assiduous in promoting Jewish missions than Roman Catholicism in the modern era, especially (in Canada) the Presbyterians and evangelical Anglicans. For this reason, Niebuhr was particularly critical of the World Council of Churches.[43]

To his Rosenzweigian perspective, Niebuhr added a pragmatic argument. Christian missions have been subverted in any case by Christian persecution, especially during the Middle Ages: "Practically nothing can purify the symbol of Christ as the image of God in the imagination of the Jew from the taint with which ages of Christian oppression in the name of Christ have tainted it."[44] His sensitivity to Jewish feelings about Christian evangelization arose not only from the insult to Judaism itself but also from his concern with antisemitism as a persistent problem in Western society. This concern was stirred in his youth by a confrontation with a pious antisemite at a family party in Germany during a visit to his father's home.[45] Curiously, however, in spite of his antipathy to Jew-hatred in all its shapes and forms, Niebuhr, in his battles with Henry Ford, never mentioned, as far as I can discover, this dark aspect of the auto magnate's moral hypocrisy. The pre-eminent American industrialist of the day, Ford was also the pre-eminent American antisemite of the day, publishing (ghost-written) Jew-baiting articles in his newspaper *The Dearborn Independent*, later reprinted in a best-selling book, *The International Jew*. The American folk-hero was as adept in the mass propagation of antisemitism as in the mass production of automobiles. Perhaps this side of Ford seemed more eccentric than sinister before the Nazi era.

In an essay on Niebuhr, A. Roy Eckardt states that America's "greatest political theologian" underestimated the unique role of Christianity in the "metastasis" of antisemitism in Western society,[46] or the transformation of Christian anti-Judaism — the "teaching of contempt"[47] — into modern secular and racial antisemitism, and its widespread dissemination. Since Niebuhr did not study the history of antisemitism as closely as specialists in the field, this criticism is probably sound. It is not likely, however, that, had he done so, he would have agreed with Eckardt's view (later modified) that the "dogma of the resurrection" is the "ideological cancer that helped...to create one Holocaust and will perhaps help to create new ones."[48] Such an attack on the heart of Christianity would not have found favour with a theologian for whom the apostolic belief in the resurrection of the body expressed "the whole genius of the Christian faith."[49] Instead of epitomizing an anti-Jewish supersessionism and triumphalism, Easter reminds the world that life can be fulfilled only beyond itself, and that sin, including the sins of the spirit such as antisemitism, can be overcome only through the hope of this fulfillment.

Niebuhr also did not agree with the view that Christian antisemitism can be nullified by purging Christianity of the deicide myth (i.e., that the Jews are guilty of a cosmic crime). Merely correcting the historical record by shifting the blame for the crucifixion from the Jews to the Romans cannot remove the "chasm between the two faiths."[50] He believed, however, that this chasm could be bridged by mutual understanding and tolerance. Yet, as long as Jews remain Jews and Christians remain Christians, the possibility of misunderstanding and intolerance remains as well. Antisemitism is a temptation that Christians must struggle constantly to resist within themselves, recognizing its historic and ideological roots in the New Testament and ancient sectarianism, and its larger human roots in the "perpetual pride of any majority dealing with any minority."[51] It is on this latter point that Niebuhr was most perceptive. Even if an *adversus Judaeos* tradition had never developed in Christian theology, the dynamics of pride and power would have combined to render the majority community tyrannical to some degree toward the minority simply because majorities do not suffer minorities gladly, no matter how tolerant their professed values. Rather than a "peculiarly Christian problem," therefore, this dimension of antisemitism represents a general human problem, to wit, "the moral capacity of collective man."[52] In their zeal to eradicate theological anti-Judaism in the sacred texts and creeds of Christendom, both post-Holocaust Jewish and Christian critics of the Christian teaching of contempt have been known to forget this insight.

At the same time, it is clear that anti-Judaism, in the form of supersessionism, has warped Christian thought since the first century: a fact that Niebuhr would not have denied. But, in his eyes, the proper relationship between Judaism and Christianity is not supersessionist but dialectical. In a supersessionist relationship, one religion replaces another as truth replaces error; in a dialectical relationship, neither replaces the other, and truth and error are found in both. If Judaism is superior to Christianity with respect to civic virtue, as Niebuhr asserted, Christianity is superior to Judaism with respect to personal virtue — the morality of the *"nth* degree."[53] Neither, however, is *really* superior to the other, and neither must view itself in this light, since the differences between them are only relative, and since triumphalist attitudes produce blindness and fanaticism. Each contains what the other has developed more fully, and, in that sense, they are reciprocal, serving to correct each other even as they contradict each other. In stating that Christianity "raises the moral pinnacle more consistently than Judaism,"[54] Niebuhr was thinking of the radical love-ethic of the Sermon on the Mount with its perfectionist injunction: the "impossible possibility."[55] This love-ethic, which is "vertical" in its impulse for perfection and "horizontal" in its impulse for community, transcends every form of law, whether Jewish or Christian (Niebuhr was frequently critical of Catholic natural law as also prone to rigidity and legalism).[56] Whether or not one accepts this interpretation of *agape* — some Christians do not[57] — Christian ethics and Jewish ethics have diverged occasionally from each other, partly as a result of the New Testament love-commandment and its stress on the outer edges of individual morality. Unlike Christianity, for example, Judaism has never developed a pacifist strain.[58] While Niebuhr rejected pacifist politics, he did see merit in the pacifist witness, as pointing to a transcendent realm of existence above and beyond the "coercion and the inequalities of the political and economic order"[59] — in other words, the Kingdom of God.

Unlike certain later Jewish and Christian theologians, Niebuhr did not draw the mass murder of the European Jews during the Nazi era into the centre of his thought, though he was fully aware of (in his own words) these "awful atrocities." "Holocaust theology," or a concern with the implications of the most terrible crime of the modern age for traditional belief, was born largely after his time. I doubt if he would have agreed with the premise that the Holocaust constitutes a rupture *nonpareil* in the Western consciousness. Yet few thinkers have addressed the problem of sin and evil personified by the killers of Auschwitz with the intellectual acumen demonstrated in Niebuhr's dissection of the human condition. Distrusting ontological thought of the Tillichian variety — it is an error, Niebuhr believed, to locate the "dark ground" of evil in the Godhead itself, making sin a "consequence of the divine nature"[60] — he took his point of departure from the biblical myth of Adam's fall and its parabolic meaning for human existence. Adam falls because the gift of freedom involves him in a profound contradiction; standing "at the juncture of nature and spirit," he is caught between them: he can become neither pure nature nor pure spirit, but must live in their everlasting tension.[61] Ambiguity, therefore, marks our human lot, together with tragedy, since it is impossible for a creature that knows its own creatureliness not to attempt to secure itself against the fate that governs all finite things. Spirit is not content to perish: consequently, Adam grows anxious, seeking a place where he cannot perish, which, of course, he cannot attain because he is Adam and not God. Hence, he falls. His anxiety, however, is not his sin, but merely (in Kierkegaardian terms) its precondition, or the "internal description of the state of temptation."[62] The sin is unbelief, or a refusal to trust God by setting oneself up as God in place of the only true God.

Adam's unbelief also points to a mystery of evil that precedes life itself. Sin rests on sin, and the temptation that leads to the fall reflects a prior disorder in the universe: "Before man fell the devil fell."[63] In the Genesis myth, the devil is depicted as the serpent, or an evil principle in the paradisean garden, who plays the role of tempter. The tempter, however, is also a fallen angel: he is Lucifer, son of the morning, who rebelled against the Most High. Evil, then, is not merely the bad fruit of human sinfulness; it is a dark shadow from a trans-human zone that no theology or philosophy can explain or fathom, and that can only be conceived mythologically. Even Kant, according to Niebuhr, caught a glimpse of this shadow in his doctrine of radical evil, in which he departed from the "moral complacency" of Enlightenment rationalism that otherwise dominates his philosophy.[64] For this reason, Christians can still speak of "original sin" (Niebuhr later regarded his defense of the term as a "pedagogical error"[65]), though not in the literalistic style of an older orthodoxy. Original sin, to Niebuhr, is an existential insight arising from a more profound understanding of human nature than conventional wisdom can achieve. It expresses a strange truth: we are destined to sin, but, since our freedom is never lost, we are responsible for our sins.[66] Our freedom, not our bondage to nature, is the instrument of our fall, and it is here that the tempter lodges his appeal. The sins of the spirit are always more heinous than the sins of the flesh, as the triumph of egotism, self-centredness and the myriad forms of pride in human affairs, is ample evidence.[67] One of these forms — the "pride of power" — leads readily to the kind of savage prometheanism that Nazi Germany, with its "maniacal will-to-power," so perfectly exemplified.[68]

This will-to-power characteristically manifests itself in the language of nation, race and soil. Nationalism, racism and antisemitism are ideological exhibitions of both an individual and collective egotism that, when fused with the might of the modern nation-state, provides a formula for catastrophe, as the twentieth century knows only too well. In Niebuhrian terms, the Holocaust and the related atrocities of the era are the deadly harvest of the "pride of nations" run amuck, or the offspring of original sin in the arena of history. When Niebuhr delivered his Gifford lectures in Edinburgh in 1939, the Final Solution had not really begun, although the "daemonic" nationalism of the Third Reich was evident enough.[69] Yet the lifelong admirer of Judaism and friend of the Jewish people was fully aware of current events in Germany, and their probable climax. "The Nazis," he wrote in 1942, "intend to decimate the Poles and to reduce other peoples to the status of helots; but they are bent upon the extermination of the Jews."[70]

To exterminate a people is the most extreme of evil deeds by any moral criterion. At the same time, the genocidal passions of Nazi Germany are misunderstood if they are assigned to National Socialism alone: "The Nazis... accentuated but they did not create racial pride."[71] Racial pride, and every other form of fanatical homogeneity, arises when the ego of a group — any group — is too insecure to permit social pluralism. This insecurity drives its leaders in dangerous directions, and the masses soon follow. Consequently, according to Niebuhr, one of the great tasks of civilization is to restrain this tendency, employing every stratagem possible to "prompt humility and charity in the life of the majority."[72] Otherwise, Nazi "tribal primitivism," or some version of the same phenomenon, becomes a virtual certainty sooner or later.[73] Hence, it is a serious mistake to imagine that the antisemitic crimes of the Nazi regime were unique to German culture: original sin is universal, and so are its effects.

The universality of original sin, and the mystery of radical evil to which it points, bestows an enigmatic character on life that defies every attempt to interpret the human epic in purely rational terms: "There are...tangents of moral meaning in history; but there are no clear or exact patterns."[74] We must live with this recognition. Faith, however, with its tokens of transfiguration beyond time and space, enables both Jews and Christians to discern the possibility of an ultimate resolution of the antinomies of life, if only in a glass darkly. In the case of Christianity, the symbol of the cross, once again paradoxically, reveals both the scandalous nature of history — the "abyss of meaninglessness" that crucifies goodness — and the divine mercy that saves us from falling into its depths. The crucifixion of the Jews in the twentieth century both confirms the scandal of history and supplies it with a new and more terrible dimension. Who, after Auschwitz, an abyss of meaninglessness deeper than any of its antecedents, can regard history as coherent, rational and intelligible? Evil is evil, and no Christian should be surprised at the diabolical ingenuity and fantastic scope of its inventions. We live in a genocidal world, and the Christian revelation itself points to this fact.

Niebuhr was much admired by many Jews, and exerted no small measure of influence on contemporary Jewish thought in America.[75] At least one modern Jewish theologian, Will Herberg, drew extensively on Niebuhr's ideas in his exposition of Jewish theology, including the doctrine of original sin.[76] Since he was a personal acquaintance of the Protestant theologian, this was not entirely surprising, but original sin with its Pauline and Augustinian connotations is not usually regard as a Jewish idea. To Herberg, as to Niebuhr, its profundity was existential rather than historical, arising from the myth of paradise lost as a myth of the self that has lost its authenticity in the act of existing. To Herberg also, the "dominion of sin" could only be broken by a "power not our own, the power of divine grace," which, however, he conceptualized in Jewish instead of Christian terms.[77] This adaptation of Christian neo-orthodoxy caused some Jewish critics to classify Herberg as a crypto-Christian who was "closer to Luther than to the rabbinic sources."[78] Whether the charge was true or false (Herberg himself believed it to be false), he was convinced that the biblical myth in either Jewish or Christian guise captures the heart of darkness more compellingly than any modern alternative.

Reinhold Niebuhr was a great man. As one of his last students, I recall his warmth and kindness as vividly as I recall his extraordinary intelligence, though I remember him as a wounded giant. He seemed to possess a special fondness for Canadians, and lost no opportunity to praise the 'Dominion of the north.' His Canadian students, in return, saw in him the personification of the best religious and political values of his own nation, and he remains an important reason why I never adopted the fashionable anti-Americanism of many Canadians then and now. Canada is not the United States, and a Canadian theologian cannot employ the same frame of reference as an American theologian, despite the fact that many issues and problems in the two societies are similar. A book on the "irony of Canadian history," for example, would not resemble Niebuhr's study of the irony of American history: the Canadian psyche, as Northrop Frye once declared, is simply too different from the American psyche in too many respects.[79] Reinhold Niebuhr was an American, and much of his writing has an American flavour, though his central theological insights cross all borders.

On the subject of Jews and Judaism, his theology is no less relevant to Jewish-Christian relations in Canada as in the United States, since the two religions are constant and since their social equilibrium is also constant, to wit, a Christian majority and a Jewish minority. The lack of an American-style civil religion in Canada, however, probably serves to create a greater distance between the Christian (largely Roman Catholic) majority and the Jewish minority, since Protestants, Catholics and Jews are not perceived as religious variations on a larger national "religion." Moreover, because of its relative size, Canadian Jewry does not possess the same degree of political influence in public affairs as American Jewry: a fact that has affected Canadian foreign policy in the Middle East and the issue of Nazi war crimes tribunals in Canada. Yet the same Jewish capacity for civic virtue that Niebuhr detected in Fred Butzel and Louis Brandeis were present in certain prominent Canadian Jews of the same era, notably the late Senator David Croll of Ontario: a man whom the American theologian surely would have admired equally. Canada never provided a forum for an antisemite as popular as Henry Ford or Father Charles Coughlin (actually, Coughlin was born and educated in Canada), but one should not forget such figures as Adrien Arcand in Quebec, and, more recently, Ernst Zündel in Ontario and James Keegstra in Alberta. Nor should Canadians forget that antisemitism has older roots in Canadian society; Goldwin Smith, for example, the much admired intellectual guru of the late Victorian era who fascinated the young William Lyon Mackenzie King, was an antisemite of no minor proportions.[80] Niebuhr, therefore, would have found abundant evidence of original sin in Canadian history, and its tribalistic configurations, had he concentrated his gaze in a northward direction.

I close with a personal memoir. Jews, Niebuhr once said in his class on the history of Christian ethics, always assume that the more pious Christians are, the more antisemitic they are likely to be. It was this comment, as much as anything else, that forced me to examine the religious convictions of my life in a new light, and that determined so much of my subsequent vocation.

NOTES

1.   Reinhold Niebuhr, *Man's Nature and His Communities: Essays on the Dynamics and Enigmas of Man's Personal and Social Existence (MNHC)* (New York: Charles Scribner's Sons, 1965): 19.

2.   Cf. Niebuhr, *Leaves From the Notebook of a Tamed Cynic (LNTC)* (New York: Meridian Books, 1957): 180–181; also "How Philanthropic Is Henry Ford?" and "Ford's Five-Day Week Shrinks," republished in *Love and Justice: Selections from the Shorter Writings of Reinhold Niebuhr*, D.B. Robertson (ed.) (Philadelphia: Westminster Press, 1957): 98–108.

3.   Richard Fox, *Reinhold Niebuhr: A Biography* (New York: Pantheon Books, 1985): 93.

4.   *MNHC*, 19.

5.   *LNTC*, 214.

6.   Niebuhr, "Jews After the War," *Love and Justice*, 138. Hereafter "Jews."

7.   ibid., 215.

8.   Niebuhr, "The Relations of Christians and Jews in Western Civilization," *Pious and Secular America* (New York: Charles Scribner's Sons, 1958): 91–94. Hereafter "Relations."

9.   *MNHC*, 17.

10.   Cf. Paul Tillich, "The Struggle Between Time and Space," *Theology of Culture* (New York: Oxford University Press, 1959): especially 38–39.

11.   George Foot Moore, *Judaism in the First Centuries of the Christian Era: The Age of the Tannaim* (1927); Travers Herford, *The Pharisees* (1924). I can find no mention of these works in Niebuhr's major writings.

12.   Niebuhr, *The Nature and Destiny of Man (NDM)* (New York: Charles Scribner's Sons, 1941): II: 39–41.

13.   David Seljak, "The Dialectical Nature of Reinhold Niebuhr's Approach to the Jews," unpublished paper, McGill University, 1987.

14.   Abraham Heschel, "A Hebrew Evaluation of Reinhold Niebuhr," in *Reinhold Niebuhr: His Religious, Social, and Political Thought*, ed. Charles W. Kegley & Robert W. Bretall (New York: Macmillan, 1956): 406 and 400.

15.   Niebuhr, "Relations," 106–107.

16.   ibid., 107.

17.   Niebuhr, *The Self and the Dramas of History (SDH)* (New York: Charles Scribner's Sons, 1955): 88.

18.   "Before God...Jew and Christian both labor at the same task. He cannot dispense with either. He has set enmity between the two for all time, and withal has most intimately bound each to each. To us [Jews] he gave eternal life by kindling the fire of the Star of his truth in our hearts. The [the Christians] he set on the eternal way by causing them to pursue the rays of that Star of his truth for all time unto the eternal end. We [Jews] thus espy in our hearts the true image of the truth, yet on the other hand we turn our backs on temporal life, and the life of the times turns away from us. They [the Christians], for their part, run after the current of time, but the truth remains at their back; though led by it, since they follow its rays, they do not see it with their eyes. The truth, the whole truth, thus belongs neither to them nor to us. For we too, though we bear it within us, must for that very reason first immerse our glance into our own interior if we would see it, and there, while we see the Star, we do not see — the rays. And the whole truth would demand not only seeing its light but also what was illuminated by it. They [the Christians], however, are in any event already destined for all time to see what is illuminated, and not the light." Franz Rosenzweig, *The Star of Redemption*, trans. William W. Hallo (Boston: Beacon Press, 1964): 415f.

19.   ibid., 329.

20.   Niebuhr, "Relations," 108.

21.   Rosenzweig, loc. cit.

22.   Niebuhr, *The Irony of American History* (New York: Charles Scribner's Sons, 1952): 70.

23.   Cf. Maurice S. Friedman, *Martin Buber: The Life of Dialogue* (New York: Harper Torchbooks, 1960): 268.

24.   Niebuhr, *SDH*, ix.

25.   ibid., 88.

26.   Niebuhr, "Relations," 104.

27.   Buber, cited in Friedman, op. cit., 262.

28.   ibid.

29.   Cf. D. Mackenzie Brown, *Ultimate Concern: Tillich in Dialogue* (New York: Harper & Row, 1965): 113–114.

30.   Niebuhr, "Martin Buber: 1878–1965," *Christianity and Crisis* 25 #12 (1965): 146.

31.   Niebuhr, "Relations," 110.

32.   Martin Buber, "Zion and Other National Concepts," *The Writings of Martin Buber*, ed. Will Herberg (New York: Meridian Books, 1956): 304.

33.   Niebuhr, "Relations," 109.

34.   Cf. Emil L. Fackenheim, *The Jewish Return into History: Reflections in the Age of Auschwitz and a New Jerusalem* (New York: Schocken Books, 1978).

35.   Niebuhr, "Relations," 108.

36.   Buber, "The Two Foci of the Jewish Soul," cited in Herberg, op. cit., 276.

37.   Ronald H. Stone, *Reinhold Niebuhr: Prophet to Politicians* (Nashville: Abingdon Press, 1972): 47.

38.   Niebuhr, *NDM* (New York: Charles Scribner's Sons, 1949): II: 71.

39.   Cf. Martin Buber, *Two Types of Faith*, trans. Norman P. Goldhawk (London: Routledge & Kegan Paul, 1951). Needless to say, Niebuhr did not agree with Buber's analysis of Jewish and Christian faith in this polemical and even anti-Christian writing.

40.   Stephen Neill, *Christian Faith and Other Faiths: The Christian Dialogue with Other Religions* (London: Oxford University Press, 1961): 27–28.

41.   Brown, op. cit., 104.

42.   Reinhold Niebuhr, "The Unsolved Religious Problem in Christian-Jewish Relations," *Christianity and Crisis* 26 #21 (1966): 282. Hereafter "Unsolved."

43.   ibid., 282–283.

44.   Niebuhr, "Relations," 108.

45. Cf. Fox, op. cit., 81.

46. A. Roy Eckardt, *Your People, My People: The Meeting of Jews and Christians* (New York: Quadrangle, 1974): 201.

47. Jules Isaac, *The Teaching of Contempt: Christian Roots of Anti-Semitism*, trans. Helen Weaver (Toronto: McGraw-Hill, 1965).

48. A. Roy Eckardt, "Covenant-Resurrection-Holocaust," *Humanizing America: A Post-Holocaust Perspective*, Second Philadelphia Conference on the Holocaust, February 16–18, 1977, page 44. See also A. Roy Eckardt & Alice L. Eckardt, *Long Night's Journey into Day: Life and Faith After the Holocaust* (Detroit: Wayne State University Press, 1982).

49. Niebuhr, "The Fulfilment of Life," *Beyond Tragedy: Essays on the Christian Interpretation of History* (New York: Charles Scribner's Sons, 1937): 290.

50. Niebuhr, "Unsolved," 280.

51. Niebuhr, "Relations," 87.

52. ibid.

53. ibid., 103.

54. ibid.

55. Niebuhr, *An Interpretation of Christian Ethics* (New York: Meridian Books, 1956), passim.

56. Niebuhr, "Love and Law in Protestantism and Catholicism," *Christian Realism and Political Problems* (New York: Charles Scribner's Sons, 1958): 154–157.

57. Cf. Daniel D. Williams, "Niebuhr and Liberalism," Kegley and Bretall, op. cit., 210–212.

58. In Jewish thought, pacifism seems to be regarded as a pious sin.

59. Niebuhr, *Reflections on the End of an Era* (New York: Charles Scribner's Sons, 1934): 112.

60. Niebuhr, *NDM* I: 254, footnote 4. Niebuhr was thinking of Jacob Böhme and Friedrich Schelling, both mentors of Tillich.

61. ibid., 181.

62. ibid., 182.

63. ibid., 180.

64. ibid., 120, footnote 12.

65. Niebuhr, *MNHC*, 23.

66.   ibid., 263.

67.   ibid.

68.   "In modern international life Great Britain with its too strong a sense of security...and Germany with its maniacal will-to-power, are perfect symbols of the different forms which pride takes among the established and the advancing social forces. The inner stability and eternal security of Great Britain has been of such long duration that she may be said to have committed the sin of Babylon and declared, 'I shall be no widow and I shall never know sorrow.' Germany on the other hand suffered from an accentuated form of inferiority long before her defeat in the World War. Her boundless contemporary self-assertion which literally transgresses all bounds previously known in religion, culture and law is a very accentuated form of the power impulse which betrays a marked inner insecurity" (ibid., 189 (footnote 7)).

69.   ibid., 219.

70.   Niebuhr, "Jews," 133.

71.   Niebuhr, *The Children of Light and the Children of Darkness: A Vindication of Democracy and a Critique of its Traditional Defense* (New York: Charles Scribner's Sons, 1944): 142.

72.   ibid., 143.

73.   Niebuhr, "Jews," 135.

74.   Niebuhr, *Faith and History: A Comparison of Christian and Modern Views of History* (New York: Charles Scribner's Sons, 1949): 132.

75.   Cf. R.G. Goldy, *The Emergence of Jewish Theology in America* (Bloomington: Indiana University Press, 1990).

76.   Will Herberg, *Judaism and Modern Man; An Interpretation of Jewish Religion* (New York: Meridian Books, 1959): 77.

77.   ibid.

78.   Cf. Emil Fackenheim, *Encounters Between Judaism and Modern Philosophy: A Preface to Future Jewish Thought* (New York: Basic Books, 1973): 184.

79.   Northrop Frye, "Canada's Emerging Identity," *Toronto Star* (June 28, 1980): B1.

80.   See Gerald Tulchinsky's essay on Goldwin Smith in my edited volume, *Antisemitism in Canada: History and Interpretation* (Waterloo, ON: Wilfrid Laurier University Press, 1992): 67–91.

BEING HUMAN BEFORE GOD
Reinhold Niebuhr in Feminist Mirrors

Aurelia Takacs Fule

INTRODUCTION

Human beings, our nature and communities are ongoing puzzles, mysteries, surprises. No wonder that some of our greatest achievements have been thoughts, theories, systems, portrayals of human beings and human nature. For Reinhold Niebuhr, the human being remained forever interesting. In Niebuhr's view the Christian faith understands the human being as created in the image of God, endowed with freedom and capacity for self-transcendence.

The human, being weak — dependent, finite, a part of creation imbedded in nature — is a unity of God-likeness and creatureliness. Both of these are present at the height of spirituality and in the humblest aspect of natural life. The evil in the human being is not the consequence of finiteness but of our refusal to admit our finiteness and to acknowledge ourselves as merely "members of a total unity of life."[1]

The majesty and the misery, the greatness and the nothingness, the farsightedness and the blindness of human beings is always before Niebuhr. He repeatedly speaks of the insignificance of the creature, involved and limited by nature and time, yet "lifted into significance by the mercy and power of God."[2] Niebuhr's treatment of the human being as an individual has been at times misinterpreted. He quotes Kierkegaard with agreement: "The paradox of faith is this, that the individual is higher than the universal, that the individual determines his relation to the universal by his relation to the absolute, not his

55

relation to the absolute by his relation to the universal."[3] Being higher than the universal does not isolate the individual. The human being by nature is social and "cannot fulfill his life within himself but only in responsible and mutual relations with his fellows."[4] Niebuhr affirmed: "The law of his nature is love, a harmonious relation of life to life in obedience to the divine center and source of his life. This law is violated when man seeks to make himself the center and source of his own life."[5]

The essence of human being is freedom. Sin is committed in that freedom. Evil is seen at the center of the human personality, in the will, in the human being's refusal to acknowledge his finitude. On a still deeper level, sin is the willful replacement of God with the self at the center of existence. This is pride. Finite and free, involved in the natural contingencies of life, we human beings try to overcome the contradictions of finitude and freedom, and either deny our finitude or hide our freedom insisting we are only creatures. To the latter, Niebuhr applies the term *sensuality*. Sensuality is always more than a natural impulse: "It always betrays some aspect of his abortive effort to solve the problem of finiteness and freedom."[6]

The moral and social dimension of sin is injustice — "The ego which falsely makes itself the center of existence in its pride....inevitably subordinates other life to its will..."[7] Particular sins have social sources and social consequences. Most of Niebuhr's attention was directed to the social consequences. Yet the essence of sin Niebuhr finds "only in the vertical dimension of the soul's relation to God."[8] The confession: "Against thee, thee only, have I sinned"[9] flows from the insight that God is the only judge of the soul.

The Cross of Christ is the assurance that judgement is not the final word of God to human beings: "There is resource in the heart of the Divine" to overcome the tragic character of life and "cure as well as punish"[10] sinful pride. In the Christian proclamation: "The life and death of Christ become the revelation of God's character...The good news of the gospel is that God takes the sinfulness of man into Himself; and overcomes in His own heart what cannot be overcome in human life, since human life remains within the vicious circle of sinful self-glorification on every level of moral advance."[11]

FEMINIST MIRRORS

The last book that Niebuhr wrote, *Man's Nature and His Communities*, was published in 1965. But his writings are republished and some of his sermons and his letters were published posthumously by Ursula M. Niebuhr. His influence is still so greatly felt that in the last three decades a number of feminists have criticized his theology. Some of the criticism raises legitimate questions, some merely indicates less than careful reading. Every criticism reminds us that we live in a world significantly different from Niebuhr's. Inclusive language, used in worship and publishing alike, may be a symbol of the change that took place in the last three decades.

Inclusive language is also relevant to our theme. It would be a mammoth yet futile undertaking to change the language Niebuhr used. From his first to his last work, he used "man" as a generic term. Since then a sufficiently large number of people in the English speaking world, primarily women, but also men, have agreed that "man" indicates male person. The major challenge of feminist theologians to Niebuhr is whether his doctrine of man excludes the experience of women.

The "experience of women" points to another change. While there has always been an element of human experience, acknowledged or not in Christian theology, an element intentionally used and noted by Niebuhr, feminist theologians give far greater weight to experience in theology than previous thinkers or schools have done. Feminists insist that "the experience of being female is significantly different from the experience of being male...that the experience of women is basic to a full understanding of what it means to be human..."[12] Some consider culture and the process of growth and development the key factors shaping masculinity and femininity, others argue that femininity and masculinity are "given" at birth.

Theology is filtered through the theologians' own human — until now mostly male — experience. When feminists consider women's experience as both the starting point and authentication of theology, experience receives added weight. Therefore, we need to look at experience with sharpened attention and ask questions hitherto not asked. We need to examine *whose* experience is described? Western? Middle class? In an industrialized or developing society? In traditional or secular society? Experience of single or married women? Of heads of family? What kind of experience? Some feminists[13] distinguish between women's *feminist* experience (liberation itself) and women's *traditional* experience (marriage and motherhood), though marriage and motherhood have been distorted by patriarchy. Other feminists consider "women's experience" a composite of what has been expected of women, i.e., the cultural and psychological role description, and the ways in which women have experienced themselves. At the initial stage of the movement for women's rights women stressed the similarity of women and men. To have the same rights to vote, own property, inherit and bequeath, or to engage in traditionally male occupations in church, state or business, women spoke of the common humanity of women and men. At a later stage women began to speak of the differences. Feminist theologians criticizing Reinhold Niebuhr's understanding of sin are an example of this.

Feminist theologies are many and diverse. They have in common with liberation theologies the stress on experience/context and the demand for liberation. The variety of feminist theologies will soon exceed the number of so-called liberation theologies. Women the world over are demanding, organizing and working for their liberation in remote rural areas and metropolitan centers. Their social, religious, political and economic settings differ as does their experience as women and their concept of liberation. While there is significant discussion among feminist theologians and ethicists on the meaning of sin and evil, and to a lesser extent on the atonement, the present task is to consider the work of those who directly address the writings of Reinhold Niebuhr.

FEMINIST REFLECTIONS ON SOCIAL ETHICS

Feminists are critical of Reinhold Niebuhr mainly in two areas: social ethics/social theory and the doctrine of sin. In both cases the dissatisfaction is rooted in some feminists' disagreement with Niebuhr's understanding of human nature, which is basic to his thinking. We will glance at the criticism of his social ethics only, as it touches his anthropology, which is considered by his feminist critics to be dualistic, individualistic and pessimistic.

Beverly Wildung Harrison is Professor of Christian Social Ethics at Union Theological Seminary in New York, in Niebuhr's own institution and department. In a paper on "Sexism and the Language of Christian Ethics" she writes:

> ...Reinhold Niebuhr gained a following for predicating his entire social ethical approach on a presumed discontinuity between the dynamics of power...in social, economic, and political life and the dynamics of power in interpersonal interactions, in face-to-face groups like the family. Niebuhr romanticized the family...He never questioned the dualism embedded in liberal political ideology between the "private" sphere, that is, the arena of those interpersonal, humane relations of the family, and the "public" sphere, those "impersonal relations" of institutions and collectivities. He did not notice that this private/public split legitimized both a capitalist mode of political-economic organization and female subjugation in personal or domestic life...He celebrated "sacrifice" as a characteristic in which he thought women excelled, and downgraded "mere" mutuality. Niebuhr was [a] prototypical liberal male chauvinist.
> Gender dualism and male supremacy condition the strongly dualistic and hierarchical character of much Christian ethics...There is *agape*...and there is *eros*...We are taught that these are fundamentally different and unrelated forms

of love and that they are in conflict...Self-assertion and self-denial are portrayed....as irreconcilable modes of being in the world.[14]

Over against Niebuhr's distinction, which Harrison deems a "presumed discontinuity" between the private and the social sphere, she points to the goal in the public sphere: "What feminists demand, in terms of transcending hierarchy and correcting inequities of power and accountability, is seen as 'unrealistic,' an effort to bring personal values into the 'impersonal' social sphere."[15]

In another essay in the same volume, "The Role of Social Theory in Religious Social Ethics," Harrison discusses the intellectual legacy of Reinhold Niebuhr in this area, a legacy she defines as "antiradical." Niebuhr's political realism bequeathed us an "ahistorical treatment of power" and a social theory characterized by a "total inability to focus the role of economic activity in society." We are left also with Niebuhr's "ongoing polemic, even diatribe, against Marx and Marxist social theory."[16] Harrison is "convinced that we must learn to treat his evaluation of Marxist social theory both as misinformed and substantively inaccurate." Harrison "concluded that he [Niebuhr] seriously misread Marx."[17]

Judith Vaughan, gave special attention to Niebuhr in her dissertation, *Sociality, Ethics and Social Change: A Critical Appraisal of Reinhold Niebuhr's Ethics in the Light of Rosemary Radford Ruether's Works*. The following quotation will introduce the problem she finds in Niebuhr in the light of Ruether:

> Niebuhr's ethical system, like his anthropology, is an expression of false consciousness which supports the very system he wants to change. The vertical and horizontal discussion, the two moralities, the two norms, the notions of sin and salvation all foster an awareness of individuals as separate and apart from others, and deny the power and responsibility that *persons-in-relation* have for creating a new humanity and a fundamentally different society in history.[18]

Vaughan contrasts this with Ruether's work: "In the ethical system based on essential sociality, sin, or the failure to transform conditions of alienation into those of communion, is of two types: the refusal to relinquish power and the refusal to claim power."[19] Although it is close to Niebuhr's will-to-power and sensuality, the roots do not go as deep; the goal, similar to Harrison's, is possible to reach: "Sin is relational, structural and personal....As alienation is overcome and a new way of being human and living together is won, sin is overcome and salvation realized."[20] And, "salvific moments are those in which alienation and oppression are overcome and relationships of mutuality and shared power are formed."[21]

In these brief selections from Harrison's and Vaughan's work we sample the thought of social ethicists whose view of human nature is not radically encumbered by sin. They reject Niebuhr's theme in *Moral Man and Immoral Society*, that collective self-regard of a group, be it class, race or nation, is far stronger and more persistent than the egoism of individuals. Without the burden of individual sin and collective egoism, they often pursue utopian visions. Niebuhr's description and comments on such visions should be recalled. One form of Messianism developed, he wrote,

> ...among the victims of early industrialism. It hoped for the kingdom of perfect justice...when the disinherited poor...would take the leap which would transform history....But we must observe that when the "poor" are blessed with historical success and acquire the power of a commissar...he does not usher in the kingdom of righteousness, but merely presides over a despotism....Evidently history solves no problems without creating new ones.[22]

FEMINIST EXPERIENCE

We will now turn to the concentrated argument which some feminist theologians aim at Niebuhr's doctrine of sin. I will consider the writings of four women, three briefly, the fourth at greater length.

While teaching at Hobart and William Smith College, Valerie Saiving published her essay, "The Human Situation: A Feminine View" in 1960 in *The Journal of Religion* and it became a trail blazer. The trail is still frequented.

Susan Nelson Dunfee of Pittsburgh Theological Seminary joined the discussion with her article "The Sin of Hiding: A Feminist Critique of Reinhold Niebuhr's Account of the Sin of Pride" and continued it in her dissertation, *Beyond Servanthood: Christianity and the Liberation of Women*.

Daphne Hampson, a British theologian, trained in her own country as well as the U.S.A., teaches in England. Her article "Reinhold Niebuhr on Sin: A Critique" is published in a collection of essays presented at a conference entitled "Reinhold Niebuhr and the Issues of Our Time" held at King's College, London in 1984.

Judith Plaskow, in her dissertation *Sex, Sin and Grace: Women's Experience and the Theologies of Reinhold Niebuhr and Paul Tillich*, presented at length "women's experience" and "women's sin," hence our special attention to her. "Women's sin" is seen by Plaskow as the "failure to take responsibility for self-actualization."[23] She "focuses...on the cultural factors shaping feminine personality."[24] Her definition of "women's experience" is the interrelation between cultural expectations and their internalization. Her analysis of "women's experience" is based on women depicted in contemporary novels, primarily in Doris Lessing's five volume *The Children of Violence*. With different novels, one would come to different conclusions, but Plaskow is free to select the novelist.

Plaskow's thesis is that since women's experiences "are continually shaped and formed by social expectations" that "present themselves as 'natural' and 'proper'...they predispose women to certain life patterns."[25] Plaskow first surveys major psychological schools that in her view contributed to the shaping of "women's experience." She then describes a woman, Martha Quest, who exhibits "women's experience." The issue is around the self and freedom. Martha Quest is the woman through whose experience Doris Lessing "painfully and perceptively charts the life history of the modern woman."[26] The story starts in the late 1930's and covers three decades. It is Martha's journey from an African farm to London, and from youth into maturity.

A week before matriculating from high school Martha develops pink eye and does not take the examination. She fails to take responsibility and begins drifting. Martha drifts into a relationship, then into marriage and motherhood. At one point she determines to leave her husband and daughter. In Plaskow's view, this may be the first real decision of Martha. Being free, Martha chooses to be a communist. Soon she drifts into a second marriage, then, estranged from her husband, falls in love and begins an affair with Thomas. Time does not permit us to follow "Martha's explorations of non-ordinary experiences" that Plaskow refers to as "experiences of transcendence."[27] These are in part experiences of union with nature, in part a taste of what Niebuhr calls the human capacity for self-transcendence.

The fifth and last volume of *The Children of Violence* finds Martha in London, "to explore further boundaries of special awareness," but she first needs to work through her past experiences "integrating the years of foolish, careless drifting."[28] She takes a job as secretary to a writer, moves into his home for a few months, and stays for twenty years. She becomes "a focal point for people and events around her." She takes "increasing responsibility for running the household." Martha, "who felt she had to leave her own daughter...become[s] the mother of a whole house of children."[29] She defines and integrates her own past self, explores her non-ordinary experiences and returns once again to the everyday. Plaskow says: "She now becomes an individual...She no longer drifts....She accepts fully the challenges and responsibilities..."[30]

Plaskow finds in Martha a certain kind of "women's experience" portraying women to whom Reinhold Niebuhr's doctrine of sin as pride and the ultimate norm of Christian life as self-giving, sacrificial love is irrelevant and hurtful because

> Martha's behavior cannot be subsumed under the category of pride...cannot be seen as the product of over-glorification of the self, for the problem is precisely that she has no self; she has not yet become a self and will not take the responsibility for becoming one. Her form of sin must be comprehended in its own terms, and that means it must be seen to have its own roots in human nature, independent of pride.[31]

These conclusions raise many issues. First, does the phrase "its own roots in human nature" come too close to positing sin in human nature? Second, do these considerations shift from the field of ethics to psychology, to sociology, to counseling? Third, would Martha be helped more by therapy than by theology? Fourth, is Martha acting voluntarily in a way germane to theological and ethical questions? Fifth, is she perhaps so fenced in by "cultural expectations" that she is not a free agent?

This is one side of the picture, but we note that Martha, who drifts, also makes decisions. She chooses not to matriculate, to leave her husband and daughter, "chooses to be a communist"[32] and begins her relationship with Thomas "...out of a need for someone who will make her what she knows she could be."[33] She not only makes choices, she makes them with reference to her felt need, even "using" someone, Thomas, to her own end. Did she choose to drift?

Plaskow also notes this other side to Martha's drifting; she cites Simone de Beauvoir with approval:

> She suggests that the failure of women ever to rebel against their lot is partially explained by certain advantages which accrue to them from their status as Other. The most obvious advantages are material ones; as long as they depend on men, women are spared the difficulty of providing for their physical comfort. But more significant, the Otherness of women also enables them to evade the necessity of having to justify and give meaning to their own lives. "Along with the ethical urge of each individual to affirm his subjective existence," as de Beauvoir says, "there is also the temptation to forgo liberty and become a thing."[34]

There are similar voices elsewhere. Susan Nelson Dunfee writes in her dissertation, *Beyond Servanthood*:

> In needing to please others women are led into conflict with our deeper need to please and name ourselves.
> The freedom to name herself is not only a freedom, it is also a risk...to choose for herself is to risk the possibility of failure, poor choice, mistake....But, in choosing the "safe option" women run the risk of not exercising our freedom,

and worse yet, we risk losing the very freedom to "dare to affirm" ourselves as subjects.[35]

Plaskow concludes: "The *imposition* of the status of Other upon women represents the external dimension of their predicament. Insofar as women accept this status for its rewards and welcome relief from the burden of freedom, they are guilty of complicity in their own oppression; they sin."[36] Since women internalize society's view of themselves, their freedom is diminished. "It would not be surprising...if sensuality and not pride were the primary female sin," says Plaskow.[37]

FEMINIST REFLECTION ON REINHOLD NIEBUHR

The first and basic charge of these feminist theologians is that Niebuhr's understanding of human nature and his doctrine of sin *are based exclusively on male experience*. Every concept Niebuhr uses they say addresses men, not women. To say that "sin is pride," that it is "man's rebellion against God," and that man "seeks to make himself the center and source of his own life,"[38] that "our inclination is to abuse our freedom, overestimate our power and significance," is the "primal sin"[39] speaks to men only. To say that "human life remains within the vicious circle of sinful self-glorification"[40] and that "the religious dimension of sin is rebellion against God...the moral dimension of sin is injustice"[41] is to overlook the experience of women according, to the theologians we are considering.

The views Saiving criticizes, she believes, "receive their most uncompromising expression in the writings of Anders Nygren and Reinhold Niebuhr," who represent "the tendency in contemporary theology to describe man's predicament as rising from his separateness and the anxiety occasioned by it and to identify sin with self-assertion."[42] It is not that women do not experience anxiety: they do. But their response is not pride and self-assertion, but fragmentation, dependence on others, even negation of the self. Such significant differences between masculine and feminine experience have been disregarded by theologians. She quotes Margaret Mead's question: Are there real differences, besides the "anatomical and physical ones but just as biologically based?"[43] Saiving assumes there are. Although not all feminists agree fully with this view, one hears echoes of her charge by many feminists. Saiving made explicit what some women have only vaguely felt. This is what we hear:

...the specifically feminine forms of sin....are better suggested by such items as triviality, distractibility and diffuseness; lack of organizing center or focus; dependence on others for one's own self-definition; tolerance at the expense of standards of excellence; inability to respect the boundaries of privacy; sentimentality; gossipy sociality, and mistrust of reason in short, underdevelopment or negation of the self.[44]

To some of us, this does not seem like a list for the confessional. Our response is more like: what a pity, what a waste. These are not sins, let alone sin as described in the Genesis story. Hampson writes: "My criticism is of Niebuhr's equation of male with human."[45] Plaskow concurs: "Niebuhr and Nygren...are guilty of identifying this important but limited male perspective with universal truth."[46] This theology "...insofar as it focuses on the sin of pride...neglects women's experience"[47] and Niebuhr's "...insistence on the primacy of pride is unfaithful and irrelevant to much of women's (and therefore, human) experience."[48]

The second charge levelled by these critics is that Niebuhr does not develop fully his concept of sin as sensuality. "Subordinating sensuality" to the primary sin of pride is problematic. Niebuhr has no doubt that "Biblical religion defines sin as primarily pride and self love."[49] The story of the Fall is a living, directing myth for Niebuhr: "The myth accurately symbolizes the consistent Biblical diagnosis of moral and historical evil,"[50] and suggests "that false pride lies at the foundation of human sin. Man sought to penetrate to the final mystery of the tree,"[51] then built the Tower of Babel, "whose top may reach unto heaven."[52] Niebuhr sees a persistent and universal self-regard in human beings that corresponds to the story of the Fall. The main line of the Christian tradition is in agreement with him. Only on its Hellenistic side is Christianity tempted to regard sin as lust and sensuality.

The human being is free and bound, limited and limitless. Seeking to solve the problem of the contradiction of finitude and freedom, the human being either denies the contingent character of his existence through pride and self-love; or escapes his freedom in sensuality. Sensuality is hiding one's freedom, and losing oneself in some aspect of natural vitalities. It is "an escape from the freedom and infinite possibilities of the spirit by becoming lost in detailed processes...and interests of existence." Niebuhr quotes Aquinas' contention that sensuality is "turning inordinately to mutable good." Inordinate love for mutable values is a result of "the primal love of self, rather than love of God."[53]

Christian theology, in both its Augustinian and Thomistic forms, regards sensuality as a derivative of the more primal sin of self-love. Sensuality represents a further confusion consequent upon the original confusion of substituting the self for God as the center of existence.[54] Niebuhr notes that "The explanations of the relation of sensuality to self-love" do not give a "psychologically convincing account."[55] He examines sensuality, referring to drunkenness, gluttony, luxurious living, sexual license (perhaps a narrow selection) but he raises very searching questions. Does the drunkard or the glutton follow self-love to the limit or is lack of moderation an attempt to escape the self? Is sensuality a desire to embrace the ego, or to escape it? Is sexual license a form of idolatry, making the self god, or is it a move of the self, seeking "escape by finding some other god"?[56] There is a little of both, he concludes, since sensuality results from the primal love of self.

Feminist theologians do not listen or do not agree. Nelson Dunfee writes: "...he fails to realize that the forms of finitude into which one can escape need not be only aspects of one's own physical cravings, but may also be loss of one's self in other finite persons, institutions and causes. Hence the sin of hiding can take the form of devotion to another."[57] Niebuhr would in fact agree! Plaskow avers "It is not entirely clear why Niebuhr is so insistent on the primacy of pride and the derivative status of sensuality,"[58] for in "...subordinating sensuality, he loses sight of it as a significant human sin and one independent of pridefulness...entirely neglecting important dimensions of the human flight from freedom."[59] Niebuhr says "...man's essence is free self-determination. His sin is the wrong use of his freedom and its consequent destruction."[60] Plaskow replies: "This statement clearly allows for the possible misuse of freedom: exaltation or abdication...Niebuhr identifies sin only with one of these alternatives....[T]here is no reason for Niebuhr to focus on the one aspect of human self-contradiction...he violates the symmetry of his account of human nature as *creaturely* freedom."[61]

Third, feminist critics assert that Niebuhr's doctrine of sin does not take account of the elusiveness of the self in women's experience. Human selfhood, in Professor Niebuhr's understanding, is a creation of the divine related to God, not through the rational faculty, but "in repentance, faith and commitment."[62] The self is creature yet free, "conscious of its finiteness and equally conscious of its pretension in not admitting its finiteness."[63] Philosophies of self-abnegation indicate "that it is impossible to deny the self by an act of will or any discipline,"[64] for "...the self is never in rational control of all unconscious stirrings of selfhood."[65] Niebuhr repeatedly refers to the paradox of self-realization through self-giving in Jesus' teachings about losing or finding life. The ideal possibility in the Christian faith is not self-negation but self-realization. It does not take place when

...the self lacks the faith and trust to subject itself to God. It seeks to establish itself independently. It seeks to find its life and thereby loses it. For the self which it asserts is less than the true self.[66]

...[S]elf-realization cannot be the intended, but only the unintended consequence of our creative relationship to others. If we intend it..."Whoever seeks to gain his life shall lose it." If we forget ourselves, however, the other side of Christ's paradox becomes true: "He who loses his life for my sake will find it."[67]

Saiving responds: "...a woman can give too much of herself, so that nothing remains of her own uniqueness; she can become merely an emptiness, almost a zero, without value to herself, to her fellow men, or, perhaps, even to God."[68] And Hampson says: "His answer of 'have faith' precisely does not tolerate the self coming to itself."[69]

Reflecting on Niebuhr's comments on Galatians 2:20 on the self-centred self that must be "crucified" to break self-centeredness and to let the "more truly real self" the new self be experienced, Hampson comments: "...this is bound to seem peculiarly unsatisfactory for women...If women's basic problem is not self-centeredness, but rather a lack of a sense of self, a scheme of salvation which consists in breaking the self, and in discontinuity with the past, may be unhelpful."[70] Plaskow states: "From the perspective of women's experience, the main problem with Niebuhr's definition of sin is...his insistence that turning away from God means turning toward the self...'*Women's sin' is precisely the failure to turn toward the self.* The sin which involves God-forgetfulness *and* self-forgetfulness is not properly called "pride" even where the word is used in its religious sense."[71]

Considering this charge, especially in the light of Martha, Lessing's leading figure, the question must be raised: is there some connection between the "self" Niebuhr understands and the "self" in sentences like "she had no self," "a woman can give too much of herself, so that nothing remains," "the failure to become a self." In this discussion, the word "self" is a verbal hook. In Niebuhr's work the term is rooted in its long use in theological tradition. The feminist use in these instances seems to come from psychological and therapeutic disciplines carrying different connotations. Bridges need to be built before these concepts can be related.

Fourth, critics also charge that Niebuhr identifies sin with self-assertion and pride, and that he also identifies love with selflessness/self-sacrifice in his doctrine of grace. These identifications are detrimental to women's self-realization. We will deal with each in turn.

(a) Self-assertion. Hampson writes: "[The woman's]...task is to become a differentiated self, a determinate individual, who may say 'I' without feeling

guilty. To tell such a woman that it is the sin of pride to seek self-fulfillment is to reinforce her form of sin: her dispersal of herself in others, her unwarranted serving of them..."[72] Saiving observes "One might expect of theologians...to support and encourage the woman who desires to be both a woman and an individual in her own right...yet theology, to the extent that it has defined the human condition on the basis of masculine experience, continues to speak of such desires as sin or temptation to sin."[73]

Niebuhr uses the terms self-assertion, self-esteem, and, at times, even assertion, in a particular way. He speaks of the ideological taint in all human rational processes and points to "man's assertion of universal significance for his particular values."[74] Discussing anxiety and sin, he says: "there is always the ideal possibility that faith would purge anxiety of the sin of the tendency towards sinful self-assertion."[75] And "The Cross...reveals the contrast between sinful self-assertion and the divine *agape*."[76] Niebuhr finds religion not simply a quest for God, but "a final battleground between God and man's self-esteem."[77] In each case the terms self-assertion or self-esteem are used negatively, twice specified as "sinful." Niebuhr speaks about human beings asserting ourselves *vis-à-vis* God, claiming the center for ourselves or claiming universal significance for our limited values. When feminists speak of self-assertion — and it is a new usage; most of us can recall when we first used it — we speak of standing up for ourselves, standing our ground, not giving in, making our intentions known to others, family, in the workplace, to friends. Niebuhr does not address this.

(b) Self-giving or Sacrificial Love. Saiving writes: "Anders Nygren and Reinhold Niebuhr...represent a tendency to identify...love with selflessness. Love is the precise opposite of sin...Love, according to these theologians, is completely self-giving, taking no thought for its own interests but seeking only the good of the other."[78] Hampson asserts that Niebuhr's "...view that...love [is] self-sacrifice...does not allow him to speak of this as a failure to assert oneself (or of a group to assert itself) or a love as involving a sense of self-worth."[79] Nelson Dunfee: "...by making self-sacrificial love the ultimate Christian virtue, one makes the sin of hiding into a virtue as well...One then becomes glorified for never truly seeking to become fully human."[80] And Plaskow: "...sacrificial love is irrelevant or even destructive for one suffering from the 'sin' of self-lack. The language of self-sacrifice conflicts with personhood and becomes destructive when it suggests that the struggle to become a centered self, to achieve full independent selfhood, is sinful. In this case, theology...serves to reinforce women's servitude."[81]

There is one slight qualification that Plaskow makes, forgetting that "Grace and Self-Acceptance" (which she quotes) was written in 1950: "By the time he wrote *Man's Nature and His Communities*, Niebuhr seems to have modified wrote *Man's Nature and His Communities*, Niebuhr seems to have modified somewhat his view of the relation between pride, self-seeking and self realization. Jesus said only that *consistent* desire for self-fulfillment is self-defeating, he now allows."[82]

Looking at the life of the Christian, Niebuhr finds that "The will of God is the norm, the life of Christ is the revelation of that will."[83] Christ's life, death, and resurrection speak of God's freedom as "the power of mercy beyond judgement."[84] Niebuhr speaks of "apprehending the Cross as the symbol of ultimate perfection"[85] and of the love of Christ that is the disclosure of divine love and a pointer to self-giving human love, the "impossible possibility." In contrast to Nygren, Niebuhr points to *agape* as the source and end of other loves, *philia* and *eros*.[86] Love as *agape* is not a simple command or obligation, but remains an "impossible possibility" approximated in moments when grace enables us to become what God calls us to be. *Agape*, revealed in Christ's self-giving, remains the ultimate norm for human beings. God speaks to the human being in the Incarnation, that reveals not only God's judgement upon the pride of man, but also "that God is Himself the victim of man's sin and pride."[87] If that is who God is, if that is what God has done, it is not surprising that we are "shattered" when we are "confronted by the power and holiness of God…the real source and center of life."[88]

Once again as on the self, now on self-assertion and self-sacrifice, the complaint cannot develop into a dialogue. Niebuhr's teaching and the feminist critique run on parallel tracks, unable to meet. Niebuhr speaks of self-assertion that places the self, not God, at the center of existence. He speaks of Christ's self-giving love as the ultimate norm for human life. Feminists recall that many women needed assertiveness training a decade or two ago. How can a dialogue develop between two such different lines of thought?

There are notes of recognition as well as protest. Plaskow sees Niebuhr's understanding of human nature as finite freedom "a potential source of insight," points to Niebuhr's reminder of the "infinite possibilities of realizing the norm of love in all personal and social relations" and his profound concern for justice.[89] Likewise, Nelson Dunfee concludes: "although Niebuhr uses the language of crucifixion and sacrifice, the self is not truly negated."[90]

Before I add my own reflection to the criticism, one feature should be noted. Changed understandings of human nature, sin and grace indicate a changed understanding of God also. Following the analysis of Saiving as well as Carol Gilligan, a developmental psychologist, Hampson points to what she considers the major difference between women's and men's experience: "Women understand relatedness; they know about the web of human interconnectedness which makes for life...Men by contrast think in terms of hierarchy and are naturally competitive."[91] Hampson is very clear on the implications of what she is saying:

> The God of the tradition...fits the male system...He is isolated, powerful, and at the top of the hierarchy. He is said to have aseity: to be entire unto himself! The God of the Old Testament is arbitrary...and he is always right. What kind of projection is this?[92]
>
> If our ideal model for human society is the web and not the hierarchy, then God as God has previously been conceived will be left stranded high and dry — at best irrelevant. God will need to be seen as involved in the web, supporting, spinning it. God is the one who moves among us, providing context for our lives. Perhaps indeed God ceases to be a separate entity.[93]
>
> God no longer competes with us, a separate entity, superior to all others but is that which is creative of our relatedness. God does not stand in contradiction to, but is commensurate with our vision of human relationships and society.[94]

This note is strongest in, but not unique to, Hampson. Other feminist theologians and ethicists who criticize Niebuhr make similar points. Plaskow notes that Niebuhr uses images and attributes of God considered masculine in our society. Vaughan is more blunt: "Hierarchicalism and the domination-subordination model permeate Niebuhr's understanding and discussion of God."[95]

Niebuhr's discussion of sin persistently points also to redemption. God overcomes in God's own heart what we cannot overcome in our life. I am left with questions. What can God do for Martha? What would redemption be for self-less women? What is redemption when God is "commensurate with our vision of human relationships?"

CONCLUDING COMMENTS

(a) On the Feminist Critique. To this reviewer it is clear that the charges we have considered are not against Reinhold Niebuhr. His writings become the occasion to argue with the main Christian tradition. Only to a limited extent is there an argument with the way Niebuhr appropriates the tradition. The basic issue is the "self" in "women's experience." Valerie Saiving in 1960 said that Niebuhr's doctrine of sin is male-defined. Feminists agreed. Though they qualified the ground of experience, they built greater structures on it. Plaskow chose Lessing's *Children of Violence* as her case-study of the underdevelopment of the self, nay, the self-lessness of women.

The work so far is done on a very limited basis: class and race distinctions, so formative of experience, are disregarded; and a great deal of white, middle class, Western women's experience is disregarded also. Surely we are not saying that women who debate planetary communications, or gene therapy, who direct major companies, run for Congress or dissect Niebuhr's doctrine of sin are strangers to pride? The value, authority and compensation given to women is universally lower than that granted to men. But the underdevelopment of the "self" in women is not, and I believe cannot, be documented as nearly universal.

Feminist theologians have taught us to consider doctrines from the perspective of the "victim" or the powerless. They have taught us that "women's experience" has features not considered by traditional theology. What we have called "human experience" was shown to be less than universal. It will take a long time before we can make a composite picture and speak once again about human nature and human experience. We have learned from the critical voices.

Many questions need to be answered. What is the perennial, transcultural difference between women and men? Does Martha Quest represent the experience of a segment of women? If she does, is self-lessness a developmental phase? Or a neurosis? Is it voluntary? Could passivity and drifting, just like action and conscious choice, be a way of replacing God with the self however elusive or fragmented the self may be? Is Martha a new kind of woman or is she already replaced by less fragmented, more centered young women, our daughters? Are women more self-less than men because of cultural expectations? because of biological difference? Because they sense that their strength may break the weaker ones, the men? Or variously, all of the above?

(b) On Reinhold Niebuhr. Professor Niebuhr's major work on human nature, his Gifford Lectures, was written just prior to the outbreak of World War II. The ideology of National Socialism, its claims rooted in inordinate pride, was an evil that Niebuhr addressed. When he discussed the shortcomings of idealism, naturalism, and romanticism and their inability to do justice to both our self-transcendence and the unity of our spirit and physical life, Niebuhr was not addressing mere ideas. He was addressing his contemporaries on the seriousness of the evil to which they had to respond.

His definition of sin as pride or sensuality has relevance for gender difference but also transcends gender difference. Pride is more likely, though not exclusively, to be the sin of the strong ones, while sensuality is often the sin of the weak, or the one weakened. He spoke more about pride than about sensuality. The latter, he noted, the church always condemned without hesitation, while pride, which is more hidden and more dangerous, had been often overlooked.

As even his most severe critics admit, Niebuhr was "absolutely supportive of women's liberation"[96] in his time, although he thought (wrongly) that women had largely succeeded. Now that we are blessed with the work of Ursula M.

Niebuhr also, giving us a further picture of both of them in *Remembering Reinhold Niebuhr*, it is even clearer how supportive he was.

What one longs to know is, what would he say to us today? His active support of unions and the civil rights movement convinces us that he would aid women's liberation. He would advise women in terms similar to his advice to Blacks in the 1950s, not to wait for men to share power. The moral dimension of sin is injustice. The ego, that false center of existence, "inevitably subordinates other life," and the oppression of women results. But it is wrong to suppose that victims of injustice are exempt from the vice of their oppressors. Niebuhr reminds us that there is a self-righteousness of the weak as well as a self-righteousness of the powerful. Beyond such help, we realize that Reinhold Niebuhr continues to interest us, not because he answers our questions; rather we turn to him because in reading his writings we are enabled to see the world with Niebuhrian insights, dialectics and balances. We also hear and share his uncompromising objection to the perfectability of human beings.

We know our world has changed, socially, culturally, politically. Discoveries of new interrelatedness and the enlargement of all fields of knowledge provide features and aspects unexpected and unconsidered a few decades ago. Such discoveries either had not yet taken place or had not entered human consciousness. In this new world *our* discoveries *also* will be provisional. As Niebuhr told us:

> The philosopher who imagines himself capable of stating a final truth merely because he has sufficient perspective upon past history to be able to detect previous philosophical errors is clearly the victim of the ignorance of his ignorance. Standing on a high pinnacle of history he forgets that this pinnacle also has a particular locus and that his perspective will seem as partial to posterity as the pathetic parochialism of previous thinkers.[97]

(c) The Tasks Before Us. First, one of the ironies of the feminist/Niebuhr diatribe is that his understanding of sin as pride is emphatically rejected as irrelevant for women while sensuality is accepted after some correction. The Roman Catholic Church centred far more on sensuality. The book of Uta Ranke-Heinemann, *Eunuchs for the Kingdom of Heaven*,[98] is a massive documentation of the oppression of women when sensuality, quickly equated with concupiscence, defines sin. We need to find ways to value and use Niebuhr's concept of pride, a concept that is so free from the weight and shadow of concupiscence.

Second, another irony, and another task. Niebuhr is accused of disregarding women's experience. That he did so is not surprising, since in his days even we women did not quite know, let alone define, the difference between men's and women's experience. But now we know that there is a difference, and that it is important. Yet the energy and imagination of Niebuhr's critics are concentrated on the experience of a segment of a particular class of white women in a handful of Western societies. Plaskow notes this limitation and considers this only a beginning[99] of a multi-faceted theological exploration. But it has remained single-faceted. Among the critics of Niebuhr, attention to the strength and commitment of African and Latina women, the figure of the Native American woman standing tall, the enduring rootedness of Asian women is missing. I sincerely hope that womanist theologians of color will also be engaged in the investigation and that the women in the work of Toni Morrison and Alice Walker, among others, will receive consideration comparable to Plaskow's attention to Martha in Lessing's novels.

Third, our task is defined by our gains through the work of feminists. We are offered a new way of looking at ourselves and the world. We are invited to survey the Christian tradition from new perspectives. Mary McClintock Fulkerson in a recent article "Sexism as Original Sin: Developing a Theacentric Discourse" considers feminist treatment of sin in the writings of Valerie Saiving, Mary Daly and Rosemary R. Ruether. She concludes: "…a new universal, the genderization of fallibility enters Christian vocabulary…as a permanent area of investigation."[100] This points toward yet more tasks. Traditional theologians, especially in the churches, need to turn their attention to feminist theologians. Many young and some not so young professional and working women and women choosing to be at home to raise children, though they may be unaware of the term, experience "genderized fallibility." If the Christian faith is to remain relevant to their lives, the church and its theologians must become familiar with women's thinking. Theology in our day must be the shared labor of women and men, colored and pale, challenging each other, building together.

The fourth and final task is one of the open questions relating to the role of the Christian tradition. Some feminists left the church, and even the Christian faith, because they believed that sexism was an integral part of the church's or Christian tradition. Those who remain are divided over how completely biblical religion can be "depatriarchalized" or whether one should just give up the effort. Some of the feminist theologians disregard or reject parts of Scripture. Feminist, traditional and liberation theologians will not be able to assist each other, nor speak a correcting word, unless they share a canon. If there is no common tradition, imagination will set the limit. It may not be surprising that some of the best feminist theological work has come from those who struggle with this issue, that is, from biblical scholars (like Phyllis Trible, Renita Weems, and Katharine Sakenfeld in Old Testament and Elisabeth Schussler-Fiorenza, Sandra M. Schneiders, Antoinette Wire and Sharon H. Ringe in New Testament). In tribute to feminist biblical scholars we close our deliberation of sin with the words of Phyllis Trible on the myth that plays so prominently in Professor Niebuhr's understanding of sin:

> Their lives are solely dependent upon God, who has, nevertheless made them responsible creatures...[T]he only "security" of the man and the woman is obedience to Yahweh God.
>
> ...[T]he tree...offers, according to the serpent...knowledge that removes the limits of humanity and merges it with divinity....[T]hroughout this scene the man has remained silent; he does not speak for obedience. His presence is passive and bland...not strength or resolve but weakness...[H]e follows his woman without question or comment. She gives fruit to him, "and-he-ate"...If the woman is intelligent, sensitive, ingenious, the man is passive, brutish and inept.
>
> ...[T]hese portrayals illustrate the wide range of human responses that participate in transgression. Both activity and passivity, initiative and acquiescence, are equal modes of lawlessness.[101]

NOTES

1.   Reinhold Niebuhr, *The Nature and Destiny of Man* (*NDM*) (New York: Charles Scribner's Sons, 1945): I: 16.

2.   ibid., 92.

3.   ibid., 75.

4.   Reinhold Niebuhr, *The Children of Light and the Children of Darkness* (New York: Charles Scribner's Sons, 1944): 4.

5.   *NDM* I: 16.

6.   ibid., 179.

7.   ibid.

8.   ibid., 257.

9.   Psalm 51.

10.   *NDM* I: 141.

11.   ibid., 142.

12.   Cynthia Campbell, *Theologies Written from Feminist Perspectives* (New York: Office of General Assembly, Presbyterian Church (U.S.A.), 1987).

13.   Carol P. Christ and Judith Plaskow, eds., *WomanSpirit Rising: A Feminist Reader in Religion* (Harper San Francisco, 1979): 1–17.

14.   Beverly Wildung Harrison, *Making the Connections: Essays in Feminist Social Ethics*, ed. Carol S. Robb (Boston, Beacon Press, 1985): 27f.

15.   ibid., 32.

16.   ibid., 59.

17.   ibid., 60.

18.   Judith Vaughn, *Sociality, Ethics and Social Change: A Critical Appraisal of Reinhold Niebuhr's Ethics in the Light of Rosemary Radford Reuther's Works* (Lanham, MD: University Press of America, 1983): 194.

19.   ibid., 193.

20.   ibid.

21.   ibid., 194.

22.   "Be Not Anxious," Sermon at Memorial Church, Harvard University, Oct. 22, 1961, in *Justice and Mercy*, ed. Ursula M. Niebuhr (New York: Harper & Row, 1974): 80.

23.   Judith Plaskow, *Sex, Sin and Grace: Women's Experience and the Theologies of Reinhold Niebuhr and Paul Tillich* (Lanham, MD: University Press of America, 1980): 3.

24.   ibid., 2.

25.   ibid., 64.

26.   ibid., 34.

27.   ibid., 44.

28.   ibid., 45.

29.   ibid.

30.   ibid., 50.

31.   ibid., 66f.

32.   ibid., 42.

33.   ibid., 43.

34.   ibid., 64.

35.   Susan Nelson Dunfee, *Beyond Servanthood: Christianity and the Liberation of Women* (Lanham, MD: University Press of America, 1989): 6f.

36.   Plaskow, op. cit., 64f.

37.   ibid., 64.

38.   *NDM* I: 16f.

39.   ibid., 92.

40.   ibid., 142.

41.   ibid., 179.

42.   Valerie Saiving, "The Human Situation: A Feminine View," *The Journal of Religion* (April 1960), University of Chicago, and reprinted in Christ and Plaskow, op. cit., 25–42. The citations appear on p. 25f.

43.   ibid., 29.

44.   ibid., 37.

45.   Daphne Hampson, "Reinhold Niebuhr on Sin: A Critique" in *Reinhold Niebuhr and the Issues of Our Time*, ed. Richard Harris (London & Oxford: Mowbray, 1986): 47.

46.   Plaskow, op. cit., l.

47.   ibid., 68.

48.   ibid., 84.

49.   *NDM* I: 228.

50.   Reinhold Niebuhr, *Faith and History (FH)* (New York: Charles Scribner's Sons, 1949): 121.

51.   Reinhold Niebuhr, *Discerning the Signs of the Times: Sermons for Today and Tomorrow* (London: S.C.M. Press, 1946): 58.

52.   ibid.

53.   *NDM* I: 185.

54.   ibid., 233.

55.   ibid.

56.   ibid.

57.   Susan Nelson Dunfee, "The Sin of Hiding: A Feminist Critique of Reinhold Niebuhr's Account of the Sin of Pride," *Soundings* 65 (Fall 1982): 316–324. Citations: 318f.

58.   Plaskow, op. cit., 62.

59.   ibid., 63.

60.   *NDM* I: 16.

61.   Plaskow, op. cit., 63.

62.   Reinhold Niebuhr, *The Self and the Dramas of History* (New York: Charles Scribner's Sons, 1955): 84.

63.   ibid., 85.

64.   Reinhold Niebuhr, *Man's Nature and His Communities* (New York: Charles Scribner's Sons, 1965): 117.

65.   ibid., 118.

66.   *NDM* I: 252.

67.   Reinhold Niebuhr, "Grace and Self-Acceptance," *The Messenger* 15 #9 (April 25, 1950): 6. *The Messenger* is the 'National Organ of the Evangelical and Reformed Church.'

68.   Saiving, op. cit., 37.

69.   Hampson, op. cit., 53.

70.   ibid., 54.

71.   Plaskow, op. cit., 151.

72.   Hampson, op. cit., 49.

73.   Saiving, op. cit., 39.

74.   *NDM* I: 35.

75.   ibid., 182f.

76.   ibid., II: 89.

77.   ibid., I: 200.

78.   Saiving, op. cit., 25f.

79.   Hampson, op. cit., 56.

80.   Nelson Dunfee, "The Sin of Hiding," 320.

81.   Plaskow, op. cit., 86–87.

82.   ibid., 89.

83.   *NDM* I: 60.

84.   *NDM* II: 71.

85.   ibid., 72.

86.   *FH* 202.

87.   *NDM* I: 148.

88.   ibid., II: 109.

89.   Plaskow, op. cit., 93.

90.   Nelson Dunfee, *Beyond Servanthood*, 109.

91.   Hampson, op. cit., 54.

92.   ibid., 56.

93.   ibid., 57.

94.   ibid., 58.

95.   Vaughan, op. cit., 122.

96.   Beverly Wildung Harrison, speaking at the Conference on Reinhold Niebuhr, at Union Theological Seminary, New York, March, 1992.

97.   *NDM* I: 195.

98.   Uta Ranke-Heinemann, *Eunuchs for the Kingdom of Heaven: Women, Sexuality and the Catholic Church* (New York: Doubleday, 1990).

99.   Plaskow, op. cit., 174.

100.   Mary McClintock Fulkerson, "Sexism as Original Sin: Developing a Theacentric Discourse," *Journal of American Academy of Religion* 59 (1991): 653–675.

101.   Phyllis Trible, *God and the Rhetoric of Sexuality* (Philadelphia: Augsburg Fortress, 1978): 107–114.

A CANADIAN SOCIALIST CHRISTIAN LOOKS AT REINHOLD NIEBUHR

Oscar Cole Arnal

The last half decade or so has witnessed a resurgence of interest, even passion, with regard to the theology of Reinhold Niebuhr. Niebuhr's eulogists are many and impressive, as are the recent published works dealing with his life and thought. As well, an entire generation of major American politicians, including such people as Adlai Stevenson, Arthur Schlesinger Jr., McGeorge Bundy and Hubert Humphrey affirmed him as a most influential figure in American political life.[1]

The purpose of this article is to deny neither Niebuhr's greatness nor his profound contributions to Christian theology and ethics. He has been an influential prophetic voice among us and, as such, deserves our continued praise. Nonetheless, it is important to be critical as well. In spite of phenomenal achievements in theology and public life, Reinhold Niebuhr can be challenged in the loci of principle and practice. The following sections will address both of these arenas as well as offer some alternative models of gospel praxis for our day.

All who theologize do so from their own historical context. Niebuhr was no exception to this. His perceptions were circumscribed by time, place and socioeconomic conditions. His mature theology has been called "political" or 'Christian Realism' and is based on classical Reformation theologies of sin and grace. Consequently his Biblical views reflected the Calvinistic and Lutheran convictions of radical sin and rescue by transcendent grace that characterized the neo-orthodox resurgence after the blood-filled trenches of "the war to end all wars." Niebuhr's profound sense of the corruption of human nature and will to power in the midst of the optimistic arrogance of North American society remains an enduring legacy of a great prophet. His voice is an outcry against cultural idolatry and self-righteousness. Beyond his use of exclusive male language, who would dare challenge Niebuhr's prophetic insight: "Man [*sic*] is mortal. That is his fate. Man pretends not to be mortal. That is his sin." In this same sermon, poignantly called "The Tower of Babel," the late 1930s Niebuhr went on to say:

> Thus man builds towers of the spirit from which he may survey larger horizons than those of his class, race and nation. This is a necessary human enterprise...But it is also inevitable that these towers should be Towers of Babel, that they should pretend to reach higher than their real height; and should claim a finality which they cannot possess...Thus sin corrupts the highest as well as the lowest achievements of human life.

For Niebuhr this primal sin, manifested in the alliance of pretension and power, is a fundamental spiritual reality. He calls this a rebellion against God which is, at bottom, "a final expression of the perennial pathos of human spirituality: its ability to detect the spurious claims of impartiality and universality in every culture except one's own."[2] Throughout Niebuhr's writings, especially in the late 1930s and early 1940s, one finds these insights about the classical doctrine of sin underscored. Whether in *Moral Man and Immoral Society* (1932) or in the Gifford Lectures a decade later (1941) called *The Nature and Destiny of Man*, one can discover this profoundly Biblical and prophetic insight regarding human and cultural pretension which the Christian tradition has called sin. This contribution of Niebuhr, in the midst of perhaps the most arrogant culture since imperial Rome, has been his most enduring legacy to us.[3]

This insight is further enhanced by the concrete character of his descriptions, whether in sermons, political pieces or theological works. In this respect Niebuhr is profoundly Biblical because his perception of sin arises from the earthy reality of human brutality and oppression habitually posturing in the dress of some higher value. Like the great Hebrew prophets, Jesus included, Niebuhr names the oppressive powers, political and religious, and calls them to account. He chastised the arrogance of bourgeois culture in its attempts to hide capitalist acquisitiveness behind the so-called eternal values of freedom, rights and liberty, and he exposed the self-righteousness of historical Christianity in its ideological alliance with ruling elites from medieval times to the present.[4] Under the title "The Idolatry of America," Niebuhr had this to say:

> Our present prosperity is actually creating a mood among our lay Christians
> that approximates the uncritical Christian adoration of the "free enterprise
> system"...The gospel cannot be preached with truth and power if it does not
> challenge the pretensions and pride, not only of individuals, but of nations,
> cultures, civilizations, economic and political systems. The good fortune of
> America and its power place it under the most grievous temptations to self-
> adulation.[5]

To culminate his insights regarding human destructiveness, he upheld the
prophetic character of the faith in these words:

> Religion, declares the modern man, is conscious of our highest social values.
> Nothing could be further from the truth. True religion is a profound uneasiness
> about our highest social values. Its uneasiness springs from the knowledge that
> the God whom it worships transcends the limits of finite man, while this same
> man is constantly tempted to forget the finiteness of his cultures and
> civilization and to pretend a finality for them which they do not have.[6]

Thus, in his assessment of human sin, Reinhold Niebuhr stands tall as one of the
many prophets who challenged and still challenge arrogance, self-righteousness
and oppression in our culture. Nevertheless, within his incisive theology are
some potential flaws which contain both elements of truth and glaring
opportunities inviting dangerous compromises with the very status quo powers
he sought to confront. Below are three of these.

First, in his description of historical sin he described the pretensions of the
oppressed and struggling classes, along with the leaders and values linked to
their cause. Most consistently criticized by him have been the Marxists and the
proletarian militants imbued with various socialist dreams. The early Niebuhr
was quick to point out the Marxists' insight in recognizing the sinful arrogance
of those who own and control the means of production; he called this "the
greatest ethical contribution which Marxian thought has made to the problem of
social life." Further he praised the industrial workforce with these words:
"Comfortable classes may continue to dream of an automatic progress in society.
They do not suffer enough from social injustice to recognize its peril to the life
of society. Only the proletarian sees how the centralization of power and
privilege in modern society proceeds so rapidly that it not only outrages the
conscience but destroys the very foundations of society." However, to this praise
Niebuhr added the critique which chastises the proletariat, Marxism and other
forms of socialism with the same prophetic critique that he applied to capitalism
and the ruling classes. These alternative forces reflect also the arrogance,
pretensions and oppressive cruelty witnessed in their "ruling class" foes. Niebuhr

pointed out the illusory idealism of democratic socialism as well as the perceived excesses of Soviet communism, critiques which became increasingly strident with the onset of the Cold War.[7] Niebuhr's insights about the sins of the marginalized and oppressed, especially in their organized and militant form, are valid, and yet that very perception, when promulgated, tends towards the kind of universalism about sin that reduces the heinous character of oppression and imperialism. By his castigation, however true, of both bourgeois and socialist pretensions, he puts himself above and beyond the fray by this tendency toward generalization. He becomes the prophetic arbiter beyond class arrogance, pointing out the sin of both oppressor and oppressed. Thus, to some extent, he sought to stand outside the struggle theologically and thus render the Biblical judgment of "a curse on both your houses." Pride and pretension notwithstanding, the Biblical prophets like Amos, Jeremiah and Jesus chose sides (Amos 2:6–7a; 4:1; 5:11–12; Jeremiah 5:26–29; 6:13–16; 9:23–24; 22:13–17; Matthew 11:4–5; Luke 4:16–21; 6:20–26; Mark 10:17–31), and they identified with the poor and oppressed classes over against the rich and powerful. In spite of Niebuhr's sensitivity there remains the temptation to speak above and outside the conflict. Not enough attention is given to his own class limitations and illusions, and more consideration needs to be devoted to the question of whose interests are served by this kind of theology. Niebuhr's incisive doctrine of sin, in so far as it names the sin of both oppressor and oppressed without full solidarity with the oppressed, is a subtle step from his earlier socialist commitments toward his postwar work as liberal apologist for American democracy and the Cold War.[8]

Second, the theology of Reinhold Niebuhr, much like its Reformation forebears, seems to be less confident in the transformative power of grace than it is in the destructive capacity of sin. Martin Luther King Jr., himself influenced by Niebuhr, summarized this critique rather nicely: "He [Niebuhr] was so involved in diagnosing (humanity's) sickness of sin that he overlooked the cure of grace."[9] His concrete description of sin's power in human life and history is not met with corresponding Biblical and historical examples of God's victory over sin. In the particular citation quoted below one can see Niebuhr's constant insistence upon the dialectical reality of the sin-grace struggle, a struggle which leaves us in the throes of profound ambiguity. Hear Niebuhr:

> The fact that God cannot overcome evil without displaying in history His purpose to take the effects of evil upon and into Himself, means that the divine mercy cannot be effective until the seriousness of sin is fully known. The knowledge that sin causes suffering in God is an indication of the seriousness of sin. It is by that knowledge that man is brought to despair....It is in this

contrition and in this appropriation of divine mercy and forgiveness that the human situation is fully understood and overcome.[10]

In fairness to Niebuhr, he does acknowledge that the impact of *agape* in human history leaves its transforming mark. It is "a resource for infinite developments towards a more perfect brotherhood in history."[11] Nonetheless, his overriding concern remained human arrogance in its messianic pretensions, an arrogance which seems to be set at bay only in self-recognition before Christ's redemptive work. His Reformation outlook appears to have ultimate confidence that the cross as "the power of God" (I Corinthians 1:24) is able fundamentally to absolve only the repentant sinner without correspondingly transforming the created order. In this position, redemption, justification and the righteousness of God, chiefly found in Paul, are understood in the context of individual rescue and haven from the dark forces of this world. In such a world view, one runs the risk of having the doctrine of salvation drowned by a profound perception of sin and Christian realism. Niebuhr, in his prophetic strength, was quick to portray Biblical brokenness in all its horror by his utilization of the canvass of human history including our own. However, in the arena of victory over sin he is driven toward inwardness, pale penultimate victories and a transcendent "out there" in some metaphysical end of history. His eschatology, mired in the dialectic of human sin and ambiguity, is itself shorn of tension. The "already now...not yet" has become the "barely now and distant yet to come." It is as if the Biblical war between the powers has become a divine retreat or perhaps a cautious advance, compromises included, until the end of history when God will pull out all the stops. The joyous transforming power of the Gospel, so pale in Niebuhr's eschatology, is significantly more transformative in major portions of canonical Jewish and Christian Scriptures.[12]

Biblical notions of salvation, shalom, reconciliation and the like are infinitely more historical and more collectively salvific than Niebuhr understood them to be. Even in Paul, the fundamental issue is not the individual sinner's justification but rather the common human brokenness, as exemplified by the particularity of Jewish and Gentile sinfulness, which is being and will be re-formed into a universal corporate reconciliation with God, with others and with all of creation (see Romans 1–3, 9–11). Throughout the Bible transformation is earthy and sensual, and it happens in history. God's promises are land and progeny (Genesis 15:1–7); God liberates, embraces and names slaves as the holy people (Exodus 20:2; Amos 3:2; Deuteronomy. 7:7–8); and God gives the landless "a land flowing with milk and honey" (Exodus 3:7–8). In sum, the promises of salvation to Israel were collective and concrete. In Israel's rallying creedal formulations grace means promise, liberation and land: these are fundamental (see Deuteronomy 26:5–9 and Joshua 24:1–15). Even when the Davidic Messiah is added to this tradition of salvation, the elements of transformation such as justice and freedom from oppression are basic (see Isaiah 9:6–7 and 11:1–9). Righteousness (what we call justification) and justice are not neatly separated into vertical and horizontal relationships but are rather ways to describe the same transforming power of God in history (see the parallel usage of these terms *tsedek* and *mishpat* in Hebrew poetry, i.e., Psalm 72:1–2; Isaiah 59:14; Amos 5:24). War will be banished from the land (Isaiah 2:4/Micah 4:3–4), and food and drink without cost are made available (Isaiah 55:1–3).[13]

The canonical New Testament is not alien to this traditional emphasis. Instead one finds continuity. In the earliest Jesus traditions one is hard pressed to find individual rescue from sin. Instead emphasis is on confrontation with demonic powers and solidarity with the poor, powerless and rejected of society. Universal love is not underscored; rather we have a Jesus who takes sides with the oppressed against the oppressors (Matthew 11:2–6; Luke 4:16–21; 11:18–20; 13:27–28; Mark 2:15–17; Luke 14:16–24; 10:38–42; Matthew 11:19; Luke 6:20–26; Mark 10:17–27; 11:15–17; 12:13–17). Jesus' parable of the Last Judgment (Matthew 25:31–46) and the condemnations and hopes recorded in the Book of Revelation (18:1–24 and 21:1–4) heighten the concrete character of this salvation. To be sure, eschatological yearnings are future-driven in the face of the tenacity of profound evil, but the community of the future stands up to power in the present (Acts 5:12–42) and shares its earthly goods in common (Acts 2:41–47; 4:32–37; II Corinthians 8:13–15). In short, the *équipe* of the eschaton, intrinsically radical, is a clear and militant alternative to the status quo and its representatives with their pretensions and their oppressive cruelties. The gospel is the victorious option now and is seen in the faces and actions of those oppressed who bring justice and wholeness into the present in the name of the future and contemporary fulfilment promised by God. That Biblical dynamism and confidence is threatened in Niebuhr's theology by his profound sense of sin.[14]

And finally, his doctrine of sin, combined with his appeals to realism in a world which predates the eschaton, shapes his understanding of Christian ethics which is characterized by the need to seek non-pretentious, penultimate compromises in a less than perfect world. However, the younger Niebuhr did not erase the radical demands of Jesus' ethic, and it is to his credit that he remained insistent upon that ideal. Further, as the prophets of old, he warned against the use of Biblical teaching to buttress a cultural and political status quo.[15] Nonetheless, in the following rather lengthy quote, can be seen a profound sense of reality along with a tendency toward domesticating Jesus' radical call to discipleship:

> The unique rigor of the gospel ethic is thus attributed to the peculiar circumstances of time and place — agrarian simplicity, for instance, as contrasted with the industrial complexities of our own day....The full dimension of human life includes not only an impossible ideal, but realities of sin and evil which are more than simple imperfections and which prove that the ideal is something more than the product of a morbidly sensitive religious fantasy....The wages of sin is death. The destruction of our contemporary civilization through its injustice and through the clash of conflicting national wills is merely one aspect and one expression of the destruction of sin in the world. Confronted with this situation humanity always faces a double task. The one is to reduce the anarchy of the world to some kind of immediately sufferable order and unity; and the other is to set these tentative and insecure unities and achievements under the criticism of the ultimate ideal.[16]

To be sure, Niebuhr's perception of the tension between Jesus' uncompromising demand and sinful human history is a real one, but there is a tendency in his ethics to relativize the radicalism of Jesus' call in the name of love seeking the realizable in the midst of human pretension. Once again, the power of substantive transformation becomes swallowed by a pragmatism that may be more middle class and American than it is Biblical. In the last analysis, Niebuhr opts for an ethics of the possible rather than the ethics of the eschaton found in Jewish and Christian Holy Writ.

II

The fame of Reinhold Niebuhr is deservedly beyond that of an extraordinarily perceptive theologian. Also he was a well-known public figure. In the years prior to the Second World War he was active in progressive and socialist circles. Though abandoning an earlier pacifist position, his socialist insights remained more tenacious. He accepted the New Deal reforms of the Roosevelt administration but not uncritically. He condemned capitalism and stood courageously against the pretensions of Henry Ford. He was a strong advocate of the union movement and its strikes at a time when such causes made him suspect in bourgeois and ecclesiastical circles. An avowed enemy of both racial segregation and fascism, Niebuhr is remembered both for his attacks against "Jim Crow" and for his provision of a haven for the renowned anti-Nazis, Paul Tillich and Dietrich Bonhoeffer. His insights were not those of an ivory-tower theologian; he was a man *engagé* in the midst of human flesh and blood. Niebuhr was one of our great prophetic activists.[17]

Tragically, there is a darker side. The prophet against the king became also the prophet for the king. The man who so eloquently cried out against the arrogance of power became, in the Cold War, an apologist of power. He who so very well denounced the religious pretensions of American imperialism was to serve as sophisticated advocate for what he had condemned earlier. This change, drastic in its practical commitments, was sophisticated and nuanced enough to represent understandable development from within his own theology. Nonetheless, the theological radical who had been under fire among church figures and intellectual colleagues was after the war lauded by many who wielded the reins of American imperialism and anticommunism. Niebuhr's movement from socialism to pragmatic American liberalism softened his earlier prophetic radicalism. Like his friend and ally, Hubert Humphrey, he opted to justify American values and foreign policy in the name of balanced realism. By so narrowing the spectrum of political options, he did his part to blunt prophetic radicalism and to limit the range of public debate in the United States. Even during the civil rights movement, he was calling for pragmatic caution while Martin Luther King Jr. and others were marching in defiance of immoral laws.[18]

Three examples may be used to highlight this critique. First of all, he became an apologist for American democracy to the point of characterizing it with transcendent values:

> Man's capacity for justice makes democracy possible; but man's inclination to injustice makes democracy necessary....Ideally democracy is a permanently valid form of social and political organization which does justice to two dimensions of human existence: to man's spiritual stature and his social character; to the uniqueness and variety of life, as well as to the common necessities of all men. Bourgeois democracy frequently exalted the individual at the expense of the community; but its emphasis upon liberty contained a valid element, which transcended its excessive individualism.[19]

As well, moderation and tolerance, essential virtues of bourgeois democracy, are given a more transcendental character in his writings. After an attack on the extremism of right and left, as if extremism were wrong in and of itself, Niebuhr defined democracy as intrinsically fair and just in its moderate balancing of interests through the protection of basic rights. Thus, he stated, "A genuine Christian contribution to the ideological conflict in democratic society must serve to mitigate, rather than aggravate the severity of the conflict; for it will prevent men from heedlessly seeking their own interests in the name of justice and from recklessly denominating value preferences, other than our own, as evil." Such an apology was not markedly different from the prevailing American liberal values of his epoch.[20]

Second, his critiques of Marxism became decidedly more strident and less nuanced than they had been in the 1930s and 1940s. Marxism, especially Soviet communism, had become the demonic evil that must be destroyed at any cost. He called Marxist communism "so odious a system of tyranny," one which is "virulent" and characterized by religious pretensions.[21] In fact, the communist danger was felt to be so eminent that it must be resisted by the United States and its allies:

> The prospects for peace are intimately related to, and derived from, the ability of the non-Communist world under the hegemony of our nation to meet the challenge of so strange and formidable an adversary. World peace requires that the dynamic of this strange political movement be contained, its ambition to control the world be frustrated, and its revolutionary ardors be tamed by firm and patient resistance.[22]

Finally, this apology for American democracy, combined with a sainted horror of Bolshevism, brought Niebuhr into the ranks of the Cold War crusaders, even to the point of his overlooking the sins of antidemocratic Third World allies. Hear his words:

> These hazards do not and must not spell the doom of democracy in its contest with Communism across the vast expanses of Asia and Africa. They do indicate that self-government is no simple alternative to Communism and that the Western powers, and particularly the hegemonic power, must exercise discrimination in their marshalling of the disparate forces of the non-Communist world. That means that we must be prepared to encounter defeat in Laos, for instance, where the social patterns make Western democracy irrelevant but dare not be complacent about any policy which threatens the democratic "heartland" of free governments in Europe. It also means that we require discriminate judgment in dealing with the various compounds of democracy and dictatorship which the cultural and economic variables across the world make inevitable. We will regard one-party systems, whether in Tunisia or Mexico, with certain sympathy and will be concerned but not desperate when a new nation, such as Ghana, develops the tyrannical and dangerous potentialities of the one-party system. We should know the difference between reversible nondemocratic regimes and those which are irreversible because their power is informed by the fanatic dogma of Communism.[23]

Gone is the prophet able to discern the idolatry in every system. The genuine hope engendered by Soviet support of Third World liberation struggles goes unacknowledged; the socioeconomic gains made in Iron Curtain Europe remain unmentioned; and U.S. support of right-wing military tyrannies are justified in the name of the anticommunist crusade. In all of this, Reinhold Niebuhr was not different from most of the liberal intelligentsia caught up in the U.S. cold war spirit. Nonetheless, he and his theology have left an important legacy for us. As a prophetic voice against human pretension and injustice he is a worthy mentor. At the same time, as one who fell under the lure of certain illusions within his own society, he must be subject to criticism.

III

There are other mentors for us, more passionately radical and Biblical, who have adopted a theology of *engagement* which repudiates nuances and pragmatism for an incarnate struggle with the oppressed of our society who march toward their and our liberation. Cross and resurrection are there both embodied and articulated, and there the God who frees slaves and establishes Jubilee calls us to follow. It is a wild and intense faith, even fanatical, and it is driven by the motor of the inrushing eschaton. It is a class theology which takes sides. Catholic liberationists call it the priority for the poor and oppressed, and it is reflected in the God of the Exodus and in Jesus preaching of God's reign.[24]

At this point I would like to suggest some very specific examples of such liberationist role models that might be useful for both personal reflection and discussion. Some come from the wider world, others from Canada. Finally, I will concentrate on those who are native to francophone Quebec. Since we are honouring one of North America's greatest theologians, it might be well to make a few initial comments about theology and theologians. All theological reflection is partisan, either covertly or overtly: in what it says and in how it says it, theology is servant of either the dominating or the dominated. The words of liberationist Otto Maduro about theological production are both prophetic and chilling. They demand serious and collective reflection. He says:

> Religious production [theology], developed in close proximity to the dominant milieux and sharing in their privileges and way of life, reproduces — *sub specie aeternitatis* — the dominant interests. Religious institutions tend to be structured in the image and likeness of the social order, and to develop — *de facto* and unconsciously — a spiritual production which will lead to the reproduction of the established order and of the privileges attached to the socially legitimate monopoly of religious production enjoyed by such

institutions. The consumption of religious products developed socially and spatially far from the milieux of the workers and peasants becomes an instrument for the sacralization of alienated labour: *opium of the people*.[25]

In short, one can see the earlier Niebuhr involved intimately with United States labour and socialism, but the later Niebuhr joined more intimately with the "shakers and makers" of American power politics. Where we are *engagés* is intimately linked to the philosophy we espouse. There is no ethereal objective neutrality in theology.

Left-wing Catholic theologians in France were acutely aware of this as early as the 1930s. Figures like Emmanuel Mounier called unashamedly for a theology of *engagement*, and in spite of some serious vacillations, he became model for theologians who emerged from the struggles of the 1930s and 1940s as precursors of today's theologians of liberation. One such figure was the Dominican Thomist Marie-Dominique Chenu. He wrote in the forge of conflict, speaking out in the name of the poor and oppressed within his own society. Like Maduro and others he challenged his church to abandon the Platonic and Gnostic theology it was utilizing to protect it from the concrete incarnation of human history. Before it was fashionable he called for an end to the oppressive silence used to hide the role of women in history and modern society. He was the defender and friend of the worker-priest movement, especially at the very moment it was being abandoned by earlier allies. And he suffered for it, being placed frequently under the interdict of silence.[26]

Dorothee Soelle is one contemporary example of such an *engagé* theologian. Her writings, simple and passionate in style, are directed toward the concerns of gospel liberation. She addresses feminist, creation, labour and peace issues not only from the standpoint of fundamental Christian faith but also from the reality of her own fierce involvement. She has been an organizer for the movement Christians for Socialism, and she is currently active in the peace movement in Germany. Whether in her personal compassion for her sisters among the poor or in her civil disobedience against capitalism and militarism, Dorothee Soelle stands as a most worthy mentor of the partisan theology so apparent in the Biblical traditions.[27] As well, there are others — James Cone, Mary Jo Leddy of the Sisters of Sion, Daniel Berrigan and numerous liberation theologians on virtually all the continents.

Examples of such radical theology are collegial as well as individual. The militant gospel is found in collectivities which embody the eschatological and concrete liberation found in sacred writ and historic struggle. Although there are numerous examples of these, I will cite only three types and concentrate on a representative sampling from post-Quiet Revolution Quebec. Rightly or wrongly

I call the first example *engagé* "think-tanks." Some U.S.-based cases include Dorothy Day's Catholic Worker movement or the Sojourner community in Washington, D.C. In Toronto exists a Christian community called the Ecumenical Coalition for Economic Justice (E.C.E.J.). Formed in 1973 as GATT-Fly this small team of activists has lived a spartan life and linked itself with grass-roots labour, farm, women, native and church groups. Its chief purpose is to do research and produce documentation to aid "poor and marginalized groups involved in struggles for economic justice."[28]

In Quebec there are similar movements, some linked to the church directly and one other which was autonomous from ecclesiastical structures. Two in the first category are the Centre de Pastorale en Milieu Ouvrier (C.P.M.O.) in Montreal and the Carrefour de Pastorale en Monde Ouvrier (C.A.P.M.O.) based in Quebec City. Both groups are oriented consciously to aid and train the church to identify with the struggles of the marginalized and poor of Quebec. Toward that end they hold regular sessions geared toward consciousness-raising and partisan militancy on behalf of the "have-nots" and the working class. For both groups this entails "class consciousness and class solidarity" through "direct action in popular movements."[29] The autonomous team (*équipe*) was the more radical Politisés Chrétiens which organized as a network (*reseau*) in Quebec in the spring of 1974. Its several hundred members included the most well-known francophone Christian militants of the 1970s and beyond. The *reseau* defined itself as "an ensemble of persons *linked to the interests of those workers* [emphasis theirs] *involved* in the struggle for their own liberation and who *gather together as 'believers'* in a common witness to the gospel of Jesus Christ." In short its members were decidedly partisan. They used Marxist analysis, were openly socialist, criticized the church's lukewarm social democracy, attacked capitalism and called for a proletarian interpretation of the Christian message. The ecclesiastical establishment was habitually cool toward the *reseau*, but it sustained both its critique and militancy until it disbanded in the early 1980s.[30]

Secondly, there are the Christian base communities, collectivities of believers among the marginalized and oppressed who gather together for worship, study, reflection and other acts of solidarity. In Quebec they are patterned after the classic models in Latin America, but they are certainly not carbon copies of these earlier examples. Called the "popular church" (*église populaire*) in Quebec it defined itself as "a community, formed of a majority of people from the popular strata and controlled by them, who identify with the exploited and oppressed and who endorse the option for their liberation." Some are led by priest militants, others by members of the laity. Still others are linked with religious orders whose vocation is incarnated among the poor and oppressed. Here in these communities can be found the blend of spirituality, worship and militancy so prevalent in a living theology of liberation.[31]

Third and last of all, I would like to highlight those women and men of avant-garde religious orders who have entered the life of the organized oppressed both in the neighbourhoods and at the factories. By way of example, the Fils de la Charité, an order created in France to minister to the industrial proletariat, sent priests into the squalor of the Pointe Saint-Charles *quartier* in Montreal. There they lived as neighbours, and there they built a base Christian community. Two of them, Ugo Benfante and Guy Cousin, undertook the vocation of full-time factory toil shortly thereafter. Their comrades elected them to union leadership positions, and in the face of violence and persecution Père Cousin sought to create a radical local over against both the Zeller's Company and its Teamster allies. Sisters and Brothers of those orders inspired by the spirituality of Charles de Foucauld are an abiding presence of compassion and justice in the ghettos of Montreal and Hull, and the Jesuits established their own presence in working class Montreal. These religious toiled with the *groupes populaires*, joined grassroots community reform movements and entered left-wing politics, all for the purpose of transforming society along socialist lines. In Hull an entire diocese opted for a liberationist approach based upon the visions of Vatican II. The Oblates sent Roger Poirier, long involved in justice issues, to train radical Catholics in community-organizing skills, and the Capuchins set up a team (*équipe*) in the midst of Hull's working class *quartier*. There they took on the alliance of federal government and real estate speculators who were stripping the poorer neighbourhoods of both life and lodging.[32]

These same orders and a number of others sent priests and religious into the factories there to toil full-time with their exploited comrades. Fathers Benfante and Cousin were mentioned already. Sister Marie-Paule Lebrun joined other marginally paid women at a Coleco plant where ironically they assembled "cabbage–patch" dolls for the up-beat children of the bourgeoisie. Dolorès Léger of the Soeurs Notre-Dame du Bon Conseil was a well-educated conscious feminist who undertook factory labour, union militancy and left-wing politics because of her gospel commitment to and with the poor. Union organizing became the lot of a number of worker-priests who were prompted to such a witness by their assembly-line comrades. One such figure was the Capuchin Benoît Fortin. He toiled as a dockloader in Quebec City's Hilton Hotel and there sought to replace a company union with a democratic and radical local of the Confédération des Syndicats Nationaux (C.S.N.). He faced harassment and threats and was fired eventually for his union activities. He took the Hilton chain to the tribunal of justice and won his case eventually before the Supreme Court of

Canada. Today his union of hotel workers is in place and throughout Quebec has a membership of about 12,000.[33] The impetus for Fortin's *engagement* is contained in the following quote:

> We must rejoin the real world of people who struggle day after day for a more just world....We must be reborn from among the poor, near to their cries, in solidarity with their struggles. Jesus has taken up the human condition; he has taken the way of the stable. We will recognize nothing of human distress if we do not live in solidarity with the most oppressed through our own flesh.[34]

It is this radical understanding of the gospel combined with a concrete and risky identification with the oppressed in their struggles that theology and Christian life must travel in our time. It is a style of discipleship that is both faithful to the tradition and profoundly relevant in a world where evil power poses as good while it crushes and casts aside the many. In short, although Reinhold Niebuhr has been among us as a great prophetic and committed voice, we must move beyond his witness. His was a theology too locked into a powerful doctrine of sin, and the prewar prophet finished his career as a postwar apologist for the Cold War and American imperialism. To the end, his thought remained nuanced and dialectical, but he had lost touch with the grass-roots forces, Christian and otherwise, who struggled for justice in the land. The faith has produced intellectual giants aplenty, and we are grateful for them. However, we need advocates who dare to live a radical and hopeful faith of transformation. The Capuchins of Quebec and elsewhere understand that by their very lives. They call it a "theology of the feet." One of their brothers Gaëtan Ouellete sums it up very well: "We must put aside thinking with our head in order to reflect with our feet, breathe with our feet and sense the deep pain of those feet that labour. We must live as the working class lives. That is our spirituality."[35]

NOTES

1.   Richard Wightman Fox, *Reinhold Niebuhr: A Biography* (New York: Pantheon, 1985): 297; Richard Harries, ed., *Reinhold Niebuhr and the Issues of Our Time* (Grand Rapids, Michigan: William B. Eerdmans Publishing Company, 1986): 183–204; Robert McAfee Brown, *The Essential Reinhold Niebuhr* (New Haven: Yale University Press, 1986): xi–xxiv.

2.   Reinhold Niebuhr, *Beyond Tragedy (BT)* (New York: Charles Scribner's Sons, 1937): 28–30. Rather than repeat continually the corrective "sic.," I put it here once to note Niebuhr's continued use of male exclusive language. In this respect, tragically, he was no different than most of his contemporaries. Perhaps it is important neither to decry nor defend him at this point. The real issue here is how we handle this language question in our lives today.

3.   Reinhold Niebuhr, *Moral Man and Immoral Society* (*MMIS*) (New York: Charles Scribner's Sons, 1960 [1932]): 1–22 and Reinhold Niebuhr, *The Nature and Destiny of Man* (*NDM*) (New York: Charles Scribner's Sons, 1964 [1941]): I: 169–203.

4.   Niebuhr, *MMIS*, 113–41 and *NDM* I: 199–203.

5.   D.B. Robertson, ed., *Love and Justice: Selections from the Shorter Writings of Reinhold Niebuhr* (Cleveland and New York: Meridian Books, 1967 [1957]): 97.

6.   Niebuhr, *BT*, 28.

7.   Niebuhr, *MMIS*, 163–8, 177–8, 192–9; *The Irony of American History* (*IAH*) (New York: Charles Scribner's Sons, 1952): 109–11, 120–3; *The Children of Light and the Children of Darkness* (*CLCD*) (New York: Charles Scribner's Sons, 1944): 31–3, 46, 57–60; "Marx and Engels on Religion," (1964) in Ronald H. Stone, ed. *Faith and Politics* (New York: George Braziller, 1968): 51–4; "Optimism, Pessimism and the Christian Faith," in Brown, *Essential*, 10–13.

8.   This characteristic of the papal social encyclicals to play a mediating position outside the fray is exposed in the trenchant work by M.-D. Chenu, *La "doctrine sociale" de l'église comme idéologie* (Paris: Cerf, 1979). The danger of oppressive generalization of the doctrine of sin is highlighted further by Daphne Hampson, who suggests that Niebuhr's conceptions do not even begin to address the notion of sin in women's experience (see "Reinhold Niebuhr on Sin: A Critique," 46–60 in Harries, *Reinhold Niebuhr*).

9.   Bill Kellermann, "Apologist of Power: The Long Shadow of Reinhold Niebuhr's Christian Realism," *Sojourners*, March, 1987, 20.

10.   Niebuhr, *NDM* (New York: Charles Scribner's Sons, 1964 [1943]): II: 56–7.

11.   ibid., 85.

12.   Niebuhr, *NDM* II: 289–301. See Jurgen Moltmann, *Religion, Revolution and the Future*, trans. by M. Douglas Meeks (New York: Charles Scribner's Sons, 1969).

13.   This very earthy character of salvation is captured by Walter Brueggemann in his studies. For one example, see *The Land* (Philadelphia: Fortress, 1977). As well, consult Norman K. Gottwald's monumental study *The Tribes of Yahweh* (Maryknoll, N.Y.: Orbis Books, 1979).

14.   In contrast to Niebuhr's pessimism and "realism," see the alternative by Kellermann in *Sojourners* (March, 1987) cited earlier.

15.   Reinhold Niebuhr, *An Interpretation of Christian Ethics* (New York: Meridian, 1960 [1935]): 23–5, 59–62.

16.   ibid., 61–62.

17.   Fox, op. cit., 88–100, 121–2, 125–6, 128–9, 136–41, 157–8, 160–1, 176–8; Paul Merkley, *Reinhold Niebuhr: A Political Account* (Montreal: McGill-Queen's University Press, 1975): 63–125, 144–50; June Bingham, *Courage to Change* (New York: Charles Scribner's Sons, 1961): 129–39, 143, 155–82, 250–2; Robertson, op. cit., 94–113, 120–32. His occasional writings in *Christian Century, Christianity and Crisis, Nation, New Republic*, etc., show this radical facet

of Niebuhr quite well during those years.

18.   "Religion," *Time* (March 8, 1948): 70–2, 74–6, 79; Kellermann, "Apologist," 15–20; Merkley, op. cit., 150–7, 169–200; Bingham, op. cit., 296–316; Fox, op. cit., 220–2, 228–40, 281–3; Harry R. Davis and Robert C. Good, eds., *Reinhold Niebuhr on Politics* (New York: Charles Scribner's Sons, 1960): 28–36, 182–92, 280–3, 318–20.

19.   Niebuhr, *CLCD*, xiii and 3.

20.   Robertson, op. cit., 68–9; Stone, op. cit., 147.

21.   Stone, op. cit., 142–3, 214.

22.   ibid., 215.

23.   ibid., 216–7.

24.   Certainly a long listing of liberation theologians (Latin American, Asian, African, Afro-American, feminist, etc) could follow, but many of these are so well-known that I would simply invite one to pick a few and dig in. For just one example of how liberation theologians deal with the classic doctrines of the faith, consult the articles of Leonardo Boff in *When Theology Listens to the Poor*, trans. by Robert R. Barr (San Francisco: Harper & Row, 1988 [1984]).

25.   Otto Maduro, "Labour and Religion according to Karl Marx," in *Work and Religion*, ed. Gregory Baum (New York: Seabury Press, 1980): 17. The italics occur in the original.

26.   Marie–Dominique Chenu, interview granted to the author, Paris, May 15, 1979; M.-D. Chenu, "Des femmes..." *Témoignage Chrétien* (6 juin 1952): 1; M.-D. Chenu, "Le Sacerdoce des prêtres-ouvriers," *Vie Intellectuelle* (février, 1954): 175–181; M.-D. Chenu (as Apostolus), "La Prière du peuple," *Quinzaine* (ler août 1953): 4–6; Père Chenu, "Les Dégagements de l'église d'après les leçons de l'histoire," *Lettre aux Communautes* (octobre, 1950): 2–8; M.-D. Chenu, "L'humanisation de la terre, dimension constitutive de l'évangile," *Lumière* 33 (décembre, 1984): 87–90; Bernard Chauveau, worker-priest, interview granted to the author, Paris, May 11, 1979; and M.-D. Chenu, *La "doctrine sociale" de l'Église comme idéologie* (Paris: Cerf, 1979). For an overview of Chenu's life and work, see *Un théologien en liberté: Jacques Duquesne interroge le Père Chenu* (Paris: Centurion, 1975) and Oscar L. Arnal, "Theology and Commitment: Marie-Dominique Chenu," *Cross Currents* 28 (1988): 64–75.

27.   Dorothee Soelle, *Revolutionary Patience* (Maryknoll, N.Y.: Orbis Books, 1977): 50. Other works of Soelle reflecting this compelling theology include: *The Strength of the Weak: Toward a Christian Feminist Identity*, trans. by Robert and Rita Kimber (Philadelphia: Westminster Press, 1984); *Suffering*, trans. by Everett R. Kalin (Philadelphia: Fortress Press, 1975); *The Window of Vulnerability: A Political Spirituality*, trans. by Linda M. Maloney (Minneapolis: Fortress Press, 1990); and, with Shirley A. Cloyes, *To Work and to Love: A Theology of Creation* (Philadelphia: Fortress Press, 1986).

28.   Ecumenical Coalition for Economic Justice, "Resources for Social Action," brochure, 1991–1992. For some data on the Catholic Worker movement and the Sojourners community, see respectively: Dorothy Day, *Loaves and Fishes* (San Francisco: Harper & Row, 1983 [1963]) and Jim Wallis, *Revive Us Again: A Sojourner's Story* (Nashville: Abingdon, 1983).

29.   For C.P.M.O.: *Jésus-Christ et son projet de libération*, juin, 1979; *Que les opprimés aient la vie* (mars, 1981); "Eglise populaire — Église du peuple," *Bulletin de liaison* (2 février, 1980): 1–2; "Église populaire — Solidarité internationale," *Bulletin de liaison* (3 novembre, 1980): 1–2; "L'Église populaire, une réalité vivante," *Bulletin de liaison* (6 novembre, 1981): 1; and interviews with those who have been C.P.M.O. directors: Claude Lefebvre, Montreal, June 28, 1988; Raymond Levac, Montreal, June 27, 1989; and Jean-Guy Casaubon, Montreal, June 10, 1988. For C.A.P.M.O.: Carrefour de Pastorale en Monde Ouvrier, "C.A.P.M.O.," brochure, 1st. 4pp. in C.A.P.M.O. records, Quebec City; "À propos du CAPMO," information piece published by C.A.P.M.O. in C.A.P.M.O.; and interviews with C.A.P.M.O. militants: Vivian Labrie, Waterloo, March 16, 1989; Jean Picher, Montreal, May 12, 1988; Jean-Paul Asselin, Montreal, May 19, 1988; Benoit FortIn, Montreal, May 13, 1988; and Paul-André Fournier, Quebec City, June 21, 1988.

30.   For material on the Politisés Chrétiens: Gregory Baum, "Politisés Chrétiens: A Christian-Marxist Network in Quebec, 1974–1982," *Studies in Political Economy* 32 (Summer, 1990): 7–16; Pierre Goldberger, Protestant member of the network, interview granted to the author, Montreal, May 8, 1989; and from the Archives of Politisés Chrétiens, Centre Saint-Pierre, Montréal: "C'est quoi le reseau des Politisés Chrétiens?" working document, septembre, 1974 and "Les Politisés Chrétiens," 1–2.

31.   Raymond Levac, *L'Église populaire en Amérique Latine et au Québec* (Montréal: C.P.M.O., mars, 1981); "Nouvelles Brèves," *Communauté* 8, 3–4 (1978): 45–46; Roger Poirier, "Un projet global pour l'Ile de Hull," *Communauté* 8, 5–6 (1978): 62–64; "Dossier: Dix ans de courant communautaire au Québec..." *Communauté* 10 (printemps, 1980): 26–27, 32–35, 40–41; "Les Communautés de Base," *Prêtres en classe ouvrière* (printemps, 1982): 1. Interviews: Labrie; Jean-Pierre Roch, Saint-Hyacinthe, May 17, 1988; Marcel Lebel, Montreal, May 17, 1988; Georges Convert and André Choquette, Montreal, May 31, 1988.

32.   "Compte Rendu – Pastorale des milieux populaires," Diocèse de Montréal (28 janvier 1978): 1–13 in Ugo Benfante, private papers; "La Pastorale des milieux populaires," Église de Montréal (22 décembre 1977): 806–808; Jacques Couture, "Trois ans de vie en quartier dans un milieu ouvrier," *Prêtres et Laïcs* XVII (août-septembre, 1967): 327–335; "Vie et travail en quartier populaire," *Dossiers "Vie Ouvrière"* 28 #128 (octobre, 1978): 485–488; "Communauté de base de Pointe St. Charles — Se redire notre histoire..." 6pp. brochure in Benfante papers; "Rendre l'église visible dans un quartier," *Pretres en classe ouvrière* (automne, 1980): 2; Roger Poirier, *Qui a volé la rue principale?* (Montréal: Éditions Départ, 1986); "A Hull, 1967–1987," 65–67 in Leon Gahier, *Avec François d'Assise* (Malonne: published by the Capuchins, 1987). Interviews granted to the author: Ugo Benfante, Fils de la Charité, Montreal, May 10, 1989; Paul-Emile Charbonneau, first bishop of the diocese of Gatineau-Hull, Montreal, June 24, 1988; Petite Soeur Claude, Longueuil, May 18, 1988; Guy Cousin, Fils de la Charité, Montreal, May 7, 1988; Jacques Couture, Jesuit, tape from Madagascar, March 13, 1989; Petit Frère Paul-André Goffart, Montreal, June 2, 1988; Claude Hardy, Capuchin, Montreal, June 22, 1988; Petite Soeur Marie-Paule Lebrun, Montreal, May 24, 1988; Gilles Morissette, Jesuit, Montreal, May 16, 1988; Isidore Ostiguy, Capuchin, Hull, May 9, 1988; Gaëtan Ouellete, Capuchin, Hull, May 10, 1988; Michel Plamandon, Capuchin, Hull, May 10, 1988; Roger Poirier, Oblate, Montreal, June 17, 1988; Petite Soeur Stephanie, Montreal, May 25, 1988; and Pierre Viau, Capuchin, Montreal, June 22, 1988.

33.   Interviews granted to the author: Sister Marie-Paule Lebrun; Dolorès Léger, Saint-Jérome, June 6, 1988; Benoît Fortin, Capuchin, Montreal, May 13, 1988; "L'Usine Coleco," *Dossiers "Vie Ouvrière"* 24 #82 (février, 1974): 115–116; from the private papers of Dolorès Léger: "Curriculum Vitae," 1–7; "La Solidarité Ouvrière" (21 août 1979): 1–12; and "Un nouveau milieu

de travail" (27 juin 1979): 1–11; "Témoignage du veçu en usine..." *Bulletin de l'Entraide Missionnaire* (1er juillet 1982): 7pp.; Stephen Cianca, "From Hotel Worker to Capuchin Provincial," *Mustard Seed* (October, 1986): 1–2, 6; "Un travailleur vs une multinationale," *Relations* (mai, 1980); "Les Travailleurs du Hilton élisent..." *Le Hiltante* (#3 in Fortin, private papers); "La glorieuse bataille d'un capuchin en 'blue jeans,'" *La Semaine* (1er décembre 1984): 52–53; and "Entreuve avec Benoît Fortin," *Vie Ouvrière* (janvier-février, 1986): 6–9.

34.   Benoît Fortin, "Quand se lève le soleil de justice," 17 in Fortin papers.

35.   Interviews granted to the author: Fortin, Ostiguy, Plamandon, Fortin and Ouellete. For a detailed example of this Capuchin theology, see Clodovis Boff, *Feet-on-the-Ground Theology*, trans. by Phillip Berryman (Maryknoll, N.Y.: Orbis Books, 1984).

IDEOLOGY AND TOLERANCE
IN THE THOUGHT OF REINHOLD NIEBUHR*

Dietz Lange

It first occurred to me as a student in Chicago in 1956 that in the thought of
Reinhold Niebuhr there was an abundant source of seminal ideas for social ethics
which had been left almost entirely untapped in the theology of my own country.
We Germans were quite numbed, as it were, by the horrible atrocities committed
by our nation during the Nazi era. As a consequence, as ethicists we have been
so completely preoccupied with coming to terms with our own past that we
failed to take note of even such outstanding foreign thinkers as Niebuhr who
could have aided us tremendously in the very task that lay before us of tackling
the problem of ideology. Instead, our ethical discussion became polarized and
frequently marred by ideological taints of its own.

On the one hand, Lutheran conservatives continued to work with the idea
of the order of creation, i.e., of organic communities supposed to represent the
will of God for society. In the eyes of most contemporaries this stance seemed,
however, to be discredited by the use that had been made of it in supporting the
Nazi cause. So there had to be an alternative. It was provided by the theology
of Karl Barth, who tried to obtain the guidelines for social ethics by drawing
analogies from God's acting in Christ.[1] That implied that ethics should be
founded neither on some sort of principle nor on a technique of compromise but

---

* This essay has since appeared in *Zeitschrift für evangelische Ethik* 38 #1 (January-March 1994),
under the title "Ideologie und Toleranz bei Reinhold Niebuhr." It is published here, with the
author's permission, in the original English version.

97

on a confession. In actual fact, this often turned out, particularly among Barth's followers, to be a highly intuitional, even emotional, ethical discourse which lacked a sober rational analysis of the facts at hand, as that was deemed to be evidence of a failure sufficiently to trust in God, or of falling back into the old trap of complacently lending theological support to the powers that be. The great and well deserved reputation of the Confessing Church whose spiritual leader Barth had been, was compounded with the leftist causes coming up in the student revolt of the late 1960s and 1970s, often becoming highly ideological in the process.

To my mind, neither of these options is valid. Rather, they represent the horns of a dilemma whose tips are the well-known twin evils of tyranny and anarchy. I have come to think of Reinhold Niebuhr's work as a guide which could go far in leading us out of this rather sterile debate, if only we would at last abandon the attitude of academic nationalism which it reflects. This can best be demonstrated, as indicated a short while ago, by referring to Niebuhr's ideas of ideology and tolerance.

In modern technical usage, the term *ideology* is unanimously understood in a derogatory sense, denoting the "false consciousness" in the Marxist sense of the word, i.e., a consciousness disguising egoistic, primarily economic, self-interest, in the service of stabilizing the power of the ruling class.[2] Niebuhr has always maintained this basic definition of the word, even as he later extended its scope beyond the realm of matters economic. Thus far, his use of the term may seem quite conventional. However, what is fascinating about it is the way in which he amalgamated the interpretation of ideology provided, not so much by Karl Marx, but by the modern sociology of knowledge, with the Christian doctrine of sin. The same holds true, analogously, for tolerance, or toleration, as ideology's antonym. Even after Niebuhr had ceased to be a Marxist, he never lost sight of the considerable element of truth in Marx's social analysis as he came to view absolutized self-interest in a very general sense to be a pervasive ingredient in all human life. To my knowledge, Niebuhr has thereby become the first theologian to make ideology one of the central concepts of his thought.

Before I enter into a more detailed analysis, one more preliminary remark might be in order. On re-reading Reinhold Niebuhr's "Intellectual Autobiography," one gains the impression that it was not only the political situation as such which evoked his preoccupation with the phenomenon of ideology. Taking into account the fact that from early on he was himself part of the American political scene, it was apparently also his own involvement in ideological prejudice at early stages of his career which forced him to ponder this problem.[3] Let me demonstrate that by two examples. During World War I,

Niebuhr energetically propagated the Americanization of citizens of German descent. In this context, he posed the rhetorical question: "Do you believe in the justice of the American cause in this great conflict?...I am willing to answer the question without equivocation," namely in the affirmative, and he did not even shrink from calling the American engagement in the hostilities a "crusade."[4] Even if this is seen against the background of the frenzy of German war propaganda and of German-American insecurities, as well as some of the balancing utterances by Niebuhr himself, this may rightly be called some sort of ideological taint. However that may be, his later book, *The Irony of American History*, can be read as one single retractation of that position. Better known is the Marxist line of thought Niebuhr pursued in the 1920s and early 1930s. Not only did he advocate class struggle at that time,[5] even though he had realized quite early that the classless society was a utopian illusion,[6] he even pleaded for a socialist revolution, albeit not with final certainty.[7] This ideological trait stood in stark contrast, by the way, to Niebuhr's own discovery in *Moral Man and Immoral Society* that because of the pervasive condition of structural evil in any society, the most that can be achieved in terms of social justice is "an uneasy balance of power" (232). This inconsistency, much commented upon, is evidenced, e.g., by the fact that Niebuhr was a member of the Socialist Party until as late as 1940, actively campaigning against Roosevelt's New Deal.[8]

Nonetheless, the germ of Niebuhr's thinking about ideology can already be found in *Moral Man and Immoral Society*, in spite of the fact that the very terminology is not utilized, unless I have overlooked something, until an article written seven years later.[9] It is as early as 1932 that Niebuhr states as a basic social fact: particular interests insinuate themselves into even the most idealistic quest for justice under the conscious or unconscious pretext of being identical with the common weal.[10] Of course, this is still a quite conventional description of the phenomenon. But in order not to overtax your patience, I shall refrain from meticulously tracing the development of the ideas of ideology and tolerance in Niebuhr's intellectual biography and limit myself to analyzing their significance in his mature thought.

IDEOLOGY

It is my thesis that Niebuhr's concept of ideology is an ingenious synthesis of Karl Mannheim's universalizing use of the term in his sociology of knowledge on the one hand and the Pauline-Augustinian-Lutheran theological tradition concerning the doctrine of sin on the other.[11] Of these two elements precedence clearly belongs to the latter, both in a temporal sense and in terms of weight.

Niebuhr's first attempt at expounding a coherent, distinctly theological doctrine of sin is to be found in *An Interpretation of Christian Ethics* (1935).[12] In this book sin is defined as "rebellion against God" insofar as "man makes pretensions of being absolute in his finiteness" (81). This amounts to his claim of being God himself (82). It is a well-known characteristic of Niebuhr's teaching, however, that, even as he began to draw more explicitly and consistently on the resources of traditional Christian theology, he never ignored the social aspect of sin as it was inculcated upon him by the Social Gospel. The pertinent question, therefore, is in which way he combined these two different views.

Looking closely at the context of the quotes cited a moment ago, one notices that he did not do this in terms of a temporal or logical sequence, as though social deviation resulted from some preceding act of revolt against God. Instead, man's rebellious claim to deity is *ipso facto* a claim to absoluteness for the social group — and thus "the root of all imperialism" (81f.). This is so because humans are not, as Niebuhr's critics have often made him appear to say, first isolated individuals before God, and second, social beings. Rather, they can never be understood apart from the relationships in which they exist. (It is true that Niebuhr's thinking on this point did not reach full clarity until his *The Self and the Dramas of History* (1955).) In other words, the religious and social aspects of sin are two sides of the same coin, and in actual human life they are inseparably interrelated. In both respects a human being is in a state of self-contradiction in that he abuses his "capacity for self-transcendence," instead of using it appropriately to view "his finite existence under the perspective of its eternal essence,"[13] i.e., of its being owed to God's creative love. Since humans are capable, in principle, of recognizing their finiteness as well as their essence, this self-contradiction is steeped in dishonesty (83).

It is obvious that even before any overt reference to the sociology of knowledge, this theological description of sin already contains most of the essential elements of Niebuhr's later theory of ideology — without so much as using the term. Taking into account the crucial importance of the doctrine of sin for Niebuhr's theology, this constitutes a hint concerning the central place to be allotted to ideology in his thought. Now, Karl Mannheim's *Ideology and Utopia* first appeared in English in 1936.[14] Niebuhr might conceivably have read it in 1939, since one characteristic idea of that book appears in an article he wrote in that year: Marxist theory is criticized for its own involvement in ideological pretension.[15] There is, however, no reference to Mannheim in this article, the first explicit quotes occur in *The Nature and Destiny of Man* (*NDM*) (I: 196f. and II: 237f.).

Mannheim's analysis of ideology starts from the Marxian definition alluded to in the introduction to the present paper. He rebukes, however, Marx's tacit assumption that the interests of the proletarian class objectively represented the common interest of society as a whole and thus were non-ideological. Second, he extends the notion beyond the boundaries of *economic* self-interest: "ideology" is an expression of the "existential" and "situational determination" of knowledge[16] which covers all aspects of living conditions in a given society. Niebuhr follows Mannheim on both counts,[17] apparently because this concept of ideology enables him empirically to corroborate his doctrine of sin and thereby lend it immediate relevance for the realm of social relations. To him, too, the bourgeois libertarian and the proletarian egalitarian view are equally tinged by self-interest and thus are ideological.[18] And what Niebuhr calls "the existential intimacy between idea and interest in human affairs"[19] is the exact equivalent to Mannheim's "situational determination." He had the wisdom, however, not to approve of Mannheim's attempt at solving the epistemological problem arising from a universalized concept of ideology, viz. his supposition of an intellectual elite capable of gradually overcoming ideological narrow-mindedness. As the German philosopher Max Horkheimer rightly suggested, this very supposition is itself highly ideological.[20] Niebuhr's objection amounts to much the same. But, unfortunately, he offers no alternative. This is due to the absence of an epistemological theory in Niebuhr's thought. As Paul Tillich once remarked: "Niebuhr does not ask, 'How do I know?'; he starts knowing. And he does not ask afterward, 'How could I know?'; but leaves the convincing power of his thought without epistemological support."[21] Niebuhr simply presupposes the existence of some limited ability of reason to acquire knowledge, just as he presupposes some "capacity for justice" even in the unredeemed sinner.[22] The only reasons he gives for so doing are that it takes an "effort to hide...ignorance by pretension,"[23] and that "false judgements depend upon true judgements for their prestige."[24] But how am I to know just which one of several conflicting judgements is true? Niebuhr is, of course, right in maintaining that ideology, and therefore also the achievement of unveiling it, is a moral affair rather than an intellectual one.[25] But this does not render superfluous the questions of which tools the will to honesty should use or by what method it should proceed to reach its goal.

This lack of epistemological interest may be due, at least in part, to the emphasis laid upon the doctrine of sin into which the concept of ideology is incorporated. So it is appropriate to take another look at this doctrine, this time at the fully developed stage it reached in Niebuhr's *magnum opus* (*NDM*). The basic form of sin, according to this book, along with the whole Augustinian tradition, is pride; one might also say, with Søren Kierkegaard, a person's will to be him- or herself[26] (i.e., to be that by oneself). Pride has its counterpart in sensuality, the will not to be oneself (ibid.). This second form of sin, however, is deemed far less important by Niebuhr. In support of his view, one may once again refer to Kierkegaard who maintains that upon closer analysis, sensuality turns out to be but a variant of the rebellion against God.[27] That rebellion is basically the refusal to accept one's self as it is willed by God "either by exalting or by debasing it." I would offer the additional suggestion that both of these forms of sin can and do occur in both men and women — contrary to Kierkegaard's opinion, by the way.

Pride is what Niebuhr called earlier the human claim to absoluteness. It is basically spiritual pride, self-deification (I: 200). But is does not have to be explicitly spiritual, e.g., self-righteousness before God (I: 201f). At any event, spiritual pride is the driving force behind the three mundane forms of pride: pride of power, intellectual and moral pride. The first of these is, in turn, the basis of the other two: the all-encompassing lust for power, be it over the world of nature or over human beings (I: 187–194). As an expression of sin, pride of power is boundless (I: 194) in that it represents the claim to divine omnipotence.

This description is obviously true not only to Reformation theology but also to the experience of the totalitarian regimes of the time, with the full inclusion of the Soviet Union, since Niebuhr had dropped the last of his Marxist delusions after the great purges of the mid-1930s. This was certainly not a nicely or even complacently "balanced" view in the sense of neutralizing the criticisms levelled at both sides. Rather, Niebuhr's frequent quoting the "plague on both your houses" implies the resolve to fight with equal fierceness the ideological idolatries on the right as well as on the left of the political spectrum, albeit with a relative moral preference for the socialist concern for the underprivileged.

Pride of power is sublimated into intellectual pride, the claim to absolute truth. It is this claim in any of its forms, even as Christian dogmatism, which is called ideology (I: 194). It is described more specifically as both the "ignorance of the finiteness of the human mind" and the "attempt to obscure the known character of human knowledge and the taint of self-interest in human truth" (I: 194f.). The lack of self-criticism which is the hallmark of ideological thinking (I: 196f.) is thus due to both ignorance and dishonesty,[28] and to both self-deception and the deception of others; it is partly conscious, partly subconscious (I: 203f.): it is "willing ignorance" (I: 205), as it were. The element of deception indicates the "vestige of truth" which is never completely absent and which accounts for ideology's being an attributable guilt rather than a blind fate (I:

203). Dishonesty must therefore be regarded as a clear indication of an uneasy conscience, however much suppressed this conscience may be.[29]

The last remark points to the fact that dishonesty is not just an instinctive reflex of some psychological state of tension. It rather serves the specific purpose of self-justification before the tribunal of public opinion. Therefore intellectual pride necessarily implies moral pride (I: 198). In this way, morality itself is inextricably tied up with sin, to the extent of being its very means (I: 199).

This is Reinhold Niebuhr's theory of ideology in outline. One always has to bear in mind, I might add, that he consistently subjected his own thinking to the impact of this criticism as well. It is not least because of this fact that he still has so much to say in our day. Of course, his thought also bears the signs of its time. One might try to challenge it from the point of view of a later generation by finding fault with its neglect of the other aspect of sin, the loss of self in vitality. That criticism is frequently put forward by contemporary feminist theology.[30] One could also argue that the potent mixture of neo-Marxist thought and unabashed hedonism concocted in the sixties by Herbert Marcuse and others was patently ideological but could certainly not be subsumed under the label of self-assertion without at least a measure of ambiguity. I would maintain, however, that this does not really affect the essence of Niebuhr's theory. This kind of criticism could reasonably call for supplementing, but not for revoking, Niebuhr's understanding. After all, as I suggested earlier, I believe one would have to agree with Kierkegaard that the will to be oneself (by oneself) and the will not to be oneself are in the last analysis but two different forms of the same human rebellion against God.

Looking back upon what we have found thus far, we can discern two distinctive features of Niebuhr's reflections on ideology which are worth noting. On the empirical plane, he succeeds in joining the individual and social aspects of ideology by means of an adroit combination of Marxist, modern sociological (Mannheim), and Freudian elements (cf. I: 34 and 42f.). The spurious ideological justification of economic, political and spiritual power is due to each individual's situational determination, which is raised to the nth power by being transferred to, and compounded in, the social group. The phenomenon is thereby characterized as being both inevitable and attributable to human responsibility, since each individual is both dependent upon, and contributes to, the conditions of the society in which he or she lives. This paradoxical result will be found to be an extremely apt description or reality by anyone who ever lived under a totalitarian regime. For Niebuhr, such a state of affairs in a society is the reflection in experience of what is meant by the doctrine of original sin on the religious plane, the antinomy of fate and guilt in man's estrangement from God (instead of some sort of biological transmission).

Whereas this theological interpretation of sin cannot claim to be something entirely new, what is fascinating in Niebuhr is the way in which he connects the two planes, experiential and religious. Another way of saying it is that Niebuhr managed to do something that few theologians in the history of Protestant thought have been able to do: he closely intertwined the so-called two realms of Lutheran theology (which are actually two modes of God's Lordship) without for one moment mixing them up and thereby hopelessly moralizing the Christian faith. God's immediate Lordship over the human heart and conscience, and God's Lordship over history which is mediated by human responsibility are thus moulded into a dialectical unity. In transferring this theological construction to a democratic model of society, Niebuhr has been able fully to unfold the critical potential which was part and parcel of Luther's original conception of that doctrine, but had remained dormant for so long in conservative Lutheran theology, even to the extent of being *de facto* eliminated by the reactionary use being made of the idea of the "order of creation."

On the other hand, in my opinion Niebuhr's theory suffers from a severe lack of clarity at one crucial point. Sin in the genuinely religious sense of the word is the depravation of the individual's relationship to God. How then does Niebuhr explain the origin of structural evil in society on that basis? He explicitly rebukes (and I think grossly misunderstands) Schleiermacher's solution which speaks of a social texture of sin, based upon a model of society which construes it basically as a product of the interaction of its members.[31] Niebuhr fails, however, to name an alternative, and thus leaves the problem unsolved. This sociological gap is the main reason for his failure to solve the thorny epistemological problem posed by a universalized concept of ideology. The only imaginable solution, or more precisely, approximation to a solution, would indeed be, in my mind, an understanding of society as a process of interaction between individuals and groups which would at least provide for the possibility of a mutual correction of ideological "blind spots." Niebuhr's later analysis of the "dialogue between the self and others"[32] could have provided the tools for such a solution. But he did not really succeed in moulding them. On the one hand, society appears as a whole toward which the individual can either look up in search for fulfilment or down in contempt for its lack of morality (I: 35). On the other hand, in the horizontal perspective Niebuhr only describes the individual's self-identification with his community in the case of conflict with some rival group (38), but concerning the internal structure of the community, he contents himself with very general terms like "dramatic patterns" or a "web of destiny for the individual" (44), without going into further detail. Communication appears to be limited to relationships between individual selves (30–33), and one does not see in which way it creates the "threads" making up that "web of destiny." Neither does Niebuhr talk much about mutual correction, nor is there some such thing as *esprit de corps*, informed by shared responsibility for the larger whole. Rather, such responsibility seems to be, at least in his theoretical thought, confined to the individual agent.

TOLERANCE

Tolerance is a concept which impressed itself on the Western mind in the meaning it acquired through the Enlightenment: granting to others the right to hold convictions, to follow customs, etc., different from those accepted by the majority. John Locke's famous *Letter Concerning Toleration* of 1689 is perhaps the most celebrated, but by no means the only pertinent, document. Tolerance is reasonable and necessary, according to Locke and many others, because of the inherent limitations of human knowledge. This is unforgettably illustrated by the well-known parable of the rings in Lessing's drama *Nathan: Man of Wisdom*. Niebuhr combines that interpretation — true to his basic synthesis of Renaissance and Reformation (II: 157–212) — with a genuinely theological one which subsequently constitutes the dominant component of his definition of the term. Tolerance thus becomes the antonym of ideology: for it is the ideological sin of intellectual pride which generates intolerance (I: 200). Conversely, tolerance implies the recognition of both "the fragmentary character of one's own wisdom" and "the guilt with which our own virtue is tainted."[33] This description represents a definite step beyond the rather conventional view of tolerance put forward in *An Interpretation of Christian Ethics*, where it is simply called a "rational ideal" (204).

Tolerance as an antidote to the ideological taint is founded on God's forgiveness (II: 217) — in the knowledge that the truth of the Gospel which proclaims that forgiveness can never become a human possession (II: 243). God's power and wisdom remain, as Luther would have said, *potentia et sapientia aliena*, God's power and wisdom, not our own (II: 107–126). Tolerance therefore requires human self-criticism which cleanses us from any pretense to absolute truth.[34]

Because of its foundation in faith, however, tolerance is not to be confused with indifference: instead, it unites humility with firm conviction, contrition with commitment.[35] This account can be traced back to Luther's idea of the lifelong dialectical unity of repentance and faith: true faith continually returns to baptism, i.e., the mortification of the old self and the creation of a new one.[36] Moreover, not only is tolerance based on forgiveness (God's toleration, as Luther sometimes puts it[37]), but it is itself forgiveness extended to others with regard to their errors and shortcomings (II: 218).

This combination of self-criticism and forgiveness has a two-fold function in Niebuhr's thought. On the one hand, it constitutes the "test of toleration," i.e., whether or not the Gospel of God's forgiveness has been rightly understood (II: 219). On the other hand, this kind of tolerance is the basis of democracy.[38] Niebuhr's Christian plea for democracy does not exclude, as it might appear, the possibility of an "ideology of democracy" as it has been exemplified in the specifically American temptation of an idealism inadvertently — or sometimes cynically — becoming imperialist under the slogan of "making the world safe for democracy." On the contrary, a considerable part of Niebuhr's political writings is devoted to this very perversion of the spirit of tolerance.[39] Nonetheless, Niebuhr's point seems to be well taken that a society, especially one which is pluralistic in ethnic, racial, and religious terms, would best be served by a mentality informed by the sort of tolerance he has in mind.

Also, Niebuhr seems right in suggesting that the spirit of humility, both historically and philosophically, is the crucial point of contact between religion — Christian religion in particular — and democracy,[40] provided the "positive" virtue of charity supplements it.[41] He is of course fully aware of the fact that the modern world can neither be called Christian in essence nor can one reasonably expect to "Christianize the social order," as Walter Rauschenbusch once suggested.[42] Niebuhr assumes, however, and not without empirical evidence, that the secular mind, apart from any specifically religious presuppositions, is capable of recognizing the limited character of all human knowledge, and thus also of competently criticizing "the false universalities of dogmatic religion" (II: 232), thereby reminding the latter of one of its own basic tenets.

Niebuhr's analysis also does justice to the actual historical roots of tolerance, both in the breakdown of the unquestioned authority of the one "ruling" Catholic church through the Reformation, and in the increasing rational scepticism toward religion itself, springing not least from the gruelling experience of the seventeenth century confessional wars as well as from the continuing intolerance of the churches and the absolutist states in the period immediately following. To be sure, the optimistic belief in progress, so characteristic of the Enlightenment, does not have a part in Niebuhr's understanding of tolerance. Rationalist scepticism, however, *is* very clearly reflected in his criticism of ideology, especially as he explicitly extends it to the Christians and their church (I: 200). The inclusion of this scepticism in a

Reformation type of piety not only turns out to be completely compatible with the essential spirit of that very piety but also helps to imbue it with a specific relevance for modern times. Niebuhr is true to both traditions when he considers all concrete forms of piety as relative, even tainted by elements of sin.[43] There is thus, for him, no difference between the church and secular society as far as the ideological taint in human reasoning is concerned, since a Christian is *simil iustus et peccator*, as Luther has it.

CONCLUSION

In conclusion, let me say that Niebuhr's exposition of ideology and tolerance is, in my opinion, one of his most remarkable contributions to twentieth century theology, and political theory as well. If I may insert a personal note at this point, Niebuhr's criticism of ideology rang more than one bell with me as the Nazi ideology and the utter disillusionment with it had been one of the most incisive experiences of my own biography. But apart from that, I am convinced that even after the eclipse of the great political ideologies that dominated the better part of this century, it has lost none of its relevance. The unblushing capitalism practised by Westerners in Eastern Europe and resurgent nationalism and tribalism in many parts of the world, and in Germany in particular, are only the most obvious cases in point.

There is but one question that remains: Is Niebuhr's analysis perhaps focused too much on the negative aspects of the problem? Ideology must be criticized, i.e., negated, and what is called for is tolerance which is based on humility and forgiveness, i.e., the negation of undue self-assertion. Niebuhr has much less to say not on whether but on how a constructive consensus is to come about. Instead he introduces somewhat too quickly his demand for institutional checks and balances at this point. These are to secure a reasonable equilibrium of power (in the sense of a balance between equality and freedom[44]), and thus to enforce a sufficient degree of tolerance. Between these two aspects, the power of institutional enforcement and the forming of a constructive basis for social action, there is the sociological gap we had already encountered earlier. There would have to be some model of social interaction, as was suggested then, without, of course, the concomitant illusion that such interactions were in any respect immune to failure. This interaction would have to be guided by some moral attitude binding the self and others together so that they form a group which *as a group* is able to act morally. But something like Josiah Royce's concept of loyalty to a common cause which plays exactly this role in Helmut Richard Niebuhr's ethics,[45] or a reference to Talcott Parson's *The Social*

System,[46] is conspicuously absent from Niebuhr's thought. It goes without saying, of course, that such a "cause" would have to be subjected to constant scrutiny. The polemic against a starry-eyed belief in progress, undoubtedly required in his day, was so predominant in Niebuhr's writings that it never for once permitted him to recognize the necessity of developing a more adequate theory of the relationship between the individual moral agent and the collective social agent, beyond the very general thesis that individual moral attitudes (or rather, immoral attitudes) are accumulated and compounded in society, however well deserved the wide acclaim this thesis has won him. That lack of a positive counterpart to the doctrine of sin in Reinhold Niebuhr's theory of social action may seem strange in view of the fact that he explicitly acknowledged that all his life he had "profited greatly from his [brother's] clearer formulations of views I came to hold in common with him."[47] Yet the contributions of the two did in fact remain distinctly different from, if not complementary to, each other. I am sure Reinhold Niebuhr would not have minded this final note which adds to the remembrance of his 100th birthday a reminder of the 30th anniversary of his brother's death.

NOTES

This paper is rendered here essentially in the form in which it was presented at the McGill Symposium, save for some improvements suggested by the comments of Professor Maurice Boutin's thoughtful critique and the ensuing discussion on that occasion. Both are hereby gratefully acknowledged. Abbreviations follow the usage established by *Theologische Realenzyklopädie.*

1.   Cf. in particular, Karl Barth, *Christengemeinde und Bürgergemeinde* (ThSt (B) 20), Zollikon 1946; and *Church and State*, trans. R. Howe (London 1939).

2.   *Christianity and Power Politics* (*CPP*) (N.Y.: Scribner's, 1940), 108–113. Cf. Karl Marx, *Die deutsche Ideologie: Kritik der neuesten deutschen Philosophie in ihren Repräsentanten Feuerbach, B. Bauer und Stirner, und des deutschen Sozialismus in seinen verscheidenen Propheten* (*Frühe Schriften*, vol. 2) ed. H.-J. Lieber and P. Furth, (Wiss. Buchgesellschaft, Darmstadt: 1971): 56, 204, 346f., 510.

3.   *Reinhold Niebuhr: His Religious, Social and Political Thought*, ed. Charles W. Kegley and R.W. Bretall (N.Y.: Macmillan, 1956): 1–23, especially pp. 8–10. This is the second volume in the *Library of Living Theology*. Hereafter *LLT*.

4.   "The Present Task of the Sunday School," (July 1918) in *Young Reinhold Niebuhr: His Early Writings 1911-1931*, ed. William G. Chrystal (St. Louis, MI: Eden Publishing House, 1977): 90f.

5.   *Does Civilization Need Religion? A Study in the Social Resources and Limitations of Religion in Modern Life* (N.Y.: Macmillan, 1927): 59f; "Is Stewardship Ethical?" (1930) in *Love and Justice: Selections from the Shorter Writings*, ed. D.B. Robertson (Philadelphia: Westminster Press, 1957): 89–94.

6.   *Moral Man and Immoral Society: A Study in Ethics and Politics (MMIS)* (N.Y.: Scribner's, 1932): 164; *Reflections on the End of an Era (REE)* (N.Y.: Scribner's, 1934): 136 and 210.

7.   *REE*, 81 and 156–162.

8.   Cf. Arthur Schlesinger, Jr. "Reinhold Niebuhr's Role in Political Thought," in *LLT* II: 126–150, 142.

9.   "Ideology and Pretense," *The Nation* 149:24 (1939): 645f. Reprinted in *CPP*.

10.   *MMIS*, 45 and 214.

11.   The basic texts are *CPP*, 107–115; *The Nature and Destiny of Man (NDM)* (N.Y.: Scribner's, 1943): I: 194–198; and *Christian Realism and Political Problems (CRPP)* (N.Y.: Scribner's, 1953): 75–94.

12.   Quoted from the "Living Age Book" edition (N.Y.: Meridian, 1953): 65–93. Page numbers refer to this edition.

13.   This terminology which seems to occur here for the first time does not necessarily stem from Tillich, who at least in his writings does not use it until a much later time.

14.   (London: Routledge and Kegan Paul). I shall quote from the 9th impression (N.Y.: Harcourt, Brace and World, 1966).

15.   *CPP*, 112. Cf. Mannheim, op. cit. 225.

16.   Mannheim, op. cit., 69 and 239. The English translation uses two different terms: "situational determination" and "existential determination" for Mannheim's *Seinsgebundenheit* and *Seinsverbundenheit*. But the German terms are synonyms that can be used interchangeably. The difference in form is to be explained by the fact that Chapter 5, which uses the second of these terms, had been published separately some time before its incorporation in the book.

17.   *NDM* II: 197 and *CRPP*, 76f.

18.   *CRPP*, 80–82 and 89f.

19.   ibid., 92. Cf. 90.

20.   *"Ein neuer Ideologiebegriff?"* in *Ideologie*, ed. K. Lenk (Luchterhand, Frankfurt: 1971): 283–303. Cf. Niebuhr, *CRPP*, 81f. and 91–94. Also Mannheim, op. cit., 262–275.

21.   "Reinhold Niebuhr's Doctrine of Knowledge," in *LLT* II: 35.

22.   *The Children of Light and the Children of Darkness: A Vindication of Democracy and a Critique of Its Traditional Defense (CLCD)* (1944; reprint, N.Y.: Scribner's, 1960): xiii.

23.   *NDM* II: 182.

24.   *CRPP*, 77.

25.   ibid., 92f.

26.   *NDM* II: 186. Page numbers in the text from this point refer to the edition mentioned in Note 11 above. Cf. Søren Kierkegaard, *Sickness Unto Death* (German ed. trans. E. Hirsch): 47–74; (Princeton: Princeton University Press, 1944): 78–107. Curiously, Niebuhr does not quote this work in the context cited, although he does mention it on another occasion (II: 171).

27.   op. cit., 66.

28.   *Faith and History: A Comparison of Christian and Modern Views of History (FH)* (N.Y.: Scribner's, 1949): 161.

29.   *NDM* I: 196f. Cf. "Christian Faith and Natural Law" (1940) in *Love and Justice*, 46–54. In *CRPP* (79) Niebuhr suggests that ideological pretense "must be regarded as at least quasi-conscious." This emphasis is certainly made in order to secure human responsibility. Nevertheless, one may doubt from an empirical point of view, whether that is an improvement.

30.   Cf., e.g., Judith E. Plaskow, *Sex, Sin and Grace: Women's Experience and the Theologies of Reinhold Niebuhr and Paul Tillich*, PhD thesis, Yale University (1976).

31.   Friedrich D.E. Schleiermacher, *The Christian Faith*, §§ 69.71 (after the second German edition). Niebuhr lumps Schleiermacher together with the Social Gospel (*NDM* I: 246), erroneously asserting that Schleiermacher lets sin originate from the social institutions.

32.   *The Self and the Dramas of History (SDH)* (N.Y.: Scribner's, 1955). Page numbers in the following sentences refer to this edition.

33.   *FH*, 234. Cf. *NDM* II: 214.

34.   *FH*, 234.

35.   *NDM* II: 219. Cf. *CLCD*, 134–137 and 150.

36.   Martin Luther, *"Sermon von dem heiligen hochwürdigen Sakrament der Taufe,"* (1519) WA 2,728,10–729,5. Cf. *De captivitate Babylonica* (1520) WA 6,535,4–10 and *FH*, 152.

37.   WA 20,146,25–36. Cf. G. Ebeling, *"Die Toleranz Gottes und die Toleranz der Vernunft,"* in *Glaube und Toleranz. Das Erbe der Aufklärung*, ed. T. Rendtorff, G. Mohn (Gütersloh, 1982): 54–73. Luther was not ready to tolerate unbelief to be sure; human toleration, for him, was motivated by love, not by faith. Cf. WA 2,431,35–37.

38.   See the chapter on Democratic toleration and community groups in *CLCD*, 119–152.

39.   Cf. *The Irony of American History* (N.Y.: Scribner's, 1952): 130–150 and *The Structure of Nations and Empires: A Study of the Recurring Patterns and Problems of the Political Order in Relation to the Unique Problems of the Nuclear Age* (N.Y.: Scribner's, 1959): 295–297.

40.   *CLCD*, 151.

41.   ibid., 137 and 143.

42.   *Christianizing the Social Order* (N.Y.: Macmillan, 1912).

43.   *CLCD*, 134 and 137.

44.   *CRPP*, 28f. and 135. Cf. *SDH*, 151, 195 and 200.

45.   See H.R. Niebuhr's *The Responsible Self: An Essay in Christian Moral Philosophy*, ed. James M. Gustafson, (San Francisco: Harper and Row, 1963): 56–60 and 79–89. Cf. also Royce's *The Philosophy of Loyalty* (N.Y.: Macmillan, 1908): 16–21.

46.   (Tavistock, 1952).

47.   *LLT* II: 4.

THE THEOLOGICAL FOUNDATIONS
OF REINHOLD NIEBUHR'S SOCIAL THOUGHT

Gordon Harland

Reinhold Niebuhr was the preeminent American "political theologian," or theologian of public affairs, in this century. For four decades prior to his death in 1971, his influence had gone out in all directions. Rarely has a theologian achieved such respect from so many diverse groups. Writing in *The New Leader* a few months after Niebuhr's death, historian Arthur Schlesinger kept coming back to this question: "Why," asked Schlesinger, did "this passionate, profound and humble believer have so penetrating an influence on so many non-believers?" He concluded that it lay in Niebuhr's "capacity to restate historical Christianity in terms that corresponded to our most searching modern themes and anxieties."[1] Such was Niebuhr's achievement in providing a Christian interpretation of the most problematic aspects of human existence, that Giles Gunn has remarked that "Niebuhr helped change the image of theologian and thus opened up opportunities for a more constructive dialogue between faith and culture, theology and literature, by devoting less of his attention to criticizing, revising and extending the traditions of theology itself as Barth, Brunner, and the others did, than to bringing the insights of those traditions to bear upon issues and problems in contemporary life."[2]

The key to this achievement was the manner in which he combined central Christian doctrines and a tragic sense of life with a passionate concern for social justice which had marked the social gospel. More specifically, his most distinctive achievement was the way in which his interpretation of such central doctrines as sin, grace, atonement and justification illuminated *both* our personal

113

and collective life. These doctrines, which are usually related only to our personal quests for forgiveness, renewal and meaning became in Niebuhr's hands the basis also for his social and political theology. Although, as Larry Rasmussen has noted, his "theology was always the controlling framework," nevertheless the felicity with which he communicated to such a great variety of audiences sometimes obscured the degree to which his thought was shaped by Christian symbols.[3]

In this paper I attempt to do two things: first, to indicate the shape of Niebuhr's theology by pointing to a few of its major themes; and second, to discuss the importance of these themes for understanding the nature of his Christian Realism, his political ethic and social critique.

THEOLOGICAL THEMES

Niebuhr's thought is focused on human nature and history. The two themes are intimately related, even intertwined, because for him, human beings are primarily historical creatures, their "real milieu is history."[4] His passionate concern — indeed, his life-long quest — was to gain an understanding of human nature that would do justice to both the radicality of human freedom and to the serious, pervasive corruption of that freedom. An understanding of both the creative and the disruptive effects of human freedom upon our communities, he constantly urged, was an indispensable resource in our attempt to build communities that are secure, free, tolerant and just.

(a) Human Nature

His interpretation of Christianity provided him with his understanding of human nature. Although the Christian view insists on our weakness and finiteness, through the doctrine of the 'image of God' it emphasizes the human capacity for self transcendence. Limited as we are by the necessities of nature and history, still the mark of our humanity is the capacity of the self "to stand as it were, above the structures and coherences of the world."[5] This radical freedom is the source of human uniqueness, our openness to the future, and the basis of our creativity. It is also the basis of human destructiveness. In *The Nature and Destiny of Man*, Niebuhr developed his understanding of human uniqueness through the metaphor the 'image of God.' It is a profoundly relational term and in *The Self and the Dramas of History* he sought to draw out the meaning of the term still further by elaborating the "dialogic life" that marks human existence. "The self," he says, "is a creature which is in constant dialogue with itself, with its neighbors, and with God according to the Biblical viewpoint."[6] Both Judaism and Christianity "interpret the self's experience with the ultimate in the final reaches of its self-awareness as a dialogue with God."[7] In this dialogue the self is judged, not for its finiteness, but for its sin and the judgment is made by a love which has the power not only to convict but also to uphold and redeem.

The language of dialogue highlights the personal nature of the relationships which mark human life but it would be a mistake to construe this after the manner of individualism. "Community," Mrs. Niebuhr has recently reminded us, was "very important" in Niebuhr's "thinking and writing."[8] The relation of the individual to the community is a large subject, one that brings into sharp focus the major problems and perils of our age, and Niebuhr's writing on the topic is extensive. Only a few brief comments can be offered here to indicate his approach.

The community is, on the one hand, the fulfillment of the individual. We have our being in relationship. To enter into true selfhood, the individual must be drawn into wider relationships. The community sustains our existence and is necessary for self-fulfillment. Moreover the community is organism as well as artifact, and over against the philosophy of individualism he would urge that "the community is as primordial as the individual,"[9] from which understanding he made his criticism of the social contract theory.

The community, nevertheless, remains the frustration of the individual. The individual's quest for ultimate meaning cannot be supplied by the morally ambiguous life of any historical community. Moreover, the understanding that human selfhood is grounded in the relationship with God can provide a significant leverage over against any institutional or political order, a matter of large significance in this technological age which facilitates concentrations of power. Niebuhr put the significance of this theological context succinctly in this way: "The problem of the individual and the community cannot be solved at all if the height is not achieved where the sovereign source and end of both individual and communal existence are discerned, and where the limits are set against the idolatrous self-worship of both individuals and communities."[10]

(b) Theology of History

Although the theological grounding of Niebuhr's understanding of human nature is clear, at no point was the Christian character of his interpretation more explicit than in his understanding of history. We may get at this understanding by first noting the significance for its framework of three terms — the unity of history, the ambiguity of history and the relationship of mystery and meaning.

The first word to be said about the Christian view is that history is conceived as a unity. All historical destiny is understood as under the sovereignty of the one God. But history is fraught with ambiguity. The people of God's choices in the Bible are not immune from idolatry. Individuals and nations are destroyed not just because they are vain and proud, but because they are also powerless. And when it is discerned that the judgment of God is being meted out, the executors of the divine judgment are frequently anything but exemplars of the divine righteousness. Faced with such moral ambiguity we are tempted, he says, either "to the despairing conclusion that there is no meaning to the total historical enterprise and that history is merely a bewildering confusion of 'death for the right cause, death for the wrong cause, paeans of victory and groans of defeat,' or that it is under a sovereignty too mysterious to conform fully to the patterns of meaning which human beings are able to construct."[11] The relationship between meaning and mystery is crucial in all Niebuhr's work. It is a theme to which he constantly returned not only in his preaching but also in his theological and political writings. There is meaning in history; there is a relationship between purpose and value. But meaning is always in a context, it is set in a penumbra of mystery, and mystery, he stresses, "does not annul meaning but enriches it."[12] These perspectives enter into and help shape Niebuhr's interpretation of history.

The core of his interpretation is a sustained reflection on the meaning of the Christ event, "an event," he writes, "through which the meaning of the whole of history is apprehended and the specific nature of the divine sovereignty of history is revealed."[13] The central focus of the Christ event, for Niebuhr, is the cross; the divine revelation is accomplished through the act of reconciliation; the atonement, he emphasized, is the content of the incarnation. And it is from this centre that he developed his theology of history; it is also here that we find the basis of his political theology. He was explicit about this: "This doctrine of Atonement and justification," he said "is the 'stone' which the builders rejected, and which must be made 'the head of the corner.' It is an absolutely essential presupposition for the understanding of human nature and human history."[14] This sweeping statement, so arresting in its boldness, is not the sort that one expects from a thinker so widely renowned for his political analysis. (Indeed this may have been one of the passages he was thinking about when he remarked in *Man's Nature and His Communities* that he would "use more sober symbols..."[15]) The doctrine was, however, utterly indispensable for Niebuhr. It gathered up so many of his themes. The doctrine presents humanity in all our complexity, our possibilities and our sin, our grandeur and our misery. At the same time, the doctrine discloses how the divine love takes our sin into itself and conquers it there, without abrogating the distinctions between good and evil upon which every healthy society depends. Indeed the central dialectic of Niebuhr's thought, the relation between love and justice, finds here, its ultimate basis. The justice of God is God's love dealing with corruption. Thus to seek love without a concern for justice is to sentimentalize and utterly distort the Gospel. But the justice of God does not exist apart from, or merely alongside, God's love. The ultimate dimension of divine justice is a love which takes into itself our violation of that same law of love. Such is the theological rootage of Niebuhr's ethics and that is why the understanding of the Cross and the doctrine of the atonement were so central to him.

At this point, I wish to mention an article by Langdon Gilkey — "Reinhold Niebuhr's Theology of History" — in my view one of the most perceptive short analyses of Niebuhr's theology that we have. The thesis of the article is that in contrast to the "temporal dialectic" of some contemporary "eschatological-political theologies," Niebuhr's thought is marked by a "vertical dialectic" in which God in past, present and future is transcendent to, yet related with, us creatures in all aspects of our being and behavior. That large and important matter need not detain us here. But Gilkey was surely right when he stressed how Niebuhr's "cross centred" theology shaped his political thought. Here is how Gilkey puts it.

> He [Niebuhr] held to a theology of atonement, justification and reconciliation as opposed to a messianic theology of a divine victory over evil men and evil orders, because he felt the former was a better *political* theology than the latter — and, note, better in terms of its possibilities for achieving justice, freedom, and humanity in history....His theology of atonement, justification, and the paradox of grace was not designed to eradicate hope for the future but precisely to eradicate the nemesis of self destructive fanaticism and the despair that arise therefrom. His theology sought to provide the most creative ground of political action possible. Even at its seemingly most impractical and theological, it was always a political theology, the theoretical ground for *praxis*.[16]

The full flavour of Niebuhr's interpretation can be gained only by following his critique of classical, modern and different Christian views of history in his major writings, in his sermons, and not least of all in his countless articles and editorials on the events of his time. His consistent attempt, however, was to make a synthesis of what he called Renaissance and Reformation emphases, that is, to do justice to the Renaissance and modern emphasis upon the meaningfulness and indeterminate possibilities of history and also to the Reformation emphasis upon the evil corruption that attends and perverts even the greatest of human achievements. Correlated with, and in many ways shaping this interpretation, was his understanding of the two facets of grace — forgiveness and the accession of resources leading to new life.

Most importantly, Niebuhr employed a wide range of theological symbols to illuminate not only our personal life but our historical and political existence. The thrust and direction of all his theologizing was to bring the resources of insight and healing in the symbols of Christian faith to bear upon the issues of the day. This leads us to a brief consideration of "Christian Realism" and his political ethic.

CHRISTIAN REALISM

'Christian Realism' is the label which best describes Niebuhr's social and political thought. Although political realism is a rather elusive concept, we may begin by noting that he himself once remarked that it "denotes the disposition to take all factors in a social and political situation, which offer resistance to established norms, into account, particularly the factors of self-interest and power."[17] In his work *Realist Thought From Weber to Kissinger*, Michael Joseph Smith assesses the thought of such major figures as Max Weber, E.H. Carr, Reinhold Niebuhr, Hans Morgenthau, George Kennan and Henry Kissinger. Smith indicates the position he thinks Niebuhr holds in this school by stating that the "range, depth, and complexity" of Niebuhr's thought make him "without question the most profound thinker of the modern realist school."[18] Our concern here is not with the development of this school of thought, nor the differences among its leading representatives; our concern is limited to those theological wellsprings which gave Niebuhr's realism its distinctive character. For, as Robert C. Good so succinctly put it,

> "Niebuhrianism," if it exists at all, is not so much a system of thought as a caste of mind. It is a complex of perspectives that, for Niebuhr, have been biblically derived and validated by experience — perspectives about human nobility and sin; human anxiety and the quest for security through power; the ambiguous role of reason, morality and religion, the nemesis of pride and power; and the persistent, disturbing intervention of a Divine "oughtness" in human undertakings.[19]

Niebuhr was a realist but he was a Christian realist, and that meant that he was continually showing how the Christian understanding could widen the vision of realists and thus provide a sounder and more humane basis for American policy. We may distinguish three closely related ways in which

Niebuhr saw the Christian perspective significantly modifying the approach of political realism.

First, he consistently argued that it could prevent the realist from conceiving the national interest too narrowly. This was particularly relevant during the period of the cold war when the temptation was strong in the United States to define the national interest in too exclusively military terms. He constantly argued indeed "that a narrow definition of the interest of the nation would lead to a defeat of that interest."[20] Even a wise self-interest must be mindful of "the mutualities between nations" and be sensitive to the needs of those with whom our human destiny is intertwined. But, and this is the crucial point, he urged that "even enlightened self interest is not sufficient alone" to prompt such concern. "It must be supported," he said, "by concern for a wider good, beyond its own interests."[21] Even "a residual loyalty to values transcending national existence," he urged in his "debate" with his esteemed friend Hans Morganthau, "may change radically the nation's conception of the breadth and quality of its 'national interest.'"[22]

The second contribution of the Christian perspective followed directly: it prods us to find the point of concurrence between the national interest and values which transcend those interests. He always emphasized that the capacity to find those points was the mark of real statemanship. Perhaps the best American example of this achievement was the Marshall Plan in which, as he put it, "a prudent self-interest was united with concern for others..."[23] Indeed, it is worth noting that several years before the institution of the Marshall Plan he had himself made a similar proposal in 1943. Looking ahead to the role of the United States after the war, he wrote: "America could function in the interest of democracy only if it were ready to give economic support to the continent without seeking to prevent the establishment of systems which sought to combine collective forms of economy with political freedom."[24]

Thirdly, the Christian perspective can help realism and its preoccupation with the national interest from falling into cynicism. He sounded this note in his critique of George Kennan's *American Diplomacy 1900-1950*. He was in full agreement with Kennan's indictment of America's "moralistic-legalistic" approach, the easy assumption of Americans that they could determine future events, and the inclination to think that the interests of other nations could be readily coordinated with their own, because those of the United Sates were moral. But Kennan's solution did not satisfy him:

> Mr. Kennan's solution for the problem of our pretentious idealism is a return
> to the concept of the national interest. He thinks that this concept should guide
> our foreign policy on the ground that we must not pretend to know more than

what is good for us. This modesty is important. But egotism is not the cure for an abstract and pretentious idealism. Preoccupation with national interest can quickly degenerate into moral cynicism even if it is originally prompted by moral modesty.[25]

Niebuhr's 'Christian Realism' remained consistent to the end but Michael Smith rightly notes that he "reshaded the emphases of his basic ideas" with the changing situation. More specifically, during the 1960s "he moved gradually from stressing the danger of moralism and simplistic idealism to underlining the limits of power and the pitfalls of a too consistent realism."[26]

Niebuhr, we have emphasized, was not only a realist, but a Christian realist. It is his Christian understanding and its explicit elaboration that sets him apart and gives his realism its distinctive character. He was explicit about that. There is in biblical faith, he said "a safeguard against both sentimentality and moral cynicism. This must be made available to the nation in the present period of critical decisions in which we cannot afford to disregard either the moral possibilities or the moral realities of our common life."[27] Kenneth Thompson concurred, and with Niebuhr specifically in mind would write: "Christian realism by illuminating the misery and grandeur of man can be a textbook for the diplomatist. [For] it can rid men of their illusions while preparing them for their finest hours."[28]

POLITICAL ETHIC

Larry Rasmussen has put the centre of Niebuhr's theology as succinctly as anyone: "Niebuhr's theology begins and ends in grace, and justification by grace through faith is the heart of his theology and his piety."[29] It is also the basis of his political ethic. Indeed, this doctrine of justification by grace, or something very much like it, is indispensable for a person like Niebuhr who sought meaning in the midst of moral ambiguity, who recognized that every statesman is daily faced with trying to realize partially incompatible goals, and that being responsible frequently involves making tragic choices. Moreover, the very struggle to secure justice itself involves the use of instruments of power, and the instruments of power are always ambiguous. Nor can innocence be maintained, or purity achieved, by withdrawing from the struggle. There is, as he frequently reminded us, no moral hiding place. But it is precisely here, in the complexity and confusion of life, that we see the genius of the Christian faith, and particularly the significance of these central, evangelical doctrines. They illuminate not only our personal circumstance, but also our social and political life. To act socially in terms of justification by grace is to know three things: first, that the Divine love which has met us in our personal lives impels us to seek a greater justice in the community; second, that the same Love that impels us to seek justice also illumines the sin we will be involved in by our efforts; and third, this doctrine also assures us of a resource of mercy to cover the evil we do in order to be responsible. This is a perspective that saves us *both* from a paralysis of will *and* from the pretension to which our righteous causes usually tempt us.

The references Niebuhr made to Abraham Lincoln on this matter are instructive. The combination in Lincoln of moral resolution and humility was what was so important, and so rare. Lincoln was resolute. But he did not allow his resolution, his moral commitment, to lead him into self-righteousness or moral rigidity. Nor, on the other hand, did he allow his great capacity for compassion to betray him into a sentimental analysis of the situation or prompt him to adopt inadequate strategies to deal with it. The doctrine of justification bids us seek this combination exemplified by Lincoln — a spirit of resolution against evil in the community with a lively awareness of "the taint of sin in the cause of devotion."

The doctrine of justification by grace does not mean that we do not take sides in the struggle for social values. It does not say "a plague on all your houses." It does not say that "since sin abounds, no significant distinctions are to be made." It is not an invitation to neutrality, nor a pious justification for being apolitical. It does mean that the faith which impels us to action keeps us aware of the fact that our cause, though relatively righteous and very important, is not absolute. This emphasis upon the transcendent dimensions of grace, far from providing an excuse to escape history, "gives us," in Niebuhr's words, "a fulcrum from which we can operate in history. It gives us a faith by which we can seek to fulfill our historic tasks without illusions and without despair."[30] Robert Good had it right when he wrote: "Niebuhr's ethic rests squarely upon the doctrine of justification by faith."[31]

TWO EXAMPLES

The manner in which Niebuhr's theological understanding shaped his political thought may be illustrated with reference to his views on democracy. He was convinced that democracy had a more compelling justification and requires a more realistic vindication than that given it by the bourgeois culture with which it has been associated in modern history. This need could be provided by the biblical understanding of human nature and the social significance of the humility, tolerance and hope which are the fruit of such faith. Certainly a free society requires some confidence in the ability of people to reach "tolerable adjustments between competing interests and to arrive at some common notions of justice which transcend all partial interests."[32] But a too consistent optimism about human nature, a failure to understand the power and persistence of sin and self-interest in life, and sentimental views about human perfectibility are not minor, innocent deficiencies. In some contexts they are perilous. Such an outlook had brought the great democracies to the brink of disaster as they faced the formidable tyrannies of Nazism and Fascism. He thus argued vigorously that a more realistic understanding of human nature, of our capacities for both good and evil, was required as a basis for democratic thought and life. He put his view in the widely quoted epigram: "Man's capacity for justice makes democracy possible; but man's inclination to injustice makes democracy necessary."[33] It is the human capacity to reach out and affirm values of the common good, and to sacrifice for them, that makes democratic life possible. But it is the same theological understanding that reminds us that no individual and no group can be good enough or wise enough to exercise absolute authority over their fellows. But more needs to be said. A healthy political life depends, however, not only upon structures and processes of accountability. It must also be constantly fed by a spirit that combines devotion to social values with the humility and tolerance that come from the recognition that our values, though of large significance, are fragmentary and tainted by our self interest. That combination is the fruit of profound religion.[34]

Although as journalist Niebuhr avoided the use of conventional religious language, his theological understanding shaped his almost weekly analysis of the responsibilities that attended what he called "America's Precarious Eminence." The long heritage of conceiving herself as the innocent nation in a wicked world, together with the deep layer of messianic consciousness in the American mind, makes it difficult for the United State to discharge the responsibilities of a hegemenous power. The heritage of the myth of mission and destiny which prompts the United States to make simple correlations between her power and her virtue, success and piety, affluence and wisdom, has ill equipped her to deal with a world that knows so much suffering, poverty, frustration and defeat. It thus became a matter of passionate concern for Niebuhr to clarify those resources of Christian understanding and spirit most necessary for the task of enabling the United States to exercise responsible leadership on the international scene.

This took many forms. He continuously reminded the nation that the anatomy of authority, the capacity to exercise leadership among nations, was dependent not only on the possession of power but also the possession of prestige. And that there were only two sources of prestige for a modern great power: a reputation for justice based upon performance and a reputation for prudence in the exercise of power.

A second way in which he sought to fulfill his task involved the *unmasking* of the deceptions and illusions to which America in her precarious eminence seemed peculiarly prone. The moral peril to which she was particularly vulnerable was what he called "the ironic tendency of virtues to turn into vices when too complacently relied upon; and of power to become vexatious if the wisdom which directs it is trusted too confidently."[35] A vertebrate biblical faith can *unmask* these ironic tendencies because of the way in which it believes "that the whole drama of human history is under the scrutiny of a divine judge who laughs at human pretensions without being hostile to human aspirations."[36]

We began our discussion with Arthur Schlesinger's question concerning the reason for Niebuhr's influence and his answer that it lay in his "capacity to restate historical Christianity in terms that corresponded to our most searching modern themes and anxieties." That is surely right. The quest for life's meaning, the struggle for social justice and the tragic choices necessitated by the age, were all placed in the illuminating, healing and hopeful context of a Christocentric faith. From that soteriological centre he developed a social ethic which combined a penetrating criticism of our subtle idolatries, a profound resource of forgiveness and renewal and the energies of an undying hope anchored not in some optimistic calculation of historical success, but in the being of God, ever present to us. Such is the theological rootage of Niebuhr's social and political thought. Such grounding is also the source of its continued relevance.

NOTES

1.   Arthur Schlesinger, Jr., "Prophet For A Secular Age," *The New Leader* 24 (January 1972).

2.   Giles Gunn, *The Interpretation of Otherness: Literature, Religion and the American Imagination* (New York: Oxford University Press, 1979): 23f.

3.   Larry Rasmussen, ed., *Reinhold Niebuhr: Theologian of Public Life* (London: Collins Publishers, 1989): 3.

4.   Reinhold Niebuhr, "Intellectual Autobiography," in *Reinhold Niebuhr: His Religious, Social and Political Thought*, ed. Charles W. Kegley and Robert W. Bretall (New York:

MacMillan Company, 1956): 18.

5.   ibid., 17.

6.   Reinhold Niebuhr, *The Self and the Dramas of History* (*SDH*) (New York: Charles Scribner's Sons, 1955): 4.

7.   ibid., 64.

8.   Ursula M. Niebuhr, *Remembering Reinhold Niebuhr: Letters of Reinhold and Ursula M. Niebuhr* (San Francisco: Harper, 1991): 412.

9.   *SDH*, 165.

10.   Reinhold Niebuhr, *The Children of Light and the Children of Darkness* (*CLCD*) (New York: Charles Scribner's Sons, 1944): 85. It is interesting to note that Wolfhart Pannenberg, in his *Anthropology in Theological Perspective*, has appropriated Niebuhr's thought at several points, but especially at this point of the relation of the individual and the community.

11.   Reinhold Niebuhr, *Faith and History* (*FH*) (New York: Charles Scribner's Sons, 1951): 132.

12.   ibid., 103.

13.   ibid., 141.

14.   Reinhold Niebuhr, *The Nature and Destiny of Man* (*NDM*) (New York: Charles Scribner's Sons, 1941): I: 148. It is interesting to compare this statement with the note in *Leaves From the Notebook of a Tamed Cynic* (*LNTC*) under the date of 1926: "We had a communion service tonight (Good Friday) and I preached on the text 'We preach Christ crucified, to the Jews a stumbling block and to the Gentiles foolishness, but to them that are called the power of God and the wisdom of God.' I don't think I ever felt greater joy in preaching a sermon. How experience and life change our perspectives! It was only a few years ago that I did not know what to make of the cross; at least I made no more of it than to recognize it as a historic fact which proved the necessity of paying a high price for our ideals. Now I see it as a symbol of ultimate reality" (*LNTC*, 85).

15.   Reinhold Niebuhr, *Man's Nature and His Communities* (*MNHC*) (New York: Charles Scribner's Sons, 1965): 24.

16.   Gilkey, "Reinhold Niebuhr's Theology of History," in *The Legacy of Reinhold Niebuhr*, ed. Nathan A. Scott, Jr. (Chicago: University of Chicago Press, 1975): 56.

17.   Reinhold Niebuhr, *Christian Realism and Political Problems* (New York: Charles Scribner's Sons, 1953): 119.

18.   Michael Joseph Smith, *Realist Thought from Weber to Kissinger* (Baton Rouge and London: Louisiana State University Press): 99.

19.   Robert C. Good, "Reinhold Niebuhr: The Political Philosopher of Christian Realism," *Cross Currents* (Summer 1961): 265.

20.   *MNHC*, 79.

21.   *FH*, 97.

22.   *MNHC*, 77.

23.   "Hybris," in *Christianity and Society* (*CS*) 16 #2 (Spring 1951): 4.

24.   "The Peril of our Foreign Policy," *CS* 8 #2 (Spring 1943): 20.

25.   "Editorial Notes," *Christianity and Crisis* (*C&C*) 11 #18 (October 29, 1951): 139.

26.   Smith, *Realist Thought from Weber to Kissinger*, 123.

27.   Harry R. Davis and Robert C. Good, *Reinhold Niebuhr on Politics* (New York: Charles Scribner's Sons, 1960): 335.

28.   K. Thompson, "Prophets and Politics," *C&C* 15 #8 (May 16, 1955): 61.

29.   Rasmussen, op. cit., 24.

30.   "Christian Otherworldliness," *CS* 9 #1 (Winter 1943): 12.

31.   Good, "Reinhold Niebuhr," 267. Niebuhr's own succinct statement of the social meaning of the doctrine is: "Justification by faith in the realm of justice means that we will not regard the pressures and counter pressures, the tensions, the overt and covert conflicts by which justice is achieved and maintained, as normative in the absolute sense; but neither will we ease our conscience by seeking to escape from involvement in them. We will know that we cannot purge ourselves of the sin and guilt in which we are involved by the moral ambiguities of politics without disavowing responsibility for the creative possibilities of justice" (*NDM* II: 284.)

32.   *CLCD*, x.

33.   ibid., xi.

34.   See *CLCD*, 151.

35.   Reinhold Niebuhr, *The Irony of American History* (New York: Charles Scribner's Sons, 1954): 133.

36.   ibid., 155.

THE CROSS AND CONTEMPORARY CULTURE*

Douglas John Hall

BETWEEN TWO INCONGRUOUS ACCOUNTS OF THE WORLD

Creativity in any field of human endeavour is always at base a mystery, but it seems to me evident that the theological contribution of Reinhold Niebuhr is bound up with a certain fundamental tension — between the faith traditions he appropriated and the spirit of the culture to which he belonged. His struggle is inseparable from the biographical-historical fact that he was at the same time thoroughly North American and thoroughly a child of the Protestant Reformation. There are those who would find no "incongruity" here, for they regard the United States of America as the Protestant culture *par excellence,* but while (as Niebuhr himself frequently noted[1]) the Calvinist influence has certainly been strong in America, the Reformation as it comes to us from the side of Luther has not. And it was Luther's reformulation of the faith that grasped, in a primary sense, the spirit of Reinhold Niebuhr.[2]

Although Lutheranism eventually became relatively strong on this continent, few historically important voices in the formation of the "New World" spoke out of Luther's reform. This is due to many practical factors, such as patterns of immigration, but the relative silence of the Lutheran tradition in the creation of "America" is due as well to the fact that what was distinctively Lutheran was in many ways at loggerheads with the whole American experiment.

* Reprinted from: Richard Harries, ed., *Reinhold Niebuhr and the Issues of Our Time* (London & Oxford: Mowbray, 1986; Grand Rapids, Michigan: William B. Eerdmans Publishing House, 1986). Used with permission.

For all his distrust of puny, sinful *anthropos,* Jean Calvin, with his christocentric triumphalism and his doctrine of election, could rather readily be co-opted by the spirit of an evolving "Americanism"[3] — as could John Wesley with his moral perfectionism. But Luther, that still-medieval man, steeped in mysticism, given to outlandish pronouncements laced with "expletives," finding always vast discrepancies between the true *gloria Dei* and the bright designs of empires, insisting upon retaining the Cross as faith's primary focus, and fearing above all what Niebuhr once identified on Luther's behalf as "the pretension of finality"[4] — this Luther could never find a comfortable home in our brave, new world. In consequence, until our own immediate epoch most American and Canadian Lutherans have kept their faith largely to themselves, nurturing it, often, within rather well-defined ethnic ghettos. Luther's emphases, where they were not sufficiently diluted, seemed thoroughly out of tune with the going worldview, like some dark tale belonging to the melancholy gothic caverns of old Europe. Enough to let that tale, suitably personalized by a Hauge or a Grundtvig, inform one's private life and keep one's sons and daughters in touch with a Past that was increasingly foreign to their social milieu.

Reinhold Niebuhr, whose own early life was marked by the generational conflict implicit in this situation, augmented by war with "the Fatherland," emerged from this crucible as a very rare bird on the American landscape. He had apprehended the essence of the European-made tradition without in the process imbibing its historical *accidens*. Informed in a rudimentary way by the core of this tradition — the 'theology of the cross' — he provided an entirely indigenous expression of it, one which took with complete seriousness the socio-political particularities of the "New World" context and entered into an ongoing dialogue with the assumptions concealed within them.

This meant that Niebuhr lived at the intersection of what had become history's most "positive" cultural philosophy and a faith tradition that from the perspective of such a culture could only seem the essence of negativity! "Pessimism," the charge regularly laid at his doorstep, is of course a naive and simply inaccurate description of Niebuhr's position — as it is of Luther's, Augustine's, Paul's or of the Hebrew prophets and wisdom writers like Job and Koheleth, all of whom contributed substantially to the tradition Niebuhr honoured and himself extended. Yet from the standpoint of an attitude towards historical existence as uncomplicatedly "positive" as modernity's, especially in its American adaptation, nothing could have been more predictable than that the truth to which Niebuhr felt himself bound would be deemed consistently "negative." After all, he insisted upon discussing sin in a society that had either reduced that profound biblical concept to bourgeois immorality or else dismissed it altogether. He even dared to reflect upon the life of the human being and human communities along the lines of "the tragic," and to enucleate a Gospel that could point "beyond tragedy" — this in a society where, as Rolf Hochhuth put it in his play *Soldiers,* the word "tragedy" is unknown: "they call it migraine."

The rejection of Niebuhr's account of reality by representatives of the official culture and church was very nearly universal.[5] That both Modernists and Fundamentalists should have spurned his rendition of the Christian message was of course to be expected. But even close associates often found him too consistently in a state of continuing struggle — too little sanctified, as it were. Understandably, this reaction to Niebuhr shows up more conspicuously in his early works, before he had become too famous to be held at a distance by persons in his immediate sphere of influence. In a moving entry in his *Leaves From the Notebook of a Tamed Cynic,* the Detroit pastor ruminates on his relations with a certain person 'H' (his brother, Helmut Richard ?) —

> Whenever I exchange thoughts with H—...I have the uneasy feeling that I belong to the forces which are destroying religion in the effort to refine it. He is as critical as I am — well, perhaps not quite so critical; but in all his critical evaluations of religious forms he preserves a robust religious vitality which I seem to lack...He has preserved a confidence in the goodness of men and the ultimate triumph of righteousness which I do not lack, but to which I do not hold so unwaveringly...
>
> I have been profoundly impressed by the Spenglerian thesis that culture is destroyed by the spirit of sophistication and I am beginning to suspect that I belong to the forces of decadence in which this sophistication is at work. I have my eye too much upon the limitations of contemporary religious life and institutions; I always see the absurdities and irrationalities in which narrow types of religion issue...
>
> Nevertheless I hate a thoroughgoing cynic. I don't want anyone to be more cynical than I am. If I am saved from cynicism at all it is by some sense of personal loyalty to the spirit and genius of Jesus; that and physical health. If I were physically anemic I would never be able to escape pessimism. This very type of morbid introspection is one of the symptoms of the disease. I can't justify myself in my perilous position except by the observation that the business of being sophisticated and naive, critical and religious, at one and the same time is as difficult as it is necessary, and only a few are able to achieve the balance. H--- says I lack a proper appreciation of the mystical values in religion. Yet I can't resist another word in self-defense. *The Modern world is so full of bunkum that it is difficult to attempt honesty in it without an undue emphasis upon the critical faculty.*[6]

The unease expressed by the young pastor in the face of his associate's piety could be a modern rendition, *mutatis mutandis,* of many things that Luther wrote in response to the apparently more secure faith of some of his associates, especially early in his career. What both the sixteenth century Reformer and the twentieth century American preacher were especially conscious of (and this will always distinguish such persons from the 'True Believers'!) was the undeniable reality of that which questions and threatens to negate belief, and the consequent difficulty of articulating one's faith without falling into more credulity and . . . "bunkum"! To anticipate a little, I would posit that the psychological basis of Luther's *theologia crucis,* if it can be distinguished from its theoretical-doctrinal basis, is precisely his commitment to "honest" reporting of what he finds in the world. Perhaps it was his peasant's incapacity for guile! "The theology of glory," writes Luther in the 21st Thesis of his Heidelberg Disputation, "has to call evil good and good evil, but the theology of the cross calls the thing what it really is." Reinhold Niebuhr's 'Christian Realism' is surely rooted in this same psychic phenomenon. It is the product of a faith which has to survive, if it is to survive at all, within a spirit that is constitutionally incapable of spiritual-intellectual self-deception. Such a spirit is not necessarily reduced to cynicism because (as Niebuhr implies in the passage cited and states openly in many places) it is graciously enabled to see *behind* the crass and ambiguous realities of existence an ultimate meaning which both transcends and uses these realities. But it will not sacrifice its dogged "honesty" about the world (say, the world of Henry Ford's assembly lines!) for the sake of achieving a more comfortable *personal* spirituality. It will not look *past* the Cross, but only *through* it. It will "call the thing what it really is," even when that kind of intellectual rigour occasions such poignant *self-criticism* as can be heard in excerpts like the one just instanced.

For Niebuhr, however, this type of "faithful realism" was if anything more painful than it was for Luther. For it is one thing to draw attention to that which negates in sixteenth century Europe, where few human beings in any case entertained very high expectations for life in this world; it is something else to do so in America during the first half of the twentieth century. Modern assumptions about history, as Niebuhr knew better than anyone, are notoriously expectant; and America was the place where it was all supposed to happen! What this means for *religion* in America is that it is under a permanent, generally unspoken but altogether effective obligation to provide the attitudinal undergirding that is essential to the psychic maintenance of "the American Dream."[7] For it is only in the last analysis a *religious* attitude — a credulity born of supra-rational conviction and continuously reaffirmed — that can achieve on the one hand the enthusiasm that is needed to "buy into" the Dream and on the other the degree of repression required to avoid facing challenges to it. One reason why every form of religion is valued in American society, its real secularity notwithstanding, lies precisely within this socio-political imperative. Without so much as mentioning the differences between them, successive American presidents can laud religious leaders as divergent as Billy Graham and Norman Vincent Peale, Jerry Falwell and Robert Schuller. But by that same token there is one type of religious faith that the dominant culture will not tolerate; and that is a prophetic faith which out of a commitment to "honesty" refuses *a priori* to contribute to the promotional and repressive functioning of the normative "cultural religion." Reinhold Niebuhr represented just such a faith.

Of course he might have pursued many of the themes that he did pursue and, so to speak, without incident — sin, the tragic, irony, the ambiguity of human motives, the corruption of power, etc. — if only he had emphasized their resolution. Between the resurrectionism of the calvinistic tradition and the progressivism of an Enlightenment faith in which *Alles hat sich aufgeklärt* there are important ideational and practical differences. But what they have in common (and therefore they could achieve such a powerful mix in American history) is a penchant for resolution. Niebuhr resisted "the pretension of finality." Certainly he believed that whatever happened God would be "with us." But he never allowed this confidence of faith to be translated into ideological certitude, and he constantly warned that God's presence never ensures the triumph of our causes.

THE LOGIC OF THE CROSS

Though Martin Luther was a major contributor to one of the two incongruous accounts of the world between which he lived, Niebuhr was no "Lutheran" in the conventional sense. He was particularly critical of the Saxon Reformer's ineptitude in the realm of social ethics and of the so-called "Two Kingdoms Theory," which, in Niebuhr's earlier years at Union Seminary, was being hardened into dogma through the rationalizations of Erlangen and other theologians sympathetic to the Nazi enterprise. He was also of course dismayed, as most sensitive students of history have become, at the later Luther's blatant anti-Judaism. In general, Niebuhr deplored the fatalism by which Luther and his followers were perennially tempted, the point at which Luther's historical realism turned into resignation and *Weltschmerz*.

Yet Niebuhr's respect for Luther's basic approach to the Faith is undeniable. Luther, he wrote in his *magnum opus*, "displays the most profound understanding of the meaning of Christian *agape*..."[8] and in a later essay entitled

simply, "Germany," he speaks of Luther's legacy as containing "in my opinion...
the most profound religious insights on ultimate questions of human
existence..."[9] Only Augustine, amongst historic theologians, plays a more
conspicuous role than Luther in Niebuhr's thought.[10]

As I have already intimated, I believe that what Professor Niebuhr gleaned
from his life-long and varied exposure to Luther was what is commonly referred
to as Luther's *theologia crucis*. So far as I am aware, Niebuhr has not used this
technical term in any of his writings; but the essential ingredients of this
minority tradition are all, as I shall attempt to show in the final part of this
statement, conspicuously present in his work.

Before considering the elements of the tradition, it would be useful to
attempt a more general explication of its character[11] — especially in an English-
speaking context where, as Ernst Käsemann has pointed out,[12] the concept
'theology of the cross' is regularly heard as if it referred narrowly to the doctrine
of the atonement. What Luther intended by this term is certainly not limited to
soteriology. It refers to a whole approach to the faith — to a spirit and method
permeating the entire theological enterprise. As a more recent exponent of this
tradition (Jürgen Moltmann) has put it succinctly, "*Theologia crucis* is not a
single chapter in theology, but the key signature for all Christian theology."[13]

No doubt Luther's own intuition was sound in that when he first
introduced the term (he did not *invent* the tradition but only named it!) he
immediately contrasted it with that other, broad theological convention which in
one form and another has dominated the faith and doctrine of Christendom,
named by Luther *theologia gloriae*. More recent parlance designates it
'triumphalism.' The theology of the cross is at its core a *critical* theology, and
the most common object of its critique is Christianity itself in its triumphalist
expressions. It is therefore not at all accidental that all of those who have stood
within this minority tradition — including Niebuhr — have been heard by their
contemporaries chiefly as *critics,* and frequently chastised for it!

But while the theology of the cross is in some ways defined by its
antithesis, it is not merely a critical theology. Even when historical circumstance
requires of its advocates that they expend most of their creative energies
criticizing the *status quo* (Kierkegaard!), the basic motivation of their critique is
a highly definitive and even "positive" understanding of the Gospel. Their
castigation of triumphalism does not mean that they simply dispense with
triumph. In a real sense, they are *preoccupied* with the triumph of divine grace,
and particularly with a manner of conveying that triumph which does justice to
its profundity and avoids the (almost unavoidable!) suggestion of so much
Christianity that "Easter" is a too easy, theoretical resolution of the human

predicament. Instead of embracing an evangelical formula in which the resurrection supersedes the cross, therefore, the advocates of this tradition locate the mystery of the divine *agape* in the cross. The cross remains the fundamental statement — both of the human condition and of the divine redemption. The function of the resurrection is that it "establishes Christ's cross as a saving event."[14] Thus what the triumphalist mentality identifies as the negative, dark and therefore at most the *penultimate* point of the Christian story ("Black Friday"!) is itself already astonishingly positive. *Omnia bona in cruce et sub cruce abscondita sunt* (Luther): everything *good* is already there — but "hidden beneath its opposite" and therefore accessible only to faith. That is to say, inaccessible to the kind of mentality that thinks of belief in terms of possessing rather than hoping, that wants to have arrived instead of being *en route,* that looks to transcendent grace for a way out of the world with its doubts and ambiguities instead of a way into it.

The cross of Jesus Christ is the paradigmatic centre of this whole mode of thought — and of course it is more than a mere paradigm. Yet it is not to be made so unique and discontinuous with every other moment in history that it loses its capacity to embody and address the human situation. It is paradigmatic in that it illuminates every other event, and the whole course of history. The problematique to which it speaks is a human one, and one of which all human beings have some awareness: How are we to live knowing that we die? — a question which, as Niebuhr frequently pointed out, is not merely about the problem of our mortality (the question which preoccupied the Greek mind) but about the *meaning* of our mortal life. In the face of all that negates "life" in the broadest biblical sense of the term, how are we to find "the courage to be" (Tillich)? Are we to become in that well-known sense "religious" and nurture some "illusion" (Freud) which offers us a triumphal world *view* at the expense of honesty about the real world? Or are we (as Ernest Becker said of Freud himself) to relinquish in the name of intellectual honesty every sort of capacity for hope, every insistence of the human spirit that truth may be more mysterious and "user friendly" than our most scientific observations of it?[15] Hans Küng has said, insightfully, that "Coping with the negative side of life is the acid test of Christian faith and non-Christian humanisms."[16] Cynical realism capitulates to the negative side. Religious and secular ideologies of triumph create simplistic or complicated theoretical victories over it. The "logic of the cross" (Niebuhr's own term) is impelled by the conviction that to abandon the earnest contemplation, analysis and transformation of the negative is to abandon humanity, and by the hope (hope against hope!) that *the negative side itself,* as with Christ's cross, already conceals a strangely positive *telos*: that life can be entered only through a heightened encounter with death, that hope is real only when it emerges "on the far side of despair" (Keats), that faith comes to be only in the struggle with existential doubt, that the City of God must be sought for in the ruins of the human city.

It is this cruciform "logic" that informs every major theo-historical judgement of Reinhold Niebuhr. He knew himself to be part of a society that had been *victimized* by a 'theology of glory' which required it to be oblivious of its own guilt and failures and, since it was also very powerful, an increasing danger within the community of nations. He believed that the only salvation for such a society was to discover a vantage-point from which to expose itself to its own inordinate pride and folly but without capitulating to the kind of despair which leads to nihilism and thus by another route to annihilation. For Niebuhr, it could be said, the whole weight of biblical faith was directed precisely towards the gaining of such a perspective: "It envisages antinomies, contradictions and tragic realities within the framework [of meaning] without succumbing to despair."[17] The Gospel of the Cross was almost designed for such a context as ours: having "lived through…centuries of hope" which "have well nigh destroyed the Christian faith as a potent force in modern culture and civilization," we find ourselves now in one of those "periods of disillusionment when the vanity of such hopes is fully revealed." This does not ensure that the Christian faith will be restored: "It has merely re-established its relevance" — namely the relevance of a system of belief that is able "to find life meaningful without placing an abortive confidence in…mere historical growth."[18] Christianity can lay claim to this relevance, not by attempting a return to the "Age of Belief," but by achieving a "new synthesis" in which the insights of biblical religion are combined with aspects of the Reformation and Renaissance to give a vision in which, on the one hand, "life in history must be recognized as filled with indeterminate possibilities," and on the other hand "that every effort and pretension to complete life, whether in collective or individual terms, that every desire to stand beyond the contradictions of history, or to eliminate the final corruptions of history must be disavowed."[19]

Thus from the vantage-point of the Cross, faith is enabled to contemplate failure without either courting it fatalistically or being reduced to despair by its prospect. As a civilization, Niebuhr thought, we do not know whether we are about to collapse or whether we are about to open into a new dimension of "world community:"

> Standing inside such a civilization our responsibilities are obvious: we must seek to fashion our common life to conform more nearly to the brotherhood of the Kingdom of God. No view of history *sub specie aeternitatis* dare beguile

us from our historical obligations. But if we should fail, as well we may, we can at least understand the failure from the perspective of the Christian faith. Insofar as we understand the failure we will not be completely involved in it, but have a vantage point beyond it. We could not deny the tragic character of what we discern but we would not be tempted to regard it as meaningless.[20]

It would be hard to find a more faithful translation into contemporary socio-historical terms of the *theologia crucis*.

INGREDIENTS OF THE TRADITION

The theology of the cross, I have insisted, implies an entire mode of thinking the faith. No brief account of any of its exemplars can exhaust the meaning of this tradition; but for the sake of concreteness we may consider briefly four characteristic features of the tradition and Niebuhr's handling of them.

(a) The Epistemological Dimension

The *theologia crucis* is first of all a theology of *faith*.[21] The *sola fide* of the Reformation is deeply present in Niebuhr's thought.[22] While he rejected the fideism of the Barthian school,[23] he was critical of hellenistic and modern expressions of belief because of their tendency "to transmute into truths of speculative reason" what can only be received by faith and expressed symbolically.[24] "The truth which is revealed in the cross is not a truth which could have been anticipated in human culture and it is not the culmination of human wisdom."[25]

Niebuhr's struggle in this respect, however, is not merely the continuing battle of Reformation Christianity against other historical forms of the faith. It is the intensely practical struggle of a North American who finds himself the inheritor of a tradition in which faith implies an ongoing dialogue with doubt (Luther's *Anfechtungen!*) in the midst of a religious community where belief seems to involve no existential struggle. Niebuhr did not find belief *easy!* Over against the American-style *theologia gloriae* which goes beyond the medieval rational acceptance of God to a faith posture which hardly even has to think in order to "believe," Niebuhr's consciousness of "the foolishness of the cross" stands out in sharp contrast. Faith is faith, not sight! "True religion must therefore be conscious of the difficulty and the absurdity of the human claiming kinship with the divine, of the temporal trafficking with the eternal. If the divine is made relevant to the human, it must transvalue our values and enter the human at the point where man is lowly rather than proud and where he is weak rather than strong."[26] Such a statement, very typical of Niebuhr, mirrors many of Luther's; but it also goes beyond Luther because it assumes the characteristic twentieth century experience of "the Absurd," and challenges Christians to think the faith within the context of what Niebuhr's friend, W.H. Auden, named "The Age of Anxiety."

(b) The Ontological Dimension

The basic ontological assumption of the theology of the cross might be stated in some such way as this: that the relation between the experienced reality we call Nature and the experienced reality we call Grace is a dialectical one, in which the dimensions of continuity and discontinuity are in constant tension. The most characteristic disagreement between Niebuhr and his long-time colleague, Paul Tillich, was that Niebuhr felt Tillich accentuated too consistently the dimension of continuity. He distrusted Tillich's whole "ontological" approach to Christian faith because of its inherent propensity to blur the distinction between Creator and Creation and thus to minimize both the reality of creaturely freedom and the radicality of divine grace.[27] "Protestant theology is right in setting grace in contradiction to nature in the sense that the vicious circle of false truth, apprehended from the standpoint of the self, must be broken and the self cannot break it. In that sense the apprehension of the truth in Christ is always a miracle; and 'flesh and blood have not revealed it unto us.'"[28]

At the same time, an undialectical emphasis upon discontinuity, while it may be desirable strategically under certain circumstances (as at Barmen in 1934), introduces the phenomenon of a God whose being and acting touches human historical existence not at all. Thus in the famous debate between Barth and Brunner, culminating in Barth's angry response, *Nein!*, Niebuhr's sympathies lay with Brunner. "...Protestant theology...is wrong in denying the 'point of contact' *(Anknüpfungspunkt)* which always exists in man by virtue of the residual element of *justitia originalis* in his being."[29]

Yet while the historic debate between the two Swiss theologians issued in a redefining of 'Orthodoxy' (Neo-Orthodoxy) that eventually incorporated many beyond Europe's boundaries, this was not the matrix in which Niebuhr's working-out of the relation between nature and grace occurred. Again we are reminded that, for him, the Reformation tradition had to express itself in a specifically "New World" context; and the temptation of Christianity in that context, while it was certainly also connected with a one-sided emphasis on the continuity factor, did not attach itself as in Europe to a political ideology which used 'Natural Theology' to undergird its racial and other theories, but was associated with theological Liberalism's tendency to sentimentalize the Gospel and thus eliminate the critical side of theology. In his preaching and other theological work, therefore, Niebuhr found it necessary again and again to draw attention to the "otherness" of the reality introduced by grace. It was this necessity which, I believe, caused the theological community to begin to regard him as an exponent of Neo-Orthodoxy — though he in fact differed significantly from the trends of this movement.[30] Reinhold Niebuhr could not have written Karl Barth's essay about "The Strange New World Within the Bible;"[31] but his consciousness of modernity's elevation of human being and of the modern Church's accommodation to that elevation made him all the same a strong spokesperson in the American scene for the ontic "distance between the human the divine."[32] While grace does in fact meet and perfect nature, there is for this tradition no faithful experience of that grace which escapes the *skandalon* of its mode of engaging the world.[33]

(c) The Soteriological Dimension

The difference between *theologia gloriae* and *theologia crucis is* the difference between salvation as resolution and salvation as engagement. A theological triumphalism which posits salvation as a *fait accompli* does not *necessarily* preclude ethics; it may produce a perfectionist ethic or an ethical passivity, depending upon whether its orientation is towards this world or "the next." But salvation interpreted as the dynamic influence of grace in the ongoing struggles of history leads necessarily to an ethic that is not merely consequential but an integral dimension of the core of the Gospel itself.

A very good case could be made, I think, for claiming that Reinhold Niebuhr was driven to his abiding vocational concern for Christian ethics because his understanding of the nature of salvation was what it was. Niebuhr understood the work of God in Christ as God's decisive participation in the historical process. This is not however the participation of a divine omnipotence which sets aside every obstacle. It is the participation of a suffering love which alters the world, not through power but through solidarity with suffering humanity: "The suffering servant does not impose goodness upon the world by his power. Rather, he suffers, being powerless, from the injustices of the powerful. He suffers most particularly from the sins of the righteous who do not understand how full of unrighteousness is all human righteousness."[34]

While ethical obedience is thus an aspect of soteriology for Niebuhr, it is not however a lapse into "works righteousness" — for Niebuhr any more than for Bonhoeffer. Niebuhr had an innate appreciation for Luther's *simul justus et peccator* which is perhaps unparalleled in the New World! It made him very impatient with Christian perfectionists, "who still do not understand the logic of the Cross. They hope that if goodness is only perfect enough its triumph in history will be assured."[35]

(d) The Eschatological Dimension

The theology of the cross sustains two difficult orientations simultaneously: a determination to be entirely "realistic" about evil in the world, and the insistence that historical existence is meaningful. Such a tradition will always be at odds therefore with two alternatives, both of them products of the triumphalist impulse: on the one hand it will reject the world view which posits a too easy triumph of the good in history; on the other it will reject the more characteristically "religious" option which abandons history in favour of a supramundane *dénouement*.

Not surprisingly then, Niebuhr found himself doing frequent battle on two fronts. The Christian Gospel "...implies a refutation...of both utopianism and a too consistent otherworldliness. Against utopianism the Christian faith insists that the final consummation of history lies beyond the conditions of the temporal process. Against otherworldliness it asserts that the consummation fulfils rather than negates the historical process."[36] Both these temptations were strongly present in Niebuhr's context, but because his *formative* experience belonged to the *first* half of this century it was the danger of triumphalistic religious and secular utopianism that preoccupied him, understandably enough. He was conscious in particular of the sin of optimism: "Faith is always imperilled on the one side by despair and on the other side by optimism. Of these two enemies of faith, optimism is the more dangerous."[37]

Whoever listens today to the pronouncements of the official optimists of our technocracy will sympathize! But for us who have survived into the last half of 'The Christian Century' (!) there is a new awareness of the hollowness of this optimism. It is precisely . . . official! That is, it cloaks a public cynicism — a covert nihilism perhaps — whose only trust is in arms not in history or God. Or if in God then in a God who is preparing to abandon the world — therefore not the God of Golgotha! Niebuhr was too sensitive a student of humanity not to notice the emergence of this new barbarism and therefore he warned Christians against the final temptation — what Bonhoeffer rightly identified as the temptation "to write this world off prematurely."[38] I suspect that it is *this* side of the eschatology of the Cross that Christians and all persons of goodwill shall have to concentrate upon from now on; for while

> the Christian faith in the goodness of God is not to be equated with a
> confidence in the virtue of man....neither is it a supernaturalism and

otherworldliness which places its hope in another world because it finds this world evil. Every distinction between an essentially good eternity and an essentially evil finiteness is foreign to the Christian faith. When Christians express their faith in such terms they have been corrupted by other types of religion. For the Christian who really understands his faith life is worth living and this world is not merely "a vale of tears." He is able to discern the goodness of creation beneath the corruptions of human sin....He will not suffer the tortures of the cynics who falsely equate their ideals with their achievements and regard their fellow men with bitterness because the latter fail to measure up to their ideals.[39]

There is no facile way for humankind to achieve the future: "The Kingdom of God must still enter the world by way of crucifixion."[40] But it is the world that God's Kingdom enters and for Christians to abandon this world is to abandon the Cross at its centre.

NOTES

1.   Niebuhr's denominational background must be traced to the "Church of the Prussian Union" (*Deutsche Evangelische Kirchenverein des Westens*) which was a union superimposed upon the Lutheran and Reformed churches of Prussia on the 300th anniversary of the Reformation by King Frederick William 111 in 1817. Gustav Niebuhr, Reinhold's father grew up within this tradition and was himself one of its shapers in the American scene. As John C. Bennett has rightly observed therefore, "Luther was an important influence in [Niebuhr's] denomination but it was not confessionally Lutheran. This explains his emphasis on Luther and the freedom with which he approached Luther" (Wm. G. Chrystal (ed.) *Young Reinhold Niebuhr: His Early Writings* (St. Louis: Eden Publishing House, 1977): 13).

2.   Cf., e.g., *The Irony of American History*: "It is particularly remarkable that the two great religious-moral traditions which informed our early life — New England Calvinism and Virginian Deism and Jeffersonianism — arrive at remarkably similar conclusions about the meaning of our national character and destiny. Calvinism may have held too pessimistic views of human nature and too mechanical views of the providential ordering of human life. But when it assessed the significance of the American experiment both its conceptions of American destiny and its appreciation of American virtue finally arrived at conclusions strikingly similar to those of Deism. Whether our nation interprets its spiritual heritage through Massachusetts or Virginia we came into existence with the sense of being a 'separated' nation which God was using to make a new beginning for mankind...Whether as in the case of the New England theocrats, our forefathers thought of our 'experiment' as primarily the creation of a new and purer church or, as in the case of Jefferson and his coterie they thought primarily of a new political community, they believed in either case that we had been called out by God to create a new humanity. We were God's 'American Israel'" (23–24).

3.   "If one were to compute [a percentage of Calvinist heritage] on the basis of all the German, Swiss, French, Dutch and Scottish people whose forebears bore the 'stamp of Geneva' in some broader sense, 85 or 90 percent would not be an extravagant estimate."

Sydney E. Ahlstrom on the influence of Calvinism in the USA, in *A Religious History of the American People* (Garden City, N.Y.: Doubleday & Co. Inc. (Image Books), 1975): I: 169. See also Sydney E. Mead, *The Lively Experiment: The Shaping of Christianity in America* (New York: Harper & Row Publishers, 1963): 142 f.

4.   *The Nature and Destiny of Man* (*NDM*) (N.Y.: Charles Scribner's, 1943): II: 185.

5.   Even today it is hard to find Christian scholars who regard Niebuhr as a *theologian*. Categorizing him as "a Christian ethicist," while it may be accurate enough in certain respects, is frequently a cloaked way of discounting him as an interpreter of the faith as a whole. Certainly he was not a *systematic* theologian, and he did not aspire to be such. But then, neither was Martin Luther! A notable exception to this generalization is George A. Lindbeck, who in his recent study, *The Nature of Doctrine: Religion and Theology in a Post-Liberal Age* (Philadelphia: The Westminster Press, 1984) writes "Perhaps the last American theologian who in practice (and in some extent in theory) made extended and effective attempts to redescribe major aspects of the contemporary scene in distinctively Christian terms was Reinhold Niebuhr" (124).

6.   (New York: Richard R. Smith, Inc, 1930): 132–133.

7.   This is not so dominant in Canada, where we possess only a "pale version" of the American Dream, and where both political and geographic realities thrust us into a struggle for survival that is not so conducive to credulity and indeed breeds a scepticism that is not always amenable to "religion."

8.   *NDM* II: 187.

9.   *Worldview* (June, 1973): 14.

10.   Responding to Richard Kroner's analysis of "The Historical Roots of Niebuhr's Thought" (in Charles W. Kegley and Robert W. Bretall (eds.) *Reinhold Niebuhr: His Religious, Social and Political Thought* (N.Y.: The Macmillan Co., 1956)), Niebuhr writes, "In regard to Professor Kroner's sympathetic account of the movement of my thought I have only a slight amendment to suggest, and that is that I was first influenced not so much by the Reformers as by the study of St. Augustine" (436–37). One may be permitted to ask, however, and especially in view of the significant differences between Protestant and Catholic analyses of Augustine, whether Niebuhr's Augustine is not rather coloured by Protestant associations!

11.   I have discussed this tradition in numerous writings, especially *Lighten our Darkness: Towards an Indigenous Theology of the Cross* (Philadelphia: Westminster Press, 1976), where I have also acknowledged my indebtedness to my great teacher, Niebuhr, for his exemplary treatment of the tradition in the North American context.

12.   "The Pauline Theology of the Cross," in *Interpretation* 24 (April, 1970): 227.

13.   Jürgen Moltmann, *The Crucified God* (London: SCM Press Ltd., 1973): 72.

14.   *Theology of Play*, trans. by Reinhard Ulrich (N.Y.: Harper & Row 1972): 30.

15.   See Ernest Becker, *The Denial of Death* (N.Y.: The Free Press, 1973).

16.   *On Being a Christian*, trans. by Edward Quinn (Glasgow: Collins, 1974): 571.

17.   *Faith and History: A Comparison of Christian and Modern Views of History (FH)* (N.Y.: Scribner's, 1959): 28–29.

18.   *NDM* II: 206-207.

19.   ibid., 207.

20.   ibid., 308.

21.   See Walter von Loewenich, *Luther's Theology of the Cross,* trans. Herbert J. A. Bouman (Belfast: Christian Journals Ltd., 1976): chapter two.

22.   "The correlate of revelation is faith. The mutual relation between the two is so close that revelation cannot be completed without faith. The revelation of God in Christ, the disclosure of God's sovereignty over life and history, the clarification of the meaning of life and history, is not completed until man is able, by faith, to apprehend the truth which is beyond his apprehension without faith" (*NDM* II: 52).

23.   "The truth is not *completely* beyond [human] apprehension; otherwise Christ could not have been expected. It *is* nevertheless beyond his apprehension or Christ would not have been rejected. It is a truth capable of apprehension by faith; but when so apprehended there is a consciousness in the heart of the believer that he has been helped to this apprehension" (ibid.).

24.   ibid., 60.

25.   ibid., 62.

26.   *The Christian Century* 100 (1983): 900–901.

27.   See "Biblical Thought and Ontological Speculation in Tillich's Theology," by Reinhold Niebuhr, in Charles W. Kegley and Robert W. Bretall, *The Theology of Paul Tillich* (N.Y.: The Macmillan Co., 1952): 216ff.

28.   *NDM* II: 64.

29.   In his footnote to this sentence, Niebuhr writes: "In this debate Brunner seems to me to be right and Barth wrong; but Barth seems to win the debate because Brunner accepts too many of Barth's presuppositions in his fundamental premises to be able to present his own position with plausibility and consistency. Barth is able to prove Brunner inconsistent but that does not necessarily prove him to be wrong" (ibid.).

30.   The foregoing footnote is typical of Niebuhr's distancing of himself even from the Brunnerian articulation of this movement.

31.   In Karl Barth, *The Word of God and the Word of Man* (N.Y.: Harper & Bros. (Harper Torchbooks), 1957).

32.   "When the Word was made flesh it not only revealed the relevance between the human and the divine but the distance between the human and the divine" (*The Christian Century*, art. cit.).

33.   "To recognize that the Cross was something more than a noble tragedy and its victim something else than a good man who died for his ideals; to behold rather that this suffering

was indicative of God's triumph over evil through a love which did not stop at involvement in the evil over which it triumphed; to see, in other words, the whole mystery of God's mercy disclosed here is to know that the crucified Lord had triumphed over death and 'when he had himself purged our sins sat down on the right hand of the Majesty on High' (Hebrews 1:3)" (*FH*, 147).

34.   *Beyond Tragedy: Essays on the Christian Interpretation of History* (*BT*) (N.Y.: Scribner's, 1937): 181.

35.   *FH*, 128.

36.   *BT*, 175.

37.   ibid., 115.

38.   *Letters and Papers from Prison* (London: SCM Press, 1971): 336f.

39.   *BT*, 132.

40.   ibid., 185.

THE CONTOURS OF NIEBUHR'S MIND

Larry L. Rasmussen

The theme of these lectures overall is Reinhold Niebuhr's understanding of power and its import for understanding our life together in society. If the Social Gospel, of which Niebuhr was both heir and critic, moved ethics somewhere near the center of Christian faith, Niebuhr moved power somewhere near the center of Christian ethics. Indeed, as a theologian and social ethicist of power, Niebuhr remains without peer.

At the same time that Niebuhr's stature is acknowledged, however, his critics abound. Their criticism puts serious questions to his 'Christian Realism' as a theological/moral orientation and the anthropology and understanding of sin and power which informs it. A cover story in *Sojourners* magazine entitled "Apologist for Power" largely dismisses Niebuhr as "a Cold War theologian" who "became...less a prophet than a priest of the present order."[1] Many a critic now nods in agreement, despite the flurry of books and articles of his friends to the contrary. Yet the larger point for us at the moment is that when we talk of Niebuhr on ethics and power, we talk of what both his defenders and critics most want to discuss.

I readily join those who want to make ethics and power the subject and to appraise Niebuhr's contributions and shortcomings. What subject could be more compelling for our life and time? If we simply take a look at the century in which Niebuhr did his work, the basic reality is everywhere the same, for better and for worse; namely, heightened human power and impact on a contracting, convulsed planet. The morally responsible use of that expanded, cumulative power is the issue for us all.

Yet I hesitate to move immediately and directly into Niebuhr's theory of power. We need to trace the contours of Niebuhr's mind overall and mark well the conceptual frame of which power is his vital subject. This first lecture, then, is the necessary introduction to Niebuhr the theologian of public life and the ethicist of power and its play in self and society.[2] What are the contours of Niebuhr's mind as his thought bears upon ethics and power? What is most helpful to know as framework for the second lecture — a description of his theory of power — and the third — a critical assessment of that?

The basic structure of Niebuhr's habit of mind was set early on and remained remarkably consistent, especially for someone whose reflection always arose from his engagement and whose engagement ranged across a broad spectrum of social issues over five tumultuous decades. At age 24 this precocious parish pastor wrote an article for *Atlantic* magazine entitled "The Nation's Crime Against the Individual." Already he regarded himself something of a publicist and he would, in due course, write more than two thousand articles on supposedly secular issues, many of them for journals like the *Atlantic*, *The Nation*, *The New Republic*. Yet the point is the play of his mind, seen already in that early piece. His thought moves there, as it does the rest of his life, between a changing, conflict-ridden social and historical reality at one pole, and a transcendent, ultimately religious vision, at the other. His characteristic dialectic is already evident — thinking which is quite tautly stretched across tensions of real/ideal, relative/absolute, time/eternity, historical change/divine steadfastness, empiricism/mystery. The basic direction and purpose of Niebuhr's reflection is already set as well: to further what he called "the ethical reconstruction of modern society." That phrase is from his very first book, now mostly forgotten, *Does Civilization Need Religion?* (1927). Theology itself, he contended first as a parish pastor, then a seminary teacher, was in the service of this ethical reconstruction. What theology does is help forge a religious imagination which sustains a commitment to public life and guides policy decisions that represent the leading edge of social justice. Written from the parish, *Does Civilization Need Religion?* includes this: "If religion cannot transform society, it must find its social function in criticizing present realities from some ideal perspective, and in presenting the ideal without corruption, so that it may sharpen the conscience and strengthen the faith of each generation" (163–164). As if to reiterate this in wiser form forty years later, Niebuhr's penultimate book, *Man's Nature and His Communities* (*MNHC*) (1965) records his "strong conviction that a realist conception of human nature should be made the servant of an ethic of progressive justice and should not be made into a bastion of conservatism, particularly a conservatism which defends unjust privileges." "I might define this conviction," he goes on in a retrospective mood, "as the guiding principle throughout my mature life of the relation of religious responsibility to political affairs" (24–25).

In brief, already by his mid-twenties Niebuhr thinks dialectically and theologically, with the purpose of reflection being to aid and abet the transformation of public life. It is important to add that this reflection happens from within the struggles of social movements and under the impact and analysis of historical events. Niebuhr's is continuously the reflection of the activist, the engaged participant, the one in the midst of the power dynamics as they are being played out. He is never the distanced ideal observer, even the deeply informed distanced ideal observer of the Enlightenment paradigm. In different words, *theoria* is a vital moment of ongoing *praxis* for Niebuhr. This is a constant from his youth onward. His comment in a 1939 article is simple and precise: "I must confess that the gradual unfolding of my theological ideas has come not so much through study as through the pressure of world events."[3] Even in his old age and in poor health, he kept up a steady stream of conversation on the pressing issues, got on the telephone to urge this cause or that, and pecked away at his trusty typewriter on yet another article or editorial which put "a realist conception of human nature" in the service "of an ethic of progressive justice." He continued, even in his last, frail years, to do what he had always done as a thinker: with an acute historical consciousness, he raided his reservoir of theological ideas for whatever illumination might be thrown on some moral and political issue for some battle to which he had committed his energy. Unfortunately for us as students of theological-ethical method, he rarely thought about *how* he thought, and didn't much care. His methodological spiral simply went its unself-conscious way as he employed Christian symbols to illumine the human drama which fascinated him, and revised and rearticulated those symbols as the drama seemed to dictate.[4] But what about the *substance* of his thought as it bears on power? Within what grand perspective does Niebuhr's treatment of power finds its place? Of first importance is the relationship of theological anthropology and politics. This will organize a brief tour of his work.

Ursula Niebuhr's introduction to Reinhold's prayers and sermons, entitled *Justice and Mercy*, includes his testimony that "I am a preacher and I like to preach, but I don't think many people are influenced by admonition. Admonitions to be more loving are on the whole irrelevant. What is relevant are analyses of the human situation that discuss the levels of human possibilities and of sin" (1). These analyses were theological for Niebuhr, and precisely these subjects — "the levels of human possibilities and of sin" — were his theological preoccupations, especially as they showed themselves in the lives of groups jockeying for position in the public square. Human nature and the making of history — here was Niebuhr's intellectual passion. Analyses of these subjects yielded relevant substance for morally-concerned, informed public action.

What were Niebuhr's key categories for analyzing human possibilities and limits, and the making of history? He was, of course, popularly regarded as a theologian of "politics" and of "sin," as a theologian of 'Christian Realism' and as a 'neo-orthodox' theologian. Each of these characterizations can be misleading, and has been. Yet each also provides the furnishings for Niebuhr's treatment of power. Each can thus escort us into his mind on our topic. We take each in turn.[5]

POLITICS

For Niebuhr politics was the continual effort to find proximate solutions for the perennial, largely insoluble problems of public life. Still, something grander than politics was behind his fascination with politics and his non-stop involvement in politics; namely, as mentioned, the making of history. Niebuhr saw human experience itself largely in terms of public drama and he always wanted to increase responsible human agency in and for that drama. Against every impulse of a religiously conservative reading of human nature to dampen the vigor of personal engagement and action, Niebuhr always responded with the sure conviction that, as children of God created in God's image, men and women are continually called upon actively to make their own history, even when foolishness, tragedy and irony will no doubt plague their efforts. Indeed, in so many ways the Gospel for Niebuhr is the continuous flow of the mercy and forgiveness of God so that we might again and again "keep on keepin' on" despite our countless foibles, despite history's recurrent tragedy and irony, and despite our inability to fashion a harmonious whole from the fragments in our hands. His was a spirituality precisely for struggle, for historically-decisive struggle in the power tussles of politics. The affirmations which grounded such struggle were two theological ones: that grace is solace and serenity in the midst of never-ending drama and struggle, and power for it; and that human agency in and for the making of history is expressive of our deepest selves as creatures who reflect God's own nature.

It is important to emphasize this, for a couple reasons. First, it is behind Niebuhr's emphasis on "human possibilities." Against the many interpretations of Niebuhr which cast him as a profound pessimist about human achievement, please note his insistence that we cannot set limits or know in advance what human beings might achieve in history. We will discuss this in more detail at a later point. The point is that, for theological reasons, Niebuhr always assumes the exercise of our powers as the subjects of history. Second, the importance of the active exercise of human powers as the medium of human self-realization (in contrast to, say, a life of contemplation) explains in part why Niebuhr invariably took the side of the subjugated, the underdog, the less powerful, the powerless. Human beings who for social and historical reasons were only the objects of history, not its subjects, the "takers" rather than the makers of history, were being robbed of the God-given human vocation to wield society-shaping power. While it is certainly the case that the present theologies of the oppressed have done their chief work after Niebuhr finished his, and thus he did not have opportunity to respond to them; and while it is the case that his own Eurocentrism meant a blind spot in his perception of important dynamics in the "Two-thirds World," at the same time the theme of the empowerment of the subjugated as agents and subjects of history, against all the forces which beat upon their dignity and render them objects, is a quintessentially Niebuhrian theme. So, too, is the theme that the arena of struggle is public and its form is political. Niebuhr was in fact a political "junky," addicted to a running commentary and involvement in the events of public life. But politics mattered so much to Niebuhr because he saw public life as the crucible where human powers contend in the forging of history itself.

We should note in passing that Niebuhr, while he can elaborate the forms of human sinfulness endlessly, never categorically assesses either power or politics negatively. The final reason is theological. That "God can perfectly combine power and goodness is to understand that power is no evil of itself," he says in *Nature and Destiny* (*NDM*) (II: 22). Like all things human, politics participates in creation's fallenness and shows the worst side of our collective propensities. But Niebuhr spends his life fighting for the acknowledgment and respectability of politics as a sphere of vital, morally-responsible human engagement. Yes, he certainly had a place for uncorrupted religious and moral vision. For this reason, he respected pure pacifism. But he had no time for Christians who were adverse to political involvement because it inevitably offended pure religious vision and entailed moral ambiguity and stain. For Niebuhr, worse than the sin of moral stain in power struggles is the sin of utter complacency and the shrinking of the self from its own history-making powers.

SIN

"Sin" is one way theologically to name the plagued efforts of human agency and power. Niebuhr is usually regarded as the consummate theologian of sin and, indeed, he remains without peer as an expositor of the self as sinner and the social consequences. His critics contend that he even "believed" in sin, especially sin as pride. But sin unfurled is considerably more than pride for Niebuhr, and begs for comment, especially when the subject is power.

Sin emerges in a kind of force field of basic insecurity for Niebuhr. It normally takes the form of fleeing from ourselves and our limitations as creatures. Much in the manner of Luther, Niebuhr says we refuse to accept the basic insecurity which is constitutional to life and our nature. Poised as we are at the juncture of finitude and freedom, earth-bound nature and a self-transcending spirit, we cannot bear the fundamental anxiety which arises with the awareness of our morality, our limits and our undefined possibilities. We are "like the sailor, climbing the mast...with the abyss of the waves beneath him and the 'crow's nest' above him...anxious about both the end toward which he strives and the abyss of nothingness into which he may fall" (*NDM* I: 185.)

With this constitutional insecurity as the pre-condition of sin, we usually flee to the myths and illusions of limitlessness and fulfillment which society offers. We do this in order to find security there, though in fact no security is to be had. We will even manufacture false ultimacies, false gods, to which we attach ourselves. What then happens is that our particular interests become identified with general interests, our piece of truth with truth itself, our parochial ways with God's. With social escalation and group reinforcement, the outcome is an unwillingness, even inability, to value the claims of other communities on the same level as ours, or to consider the interests of others on a par with our own. We consequently take advantage of other life, to its detriment and our supposed security and gain. To use the language of religion and ethics which Niebuhr did, sin expresses itself in two ways — as idolatry and injustice, and both are compounded by ideology.[6]

Fleeing from ourselves frequently takes the form of assertion and pretense, of what Niebuhr, moving in Augustine's wake, detailed as forms of "pride" — the pride of power and glory, intellectual pride, moral pride, and religious pride. But sin for Niebuhr was also the self's dissolution, and not only its overweening reach. He chose an unfortunate term for this — sensuality; but the notion is crucial. It means we often evade the burden of being a free and responsible self by drowning ourselves, as Niebuhr says, "in some aspect of the world's vitalities" — sexual compulsions, addictions, indulgences, and various pathologies that arise, not from too high an estimation of ourselves, but too low. Sin as sensuality manifests itself as the lack of harmony *within* the self, rather than the effort to center all life *around* the self (pride). It is a weak self's fear *of* freedom and fear of its own powers, rather than the aggressive self's abuse of freedom and its own powers. Its most corrupt forms are, as he so crisply put it, "not a flight to a false god but to nothingness" (*NDM* I: 237).

I am keenly aware of the proportions in Niebuhr's famed discussions of sin. He spoke to the powerful, from within circles of power, more than he did to the powerless, even when he took their side. He therefore treated the sins of the powerful, above all their overreach and self-deception, and neglected the evasions of freedom and moral responsibility in opiates of various kinds on the part of those who had little social power or opportunity. He never really understood the utterly defeated, even when his good pastor's heart felt compassion for them and he took up their cause. It is nonetheless important to underscore both pride *and* sensuality, lest we truncate Niebuhr's contribution. Grounded in the very nature of the human spirit itself, sin is manifest in both the imperial reach of an expansive self which does not respect limits, and in the evasions of a diminished self which does not honor its possibilities. In the terms of our topic, sin is manifest both in the abuse of power and the failure to relinquish and share power, and in the failure to claim power on the part of a denigrated self unsure of its own agency and/or unable to exercise it.

REALISM

Realism is another term essential to Niebuhr's discussion of ethics and power. As with all his key categories, the reference is to some dimension of the human self. In this case, realism means a kind of wisdom which grows from the knowledge that while human nature exhibits both self-regarding and other-regarding, or social, impulses, the former are generally stronger than the latter. Moreover, self-regarding impulses are compounded and intensified in the lives of groups, along lines of ethnicity, class, race, gender, nationality, creed, or other "we/they" social dynamics. This in turn means that relations between groups will be determined "by the proportion of power which each group possesses at least as much as by any rational and moral appraisal of the comparative needs and claims of each group" (*Moral Man and Immoral Society* (*MMIS*), xxiii). So, to jump ahead into the next lecture, a decent life in society is less dependent upon, say, a good education system or an ethically sensitive religion than it is upon structural checks and balances whereby the different groups in society have some measure of equality *vis à vis* one another. This is why Niebuhr consciously gives the nod to justice over love as the reigning moral norm for life in society.

Niebuhr is serious when he attaches "Christian" to "realism." Realism means he takes the factors of self-interest and power into special account for matters of public life. But "Christian" means this realistic analysis is set in a dialectical framework with the ideal, the eternal, and the infinite. It means justice is more than the organization of power; it is a social quest judged by and qualified by everlasting love and mercy. "Christian" added to realism also means we may yet be lured to higher achievements than any attained to date. Yes, Niebuhr always distanced himself from idealists who expected more from history than, in his judgment, human nature permits. He had no time for the sentimental or naïve, and scorned them, usually with good humor and always with compassion. But he also distanced himself from those whose realism slid into pessimism and cynicism because they did not understand human possibilities well enough or the human and divine sources available for human and social renewal, even renewal by societies in a period of decline. In any case, realism never meant "the moral justification" of "the power of self-interest in human society" (*Children of Light and Children of Darkness (CLCD)*, 41), as it often did and does for advocates of straightforward *realpolitik*. And Niebuhr's "realism" certainly never meant resignation. He was as incapable of that as he was of sloth. In a word, "Christian" in Niebuhr's 'Christian Realism' signalled hope, grace, forgiveness, and the power, he says in a discussion of justification by grace through faith, "to recognize the higher possibilities of justice in every historic situation" (*NDM* II: 284), as well as the power to taste that love and communion which he insisted is the very "law" of our being itself. More on this in the second lecture, as it bears on social power and its redemption.

'Neo-orthodox' and 'liberal,' as tags for Niebuhr, finish our tour of the furrows of his mind. "Neo-orthodox" is incorrect as applied to Niebuhr. He knew it was and said so, preferring to characterize his own theology as a synthesis of Reformation and Renaissance themes, together with some modern Protestant liberal ones. But 'neo-orthodox' is a mistake which has some merit, if it refers to the Augustinian tradition as mediated by Calvin and Luther and modified by nineteenth and twentieth century experience. Then neo-orthodox describes Niebuhr's revulsion against acculturated religion and the cultural optimism that issued in a reading of Western history as progress and the extension of Western civilization as a global good. Neo-orthodox also describes his effort never to fuse religion and politics, yet to relate them in such a way that religion is a power for sharp cultural criticism *sub specie aeternitatis* and a motivating force to transform both self and society. Neo-orthodoxy certainly describes his rejection of belief in human perfectibility and his awareness of the often perverse and ironic consequences of human decisions, including well-intentioned ones. At the same time neo-orthodoxy underscores human freedom and the capacity for transcendence, even when all those "indeterminate possibilities" of human striving will be marked with an irascible sinfulness. In social ethics, neo-orthodox underscores his conviction that a morally-measured coercion is necessary for advancing as well as securing social justice. Finally, and most important, neo-orthodox describes Niebuhr's God. His was largely Luther's "hidden God" (*deus absconditus*) of justice and mercy. Things are never quite what they seem, and God is so very often present *sub contrario* ("under the sign of the opposite"). The cross itself is the supreme instance of the hiddenness of God *sub contrario*. Saving power is hidden in weakness, true strength in humility and sacrifice, and the receiving of life in the letting go of it. The eternal, transcendent God is indeed present in changing history but must be discerned amidst the ambiguous, paradoxical history of which we are a part. And God is only known indirectly and partially.

Niebuhr said that in the last analysis he was a "liberal." Yet he is best known as the demolisher of liberal tenets and culture. Indeed he was. I cite just one typically blunt rejection of "the articles of the [liberal] credo" he finds fallacious:

• That injustice is caused by ignorance and will yield to education and greater intelligence.

• That civilization is becoming gradually more moral and that it is a sin to challenge either the inevitability or the efficacy of gradualness.

• That the character of individuals rather than social systems and arrangements is the guarantee of justice in society.

• That appeals to love, justice, good-will and brotherhood are bound to be efficacious in the end. If they have not been so to date we must have more appeals to love, justice, good-will and brotherhood.

• That goodness makes for happiness and that the increasing knowledge of this fact will overcome human selfishness and greed.

• That wars are stupid and can therefore only be caused by people who are more stupid than those who recognize the stupidity of war.[7]

Liberalism was what Niebuhr sometimes called "soft utopianism" and "faith in man" and in "history," and he rejected it as a faith and a culture. At the same time basic elements of Protestant theological and ethical liberalism were rooted deeply in Niebuhr, as was Anglo-American political liberalism. We take these in turn.

The theological liberalism was mediated largely by his father and the early influence on Niebuhr of Troeltsch and Harnack. Niebuhr's own starting point in both theology and ethics was the starting point of this liberalism; namely, with human needs, powers, and responsibilities. Niebuhr's thought itself moved from lived human experience and historical consciousness into the knowledge of God, rather than the reverse (neo-orthodoxy's preference). His Jesus was also liberalism's. Jesus was a person of deep, personal, free and utter trust in God who lived out that trust without compromise and with singleminded moral vigor, even heroism. Niebuhr's picture of the Kingdom of God was also liberalism's — a vision of an ideal ethical and religious reality in which all the values of pure spirituality are realized and a vision which functions as a judge upon all our strivings, as well as a lure for them. Yet neither Jesus nor the Kingdom furnish any more than the rudiments of a Christian social ethic. The day-to-day substance of a Christian social ethic will thus have to be worked out by us amidst our reality — this was liberalism's conviction, and Niebuhr's. He also retained liberalism's view of religion as a power for social struggle and transformation. He could lambast the Social Gospel for its naïveté about sin and power, but he never abandoned its goal of social transformation nor its conviction that religion's power could be real energy directed to social change.

Niebuhr was a liberal in the Anglo-Saxon political sense as well. He shared its model of society as a marketplace of competing interests and powers. His own regulative principles of justice were liberalism's — namely, equality and liberty. His social strategy was also liberalism's — justice is furthered by increasing the power of marginal groups within the context of democracy as the polity. Lastly, while Niebuhr dismissed liberalism's sentimentality — its trust that love and good-will could harmonize social relations — he affirmed its pragmatism, its pluralism, its prizing of tolerance, its social experimentation, and its rejection of absolutisms of all kinds.

To close — abruptly. While none of the facets of Niebuhr's thought we have sketched — his notions of politics, sin, realism, neo-orthodoxy and liberalism — is yet his theory and ethic of power, everything we have touched upon gives his theology and ethic of power the particular shape and substance it has. This long introduction thus seemed the proverbial "scratch" from which to start. The reader is supposed to be a little frustrated with it, frustrated that we have only come to the water's edge and have not yet plunged into social power and its redemption — the second lecture — nor an appraisal of Niebuhr on power — the third and last.

NOTES

(A General Bibliography for these *Birks* Lectures begins on page 183.)

1.   Bill Kellerman, "Apologist of Power," *Sojourners* 16 #5 (1987): 14–20.

2.   Let me only note as an aside that U.S. society does not commonly generate intellectuals as common fixtures of public life, and U.S. society almost never generates *theological-moral* reflection on the role of its considerable power in the world as a matter of public discourse. Niebuhr and Martin Luther King are rare and welcome exceptions.

3.   "Ten Years That Shook My World," *The Christian Century* 56 (1939): 546.

4.   An amusing aside: at a seminar at the Cathedral of St. John the Divine held in Niebuhr's honor, Tillich remarked; "Reinie never tells us how he knows; he just starts knowing."

5.   The treatment of these basic Niebuhrian categories draws heavily from my "Introduction" to *Reinhold Niebuhr: Theologian of Public Life*, ed. Larry Rasmussen (Minneapolis: Fortress Press edition, 1991).

6.   For him, ideology is reason in the service of self-interest, especially collective self-interest, serving in ways which lead to or intensify self-deception, especially collective self-deception.

7.   "The Blindness of Liberalism," *Radical Religion* 1 (Autumn, 1936): 4f.

NIEBUHR'S THEORY OF POWER
Social Power and its Redemption

Larry L. Rasmussen

Reinhold Niebuhr's most fully developed essay in social ethics was his monograph on democracy, *The Children of Light and the Children of Darkness* (*CLCD*). In it he contrasts moral idealism and cynicism and argues that neither of itself serves the cause of democracy well. The idealism and innocence of "the children of light" is the source of the usual defense for democracy, conceiving it to be the polity which an enlightened and self-directed citizenry deserve. Examples of this perspective are legion. I choose but one; a line from Harry Truman's U.S. Presidential Inaugural of 1949: "Democracy is based on the conviction that man has the moral and intellectual capacity, as well as the inalienable right, to govern himself with reason and justice."[1] The source of twentieth century totalitarianisms, by contrast, is the moral cynicism of "the children of darkness."[2]

Yet democracy, he argues, is on extremely shaky grounds if it depends upon moral idealism and assumes human goodness and moral progress. The power of individual and collective egotism is no less present in democracy than any other polity. Any genius democracy might have, Niebuhr argues, is the felicitous combination of the free exercise of human agency across the entire populace and structural arrangements that rest in a healthy suspicion of concentrated power. Differently said, democracy draws upon moral idealism while entertaining serious doubt about that idealism. It works from the possibilities humans achieve, or might achieve, in their exercise of human powers while simultaneously placing restraints upon the exercise of those

155

powers. It affirms that we are moral creatures and can achieve a degree of community and harmony (i.e., children of light) while also contending that we are sufficiently self-serving that wise communities always check the will-to-power. Thus the famous epigram that "Man's capacity for justice makes democracy possible; but man's inclination to injustice makes democracy necessary" (*CLCD*, xiii).

The purpose of this lecture is not to explicate Niebuhr's defense of democracy, however, but his understanding of power, especially his understanding of power in society and its redemption. I begin with Niebuhr on democracy, however, because it gathers the substance we wish to address. That substance consists of, first, the focal points in Niebuhr's theory of power — namely, the organization and balance of power — and, second, his consistent concern to view power in moral and religious perspective and to enhance power's possibilities for socially redemptive action by appropriating religious and moral resources. For Niebuhr, the relationship of power — its organization and balance — to evil and injustice is disarmingly simple. The last sentences in the paragraph with the famous epigram read as follows: "If men are inclined to deal unjustly with their fellows, the possession of power aggravates this inclination. That is why irresponsible and uncontrolled power is the greatest source of injustice" (xiii–xiv). The answer to the question of his 1953 essay, "Why Is Communism So Evil?" runs in the same vein: "...the relation of absolute power to complete defencelessness is the basic cause of all the evils of communism..." (*Christian Realism and Political Problems*, 36). Niebuhr in fact came to reject his own earlier Marxist socialism because, as he said even while yet attracted to it: "A society which establishes an economic equilibrium through social ownership" may "create a new disproportion of power through the necessity of strengthening the political force which holds economic power in check" (Brown 52, citing *Reflections on the End of an Era (REE)*, 83).

We begin, then, with Niebuhr's basic concern for power and his basic conviction about it. What drives his abiding interest in power is social justice and injustice. His concern for power is essentially a moral one. And his basic conviction is that the misorganization of power and its imbalance is the social source of evil and injustice. About the best social arrangements we can muster, he thinks, are those which permit the non-violent organization of countervailing power so that all groups in society share both social burdens and benefits in roughly equal measure. For this reason Niebuhr tirelessly defended democracy. By embodying "the principle of resistance to government within the principle of government itself" (*NDM* (1943): II: 268), democracy provides the space for citizens to organize power in their own interests and against the unchecked power of others. Since we apparently are not able to dispense with coercion in society altogether, democracy is preferred because it comes closest to "mutual coercion mutually agreed upon."[3]

It is important to add that precisely the organization and balance of power (or its misorganization and imbalance) is the reason Niebuhr now and again railed at the naïveté and self-delusion of powerful democratic nations, like the U.S. and Great Britain. They failed to recognized the sure imperialism which flowed from disproportions of power between more powerful nations and less powerful, whether their domestic polities were democratic or not. Indeed, the very moral idealism which bolstered their case for democracy often served not only to justify their imperialism but intensify it. As Niebuhr was wont to say against all idealists, power operating behind a screen of acclaimed ideal ends is frequently more self-delusory and sometimes even more evil than purely cynical and open defiance of moral ends. This is perhaps the equivalent for ethics of Luther's remark that oftentimes the curses of the ungodly are more pleasing to God than the alleluias of the pious.

Locating the focal points of Niebuhr's notion of power in its organization and balance is not yet to understand it, however. Understanding it means, as always with Niebuhr, understanding human nature. In this case, it means above all analyzing human nature as expressed in our life as citizens in society contending in the public square.

We cannot of course unravel Niebuhr's famed "doctrine of man" layer by layer. Some other tack must be taken and I am simply going to list and comment upon essential Niebuhrian "theses" on human power and human nature in society. Most of the following are from his first blockbuster treatise, *Moral Man and Immoral Society* (*MMIS*) (1932). This volume laid out the basic elements of his social theory, at the heart of which is his theory of power and its relation to morality and religion. There were changes later but no genuine retractions.

The background and purpose of *MMIS* are important. Writing in the midst of the Great Depression and against the background of both secular and religious liberalism and idealism, Niebuhr wants to confront liberalism and idealism with the reality of power in social relationships and the bracketed capacity of human beings to deal morally and rationally with power. At the same time, he will not accept an amoral and utterly utilitarian politics. So he seeks a relationship of religion, morality and power that is realistic about power and human nature that will also serve his own passion — a progressive, religiously grounded justice. He wants to preserve moral values in politics *and* garner secular and religious power for a social justice struggle that is informed both by human possibilities and human limits. Niebuhr knows full well he is flying in the face of U.S.

American cultural confidence and innocence. He knows that the vision he is deploying is a tragic perspective "stamped with a Christian imprimatur"[4] and that the American bourgeoisie has no real "feel" for either a tragic perspective or human limits. He knows his views will be dismissed by many, including many sincere Christian thinkers, as doomsaying pessimism. He nonetheless argues for precisely this tragic but graced perspective as the pragmatic framework for a sharp moral critique and a charged social struggle which takes as its task the organization of the disadvantaged. With this backdrop in mind, we turn to Niebuhr's rather striking contentions about power in society:

- That "there is no ethical force strong enough to place inner checks upon the use of power if its quantity is inordinate" (164). This is Niebuhr's way of stating Acton's law that power tends to corrupt and absolute power absolutely. The clear implication is that only the organization of countervailing power avails to check injustice. Niebuhr does say that "social intelligence and moral goodwill" may sometimes "mitigate the brutalities of social conflict," but his forceful conclusion is still that "when collective power...exploits weakness, it can never be dislodged unless power is raised against it" (Brown 47, citing *MMIS*, xxiii, 3–4, xii). We could note here the spirited exchange that went on for years between Niebuhr and John Dewey. Both Niebuhr and Dewey knew the social order is largely dominated by force of one kind or another. But Niebuhr thought Dewey naïve in believing that conflicting claims can usually be adjusted through discussion and education. The rational arbitration of social conflict is usually unavailing, Niebuhr said, because reason won't control force. Reason is itself a fragile instrument already serving self-interest and tainted by it. When power is inordinate, neither moral appeal nor reason is a significant check or means for transformation.[5]

- That it is "impossible to transfer an ethic of personal relations uncritically to the field of inter-group relations" (173). The moral resources of large human collectivities are fewer than those of individuals and small groups of persons in face-to-face relationships.

- That a positive moral continuum exists, *from* the moral ideal of relatively "disinterested" love, achievable in highest, but never perfect, degree by self-sacrificing and other-regarding individuals and intimate groups, *to* social justice, achievable, via an always precarious and tenuous balance of power, by competing collectivities. This continuum parallels the continuum of greater moral resources for individuals than for groups.

- That both social gradations and unjust consequences flow from imbalances or disproportions of power.

• That while "any kind of social power develops social inequality," (8) all social cooperation on a larger scale than the most intimate groups requires a measure of coercion. Coercion, then, is both a social necessity and a social danger. The same force which makes for social peace makes for injustice. Niebuhr repeats this point with some force in *NDM*: "The basic paradox of history...[is that] the creative and destructive possibilities of human history are inextricably intermingled. The very power which organizes human society and establishes justice, also generates injustice by its preponderance of power" (II: 21).

• That social justice is not possible apart from coercion, and since countervailing power is needed to check or destroy oppressive power, the question is how to make new power constellations moral.

• That the most pervasive, effective, and common uses of power are covert. They are subtly socialized and institutionalized. Most citizens in a democracy are unaware of the degree of coercion present. (The exceptions are alienated minorities.)

• That the disinherited have more of a right to fight for their (violated) rights than the powerful have to extend theirs, and that it is thus possible to distinguish between morally justified and morally unjustified self-interest or self-seeking.

• That the social privileges generated by disproportionate power need not be economic in origin but usually are, and that "economic power is more basic than political power" (210).

• That religion normally intensifies power dynamics. Religious humility and self-deprecation will tend to foster sacrifice of power and intensify powerlessness. Religious pride and its "cosmic" affirmation of the self and its communities tends to foster extremism, fanaticism and absolutism. "Religion is...humility before the absolute and self-assertion in terms of the absolute" (64). Religious vitality will therefore invariably strengthen power dynamics, whatever their particular character and direction may be.

• That "non-violent coercion and resistance...is a type of coercion which offers the largest opportunities for a harmonious relationship which the moral and rational factors in social life. It does not destroy the process of a moral and rational adjustment of interest to interest completely during the course of resistance" (251). "There is no problem of political life to which religious imagination can make a larger contribution than this problem of developing non-violent resistance" (254).

Since Niebuhr's attack on absolute pacifism and his campaign to resist fascism by force has obscured his call for developing forms of non-violent resistance, I want to elaborate on it, not least because precisely here lies, in his judgment, the place to relate religious and moral factors redemptively to power. At least we should not be surprised when Niebuhr writes, as he did in 1967: "I think, as a rather dedicated anti-pacifist, that Dr. King's conception of the nonviolent resistance to evil is a real contribution to our civil, moral and political life" (Stone 234, citing the foreword to King's published address on Vietnam at Riverside Church). The reasons have already been alluded to: non-violence retains the presence of all parties as parties to a settlement in which they are respected and in which "moral and rational adjustment of interest to interest" is still part of the process. The spiral of violence and its action/reaction pattern of intensifying deadliness is not set in motion but disciplined by refusing to use deadly force as a means. Niebuhr is sensitive here in ways his critics have sometimes overlooked. The means of force invariably are transferred to the ends as he noted even in his most "apocalyptic" and Marxist writing, *REE*: "One of the pathetic aspects of human history is that the instruments of judgment which it uses to destroy particular vices must belong to the same category of the vice to be able to destroy it. Thus some evil, which is to be destroyed, is always transferred to the instrument of its destruction and thereby perpetuated" (Stone 193, citing *REE*, 94).

Niebuhr, criticizing Gandhi, argued that non-violent resistance was also a form of coercive power and was potentially effective for that reason. It, too, could be a destructive means which transferred evil. But it was less likely to do so and more likely to keep open the way for a more just resolution of inevitable social conflict and the redress of power. In any event, and contrary to some impressions of Niebuhr, he rejected what he called "a purely tragic view of life" in which "destructiveness is…an inevitable consequence of human creativity. It is not invariably necessary to do evil in order that we may do good" (Stone 195, citing *The Irony of Americam History (IAH)*, 157). Non-violent coercion is the means more likely to do good. It might be added that Niebuhr's 1932 volume, *MMIS*, practically laid out the full strategy later used in the Civil Rights Movement. And if one looks at the Niebuhr writings and actions on race from 1925–1971, the following forms of persuasion and force are found: "moral teaching, education, economic boycott, study commissions, civil rights legislation, cooperative economic organization, antipoverty legislation, church action, writing, rallies, and demonstrations" (Stone 237). Niebuhr considered race relations America's national shame and most intransigent sin. The poverty, poor housing, and unemployment of African-Americans, he wrote in 1968, is "due to a complacent self-satisfaction about our American democracy" (Stone 237, citing "The Negro Minority," 55), a complacency which he traced from the nation's founding documents up through the inadequate response to the rage and riots of 1966–68. Ronald Stone comments that on this and other matters the "reuniting of Niebuhr's [non-violent] strategies with religious imagination appropriate for the 1990s remains the task of the churches" (Stone 237).

• That power impulses in society are finally impulses of persistent human nature and will themselves persist, whatever the forms of social organization. There simply is no sharp line between the will-to-live and the will-to-power. The human spirit is a "curious mixture of fear of extinction and love of power" (*MMIS*, 42). This means that an imperial reach easily attaches itself to our efforts to preserve life and to foster and defend ways of life. Even the will to survive itself cannot be disentangled from what the "two forms of its spiritualization," namely, "the will to self-realization" and the "will to power" (*CLCD* 18). The fact that these "wills" — the will to survive, to realize one's self, and to exercise power — are always mixed and compounded with each other "on every level of human life... makes the simple distinctions between good and evil, between selfishness and altruism" invalid (*CLCD* 21). It also means that power is a part of virtually every dynamic of our lives. As Charles Brown, interpreting Niebuhr, notes: "Seeing perils in nature and history, humans seek security by enhancing their power; seeing their smallness, they seek compensation by pretensions of power" (Brown 115). On a light note, I can assure you in passing that Niebuhr would have appreciated the title of Ashley Brilliant's little collection: *All I Want Is a Warm Bed, A Kind Word, and Unlimited Power*.

• That, in the end, power itself is the product of spirit. It never exists "without an ally of physical force but it is always more than physical compulsion" (*NDM* II: 20). Power engages and expresses all the vitalities of life, including mind and heart. "Reason" and "force" may perhaps be regarded as "end points" on a spectrum of human spirituality and vitality but in fact no sharp distinction can be made between them in the play of human power in society. Because power is as much a matter of spirit as of physical force, engaging our human vitalities at many levels, only a few human conflicts are waged at the level of survival. Most are on other levels. All involve power.

As mentioned, Niebuhr later modified some elements of his convictions about human nature, religion, morality and power. He upgraded somewhat the creative moral accomplishments possible for human groups and their collective ambition at the same time that he tempered his earlier estimate of the moral performance of individuals and their circles of intimacy. He commented late in life that the title of his early work might better have been *Not So Moral Man in His Less Moral Communities*. On at least one occasion he nearly erased the differences he so pushed in *MMIS*, the differences between the morality and power dynamics of intimate circles and those of mass scale: "The most terrific social conflicts actually occur," he wrote in 1935, "in intimate communities in which intensity of social cohesion accentuates the social distance of various groups and individuals....Even when [they are] less pronounced than the imperialism of groups [they] may be more deadly for operating at close range" (*Interpretation of Christian Ethics*, 115–116). Despite these acknowledgments, Niebuhr never really pursued the similarities which bridge from the private and intimate to the public and collective. He did not study, for example, the relationship of power dynamics in families to public conflicts in society and among nations. This has led to significant criticism of his thinking about human nature, justice and power (as we shall see in the third lecture). I only add that his underlying assertion about the need for countervailing power is not thereby changed, and his best critics still stand by his own unaltered conclusion that in the struggle for justice the key is the increase of power in the ranks of the victims of injustice, wherever they are.

In later discussions of power, Niebuhr also modified his contention that "economic power is more basic than political power." He undertook systematic comparative studies of "nations and empires" and concluded that there were times and places when, for example, priestly and military power — and especially priestly and military power together — were "more basic" than economic power. He nonetheless went on to say that our era is most shaped by the creative energies of the bourgeoisie. Ours is an era dominated by "economic man." For the modern world, then, economic power *is* the single most powerful of the forces shaping our life together. On this point *NDM* largely echoes *MMIS*, even when the later Niebuhr is more aware that his earlier view suffered from a false universalism. Along with both Marx and the capitalists, he had wrongly surmised that economic power had always been socially determinative. A few sentences in *NDM* are worth citing as an indication of both continuity in Niebuhr's view and developing nuances: "It may be taken as axiomatic that great disproportions of power lead to injustice, whatever may be the efforts to mitigate it. Thus the concentration of economic power in modern technical society has made for injustice, while the diffusion of political power has made for justice" (II: 262).[6]

The mention of political power returns us briefly to the basic foci in Niebuhr's theory of power — the organization of power and its balance. Niebuhr says with regularity that there are always two aspects of power in human communities, a central organizing principle and power, and the balance of vitalities and forces in any given social situation. The first, the "central organizing...power," belongs to the polity and instrumentality to the state; the second belongs to the give-and-take of the varied human collectivities that make up society. The organization of power and the dynamic balancing of power are *not* separate in any discrete sense, any more than state and society can be understood, much less lived, in abstraction one from the other. Nonetheless, because political power is the fundamental power to shape and govern the "polis," Niebuhr is led to treat political power separately and lift up the organization of power as a factor distinct from its balance. Any moral or social advance in human community has to attend to *both* the organization — or structuring — of power and the balance of power. A good constitution and good laws are vital, but they cannot compensate for deficient socialization of the citizenry, for a healthy, participatory culture, or for a variety of more-or-less balanced forces in society. On the other hand, formation of character and attention to civic virtue and its exercise in public life cannot of itself substitute for sound structure and good law. Even healthy contending forces of civil society do not provide ipso facto their own framework and governance.

Most treatments of Niebuhr on power stop with his case for democracy and the balance of power and with his sophisticated power analysis as based in his social anthropology. They close with appreciation for his insights from human nature into the need for checks-and-balances and the organization of countervailing power against the concentrations of power. That is quite understandable, since Niebuhr argues that forcefully and with few qualifications. Listen to this passage from *NDM*:

> The domination of one life by another is avoided most successfully by an equilibrium of power and vitalities, so that weakness does not invite enslavement by the strong. Without a tolerable equilibrium no moral or social restraints ever succeed completely in preventing injustice and enslavement. In this sense an equilibrium of vitality is an approximation of brotherhood within the limits of conditions imposed by human selfishness (II: 265).

But to stop here is a serious mistake, even an injustice to Niebuhr. To begin with, balancing power is not enough. Niebuhr in fact explicitly rejects it, even in the very next sentence of the passage just read:

> But an equilibrium of power is not brotherhood. The restraint of the will-to-power of one member of the community by the counter-pressure of power by another member results in a condition of tension. All tension is covert or potential conflict. The principle of the equilibrium of power is thus a principle of justice in so far as it prevents domination and enslavement; but it is a principle of anarchy and conflict in so far as its tensions, if unresolved, result in overt conflict (ibid.).[7]

Why this tenuous power equilibrium never holds rests in the nature of human nature itself: "No participant in a balance is ever quite satisfied with its own position," Niebuhr writes. "Every center of power will seek to improve its position; and every such effort will be regarded by the others as an attempt to disturb the equilibrium. There is sufficient mistrust…to make it quite certain that a mere equilibrium…will not suffice to preserve the peace" (*CLCD* 175). Differently said, the insecurities of any age, and the endless jockeying for a more secure and satisfactory position, are enlargements of the insecurities of the self.

Still, the chief objection to balance of power as a goal and endpoint is not its social unsustainability as such. A "realistic" theory is deficient because it shortcuts Niebuhr's own project of relating religion, morality and power positively and in a manner which does more than merely "balance" power. He wants power to serve socially progressive ends, of course. But within the possibilities given human beings, he also wants to reveal a redemptive dynamic in social power dynamics themselves. His interest is social power and its possibilities for a redemptive dimension in the making of history. His interest is discerning God's own struggles within the human exercise of power. This is far more than balancing power and Niebuhr contested against all who would reduce politics to a stark struggle for power, even balanced power, and no more. To his mind the reason is dictated by the religiously-driven human spirit itself. Let us finish, then, with this question: What does Niebuhr's account of a religious component, and more specifically of Christian faith, bring to his theory of power?

In Christopher Lasch's opus, *The True and Only Heaven: Progress and Its Critics*, chapter nine is entitled "The Spiritual Discipline Against Resentment" (369ff.). The chapter draws heavily from Niebuhr. "The spiritual discipline against resentment" is itself a phrase from *MMIS* and arises amidst themes we have already identified — that "social cohesion is impossible without coercion,"

"coercion is impossible without the creation of social injustice," "the destruction of injustice is impossible without the use of further coercion," and thus we are caught up "in an endless cycle of social conflict" (*MMIS*, cited from Lasch 377). Lasch goes to say what we have already also noted, that while power is inescapably involved in making justice, it makes injustice as well and thus an uneasy balance of power through systems of checks and balances is about the best we can manage under the conditions of sin. But for Niebuhr the recognition of the inescapable role of power as coercion in society defined the problem, not the solution (Lasch 376f.). And his concern and issue is how to humanize inevitable conflict, set its face toward justice, and further moral values and even a redemptive spirit in the process. This is the precise context in which his phrase, "the spiritual discipline against resentment," arises.

To what does it point? Let me signal the way by recalling Niebuhr's judgments about two U.S. Americans. He found Abraham Lincoln both the U.S.'s best politician and its best public theologian, and he regarded Martin Luther King, Jr. the most creative Protestant of the 20th century. The reason for his positive assessment was their preservation of religious and moral values in and as part of the conflict-ridden power dynamics of social struggles. Their politics and exercise of power included "the spiritual discipline against resentment" as an expression of these values.

But what are these values in their politics — more precisely, their making of history — and how are they manifest in Niebuhr's theory of power? We must begin in an apparently unlikely place — Niebuhr as the critic of the Enlightenment legacy in both its liberal bourgeois and Marxist renditions. For him, liberals and socialists made the same mistake. Namely, the errant assumption that life in society could be guided by a universal rationality based in a universal humanity. If I may cite a student of Niebuhr's, Charles West, from a recent issue of *Christianity and Crisis*: West is writing about the breakdown of Eastern European nations. His analysis and conclusion are utterly Niebuhrian.

> The breakdown will be addressed at its heart only when a new concept of the relation between political and ethnic community emerges to capture the imagination of the people. Marxism-Leninism could create, at best, solidarity, not community. Western individualist, free-enterprise liberalism leaves communal identity and values completely to one side. Both are ideologies of universal humanity that leaves a whole dimension of human living out of account (52 (1992), 278).

The "dimension of human living" left "out of account" is what makes community community; namely, the power of particularity. The power and driving force of family, race, ethnic identity, culture, religious community, nation, sexuality, language. Yes, Niebuhr traced the immorality of groups and the endless renewal of social conflict to this particularism that makes for community itself. This was the thrust of *MMIS* which continues as a theme on into his penultimate book, *MNHC*. But Niebuhr also found liberals and Marxists utterly naïve about transcending the power of particularity. They both make the fatal mistake of dismissing the "organic unities of family, race, and nation as irrational idiosyncrasies which a more perfect rationality will destroy" (Lasch 274, citing Niebuhr). Somehow the market and/or the state were supposed to rid the world of the plague of locality and traditional identity, and render some world synthesis which would redound to the common good of all. It would be difficult, Niebuhr wrote, "to find a more perfect and naïve expression of the modern illusion that human reason will be able to become the complete master of all the contingent, irrational, and illogical forces of the natural world which underlie and condition all human culture" (Lasch 375, citing Niebuhr). To repeat: Niebuhr was not denying the negative power of particularism. After all, he was battling not just Stalinism and liberalism, but the vehement racist fascism of Hitler's community of Aryan blood and soil (*Blut und Boden*). He fully understood a particularistic community's power for evil. What he was denying was that particularistic identity could be eliminated or even overlooked. It could be suppressed, perhaps, for a season. But then it would likely explode when the historical chance arose, resulting, as Niebuhr says, "in desperate and demonic affirmations of the imperiled values" inextricably associated with community particularism.

Niebuhr's own alternative to a liberal capitalist and socialist rationality was always to understand the human self in what he called "dramatic-historical" terms, or what he simply identified as the "biblical" perspective. Human selves and their restless freedom will always escape and shatter all the rational schemes by which we try to understand ourselves and control the course of history. Niebuhr would not have been the least bit surprised first to witness the collapse, largely from within, of rationalistic establishment socialism, and then the disillusionment for millions of its competitor and successor, messianic capitalism. He would have identified anew what he had long contended, that these are in fact contentious *siblings*, both the offspring of the same Western technocratic prometheanism and both sharers in the same Enlightenment illusion about shedding dramatic-historical particularisms in favor of a grand cosmopolitan scheme. To cite Niebuhr directly: "Human beings do not live in abstract universal societies. They live in historic communities; and the peace, order, and justice of such communities, such as it is, is the product of ages of development..." (Brown 62, citing a lecture of Niebuhr, "English and German Mentality— A Study in National Traits").

But if the Enlightenment quest for a rational universalism, stripped of the narrow loyalties of particular times and places and peoples, is unavailing; if we are who we are only in concrete and varied and conflicting and conflicted communities, what then? What solution is there to "the endless cycle of social conflict?" The awareness of ourselves as "dramatic-historical" is a recognition, not a solution.

We have already seen the large portion of Niebuhr's practical answer rooted in his own liberalism: an organization of society which affords the best opportunity for checks and balances and the continual organization of countervailing power, a structure accommodating the freedom of the restless self but pressing for equality in every way possible. We could go on, as he himself does, to make a strong case for the liberal Enlightenment value of tolerance. Yet all this falls painfully short, Niebuhr knows. In response he argues for a religious and moral tempering of our exercise of power. The roots are theological for him and the outcome intersects attitudes, actions and policies themselves.

Let me begin with Niebuhr on forgiveness. It is forgiveness, not tolerance, which provides the corrective to the egotism and self-righteousness of groups, anchored as this is in the stubborn limits of their irrepressible particularity. Forgiveness is far more difficult than tolerance, but also far more profound. It lets contending groups battle passionately without denying one another's humanity and foreclosing on a genuine chance for new beginnings. Forgiveness as a component of the power dynamic itself is, in Niebuhr's terms, an example of engaging in social struggles "with a religious reservation" (Lasch 376, citing Niebuhr). Specifically, it illustrates "the spiritual discipline against resentment" and was exemplified by Lincoln's capacity to carry on a tragic conflict "with malice toward none" and a deep sense of his own and society's sinfulness. It was exemplified with similar power by Martin Luther King's capacity to use a means of struggle — non-violent coercion — which affirmed the humanity of all participants and retained a space for all, friend and enemy alike, to be in on tough negotiated conclusions together and difficult new starts together. Against both capitalists and socialists, Niebuhr is certain that the sources of social conflict themselves will never be eradicated. So it is, in his words, "more important to preserve the spirit of forgiveness amidst the struggles than to seek islands of neutrality" (Lasch 376, citing Niebuhr).[8] It is important as well to draw upon and channel the power of particularity and otherness, rather than suppress it.

Incidentally, quite independently of Niebuhr, the renowned political philosopher Hannah Arendt makes a similar, and intriguing, case for the political necessity of forgiveness. In *The Human Condition* (*HC*) she focuses one section on "action" and in it discusses the dilemma of action as the irreversibility and unpredictability of the process it sets in motion and furthers. "The possible redemption from the predicament of irreversibility," she writes, "— of being unable to undo what one has done though one did not, and could not, have known what he was doing — is the faculty of forgiving" (*HC* 237). Forgiveness, she argues, "is the only reaction which does not merely re-act but acts anew and unexpectedly, unconditioned by the act which provoked it and therefore freeing from its consequences both the one who forgives and the one who is forgiven" (*HC* 241). Differently said, only forgiveness permits action at its most profound, which is action as the capacity to initiate new beginnings amidst inevitable human conflict. Indeed, only through the "mutual release" offered by forgiveness, Arendt says, can people "remain free agents, only by constant willingness to change their minds and start again can they be trusted with so great a power as that to begin something new" (*HC* 240). Forgiveness, especially as freedom from vengeance, breaks the "automatism" (*HC* 241) of action/re-action that builds the spiral of injustice and violence. Though not a Christian, she cites Jesus of Nazareth as "the discoverer of the role of forgiveness in the realm of human affairs" (*HC* 238) even when there are some soundings elsewhere among students of power.

I offer but two illustrations of the working of forgiveness in Niebuhr's discussions. The first is at the level of our most basic dispositions, our bearing and orientation as we confront conflict, especially among groups. It is not to the stark individual that Niebuhr writes a famous little meditation on the theological virtues. The following paragraph is from the book, *The Irony of American History* (*IAH*), in a chapter entitled "Happiness, Prosperity and Virtue." Niebuhr says dominant U.S. American culture sets itself up for disappointment by assuming that happiness will attend prosperity and that the incongruities and disharmonies can be overcome, that life is a problem to be solved. None of our strategies can overcome the fragmentary character of human existence. Thus, he says, "the final wisdom of life requires, not the annulment of incongruity but the achievement of serenity within and above it" (*IAH* 63). Then this:

> Nothing that is worth doing can be achieved in our lifetime; therefore we must be saved by hope. Nothing which is true or beautiful or good makes complete sense in any immediate context of history; therefore we must be saved by faith. Nothing we do, however virtuous, can be accomplished alone; therefore we are saved by love. No virtuous act is quite as virtuous from the standpoint off our

friend or foe as it is from our standpoint. Therefore we must be saved by the
final form of love which is forgiveness (*IAH* 63).

Forgiveness, then, is part of a whole spirituality which Niebuhr brings to the
exercise of power and which tempers it with wisdom and mercy. It also has its
impact directly on policies, which is my second illustration. The very person
who rallied for U.S. participation in WWII and who generally supported
President Roosevelt's conduct of the war opposed certain of Roosevelt's wartime
policies and promoted others, around four issues. Listen for the presence of
mercy and forgiveness in these. First, he disagreed with the policy of saturation
bombing. Second, he opposed the policy of demanding unconditional surrender
of Japan and Germany. Third, he opposed, criticized, and organized against the
policy of interning Japanese-Americans. And fourth, he urged positive steps by
government for the rebuilding of countries destroyed in the war, including the
enemies (Stone 129). In arguing these, he often recalled the costs to everyone,
victor and vanquished alike, of the spirit of vengeance which had, in effect, lost
the peace after WWI at Versailles (Stone 130). Forgiveness means the tempering
of mercy in the exercise of power, including the formulation of policy, and it
means genuine new beginnings in the place of entrapment and despair.

Niebuhr's "religious reservation" is even more than forgiveness, however.
I have chosen the spirit of forgiveness as a crucial dimension but it is only, as
intimated, part of an entire "spirituality" of social struggle which was integral to
Niebuhr's theory of redemptive social power. Time forbids elaboration, so I will
close by simply reading two passages in the mother tongue! I remind you the
context is that a formal organization and balance of power is not enough as
either the theory or practice of power.

The first passage is from *NDM* (II: 284):

> There is no possibility of making history completely safe against either
> occasional conflicts of vital interests (war) or against the misuse of the power
> which is intended to prevent such conflict of interests (tyranny). To understand
> this is to labor for higher justice in terms of the experience of justification by
> faith. Justification by faith in the realm of justice means that we will not regard
> the pressures and counter pressures, the tensions, the overt and the covert
> conflicts by which justice is achieved and maintained, as normative in the
> absolute sense; but neither will we ease our conscience by seeking to escape
> from involvement in them. We will know that we cannot purge ourselves of the
> sin and guilt in which we are involved by the moral ambiguities of politics
> without also disavowing responsibility for the creative possibilities of justice.

The second passage was written in 1944 but seems poised for 1994. It is
the conclusion of the book with which we began, *CLCD* (188–190):

The Christian faith finds the final clue to the meaning of life and history in the Christ whose goodness is at once the virtue which man ought, but does not, achieve in history, and the revelation of a divine mercy which understands and resolves the perpetual contradictions in which history is involved, even on the highest reaches of human achievements. From the standpoint of such a faith it is possible to deal with the ultimate social problem of human history: the creation of community in world dimensions. The insistence of the Christian faith that the love of Christ is the final norm of human existence must express itself socially in unwillingness to stop short of the whole human community in expressing our sense of moral responsibility for the life and welfare of others. The understanding of the Christian faith that the highest achievements of human life are infected with sinful corruption will help men to be prepared for new corruptions on the level of world community which drive simpler idealists to despair. The hope of Christian faith that the divine power which bears history can complete what even the highest human striving must leave incomplete, and can purify the corruptions which appear in even the purest human aspirations, is an indispensable prerequisite for diligent fulfilment of our historic tasks. Without it we are driven to alternate moods of sentimentality and despair; trusting human powers too much in one moment and losing all faith in the meaning of life when we discover the limits of human possibilities.

The world community, toward which all historical forces seem to be driving us, is mankind's final possibility and impossibility. The task of achieving it must be interpreted from the standpoint of a faith which understands the fragmentary and broken character of all historic achievements and yet has confidence in their meaning because it knows their completion to be in the hands of a Divine Power, whose resources are greater than those of men, and whose suffering love can overcome the corruptions of man's achievements, without negating the significance of our striving.

I close with this summary. Niebuhr's picture of justice-making power in society is mutual coercion mutually agreed upon and enforced. But this is not his full theory of power and it is ironic that Christians were so appreciative of Niebuhr for teaching them the positive use of power, and secular humanists were so grateful for learning sophisticated power analysis within a meaningful moral framework, that neither realized what Niebuhr himself pursued with all his might and much of his piety. His full theory of power invests the passion for justice through power with the religious and moral power of humility, mercy and an ultimate trust in a divine suffering power who brings our important, but feeble and partial, efforts to completion. This is Niebuhr's experience and goal, namely, social power tasting of redemption itself.

Notes

(A General Bibliography for these *Birks* lectures begins on page 183.)

1.   Cited from J. Ronald Engel, "Sustainable Development: A New Global Ethic?" *The Egg: An Eco-Justice Quarterly* 12 #1 (Winter 1991–92): 4.

2.   Niebuhr is writing in 1944 and discussing fascism and Stalinism.

3.   The phrase is Garrett Hardin's, not Niebuhr's, but its substance is the wisdom of Niebuhr's "children of light" and "children of darkness" together.

4.   The phrase is Cornel West's in *The American Evasion of Philosophy* (Madison, WI: University of Wisconsin Press, 1989): 150.

5.   Ronald Stone, to whom this discussion of Niebuhr and Dewey is indebted, notes that Dewey, unlike Niebuhr, did not recognize the dynamic evils of Hitlerism and Stalinism even when they were rather conspicuously on the rise. See his *Professor Reinhold Niebuhr* (Louisville: Westminster/John Knox Press, 1992): 211–213.

6.   I must interject here that the appropriation of Niebuhr by neo-conservatives championing democratic capitalism is a serious case of not having "eyes to see and ears to hear" Niebuhr's nuances about dangerous concentrations of economic and political power.

7.   Niebuhr writes elsewhere in like manner, that "the realistic school of international thought believes that world politics cannot rise higher than the balance-of-power principle. The balance-of-power theory of world politics, seeing no possibility of a genuine unity of nations, seeks to construct the most adequate possible mechanism for equilibrating power on a world scale. Such a policy...can undoubtedly mitigate anarchy. A balance of power is in fact a kind of managed anarchy. But it is a system in which anarchy invariably overcomes the management in the end" (*CLCD* 173–174).

8.   Incidentally, Hannah Arendt's argument was that action at its most profound was the capacity to initiate new beginnings and that, given ongoing human conflict, this capacity was finally grounded in forgiveness. What is intriguing is that while Niebuhr argues as a committed Christian theologian, Arendt makes a straightforward "secular" case.

NIEBUHR ON POWER
Assessment and Critique

Larry L. Rasmussen

Most of the time Niebuhr means by "power" the varied nonviolent and violent forms of coercion, pressure, force, persuasion, in society. This power will be perennially important, he contends, because of two enduring characteristics of human nature. One is the unity of body and soul, vitality and reason, feeling and thought, spirit and matter. All our own powers of body, mind and spirit are engaged when our life in society is the issue. The other is the unremitting tendency to consider a common problem from the standpoint of our own limited interest, what Niebuhr often calls "inordinate self-love" and sometimes "original sin." "Through [original sin] one may understand," he writes,

> that no matter how wide the perspectives which the human mind may reach, how broad the loyalties which the human imagination may conceive, how universal the community which human statecraft may organize, or how pure the aspirations of the saintliest idealists may be, there is no level of human moral or social achievement in which there is not some corruption of inordinate self-love" (*CLCD* 16–17).

Indeed, for Niebuhr "evil" is "the assertion of some self-interest without regard to the whole," whether the whole "be conceived as the immediate community, or the total community of [humankind], or the total order of the world", while "good" is always "the harmony of the whole on various levels" (*CLCD* 9).

173

When we combine these characteristics, as life does — our partial and skewed interests and the unity of body, soul, and mind — the outcome is twofold. We will pursue egoistic pursuits with the resources at our disposal, including the forms of power available. And we will try to place social restraints on such pursuits by others. This will also require and draw from the many forms of power. The forms of power used to extend our own and restrain others will include "spiritual" forms, a matter which leads Niebuhr to an insight such as this: "All civilized relations are governed more by spiritual, rather than physical, facets of power. It is significant that they are not, for that reason, naturally more just" (*NDM* II: 261). The subtle colonization of mind and spirit can sometimes be as unjust as brute territorial occupation, and more difficult to throw off.

In a word, lasting patterns in human nature itself are the reason that we will always exercise and contend with power in society, the reason that power comes in varied forms which reflect in myriad ways the unity of body, mind, and spirit, and the reason that power establishes justice and injustice alike, mixing them in complicated and fascinating ways.

With this as introduction, and the two previous lectures as background and substance, what do we make of Niebuhr on power? How do we assess his massive contribution as a theologian, social theorist, and ethicist of power? I will first register his critics' views, then conclude with my own.

We have already anticipated some of the criticisms. But we need to elaborate them now. Beverly Harrison, for example, rejects Niebuhr's "presumed discontinuity between the dynamics of power existing in social, economic, and political life, and the dynamics of power in interpersonal interactions, in face to face groups like the family" (Harrison 27). Niebuhr made this discontinuity his thesis in *MMIS*. He modified it somewhat but never retracted it. More significantly, his liberalism, and the culture's, largely assumed an important version of it when it distinguished public life from private and largely left the basic moral formation of persons to families and the other intimate communities of the private domain. Like most liberals, Niebuhr also tended to ignore these communities when the subject was how power functioned in society. Again like most liberals, at least male liberals, he tended to romanticize home and neighborhood and school and simply assume that they were doing reasonably well what they were supposed to be doing as society's base communities of personal moral formation.

In my country now it is obvious that these communities are in crisis. It is a crisis of basic moral formation that runs the gamut of the populace. It is also very clear that for the basic formation of human character and conscience no line neatly divides public and private domains. From a social-psychological point of view, there is no sharp discontinuity of domains for the patterning of moral formation *and the power dynamics* which are part and parcel of it. This is not to deny that people may meaningfully distinguish economic, political and cultural spheres of society, or distinguish "public" from "private," but *at the level of moral formation*, such distinctions do not pertain. To quote Beverly Harrison again, in her essay on Niebuhr's social theory: "Unjust social relations are reproduced in most families; yet we rarely pause to wonder why a sense of justice is so poorly developed in the sensibilities of people in society" (Harrison 27).

Niebuhr, too, rarely paused to ponder this, and instead largely overlooked the socialization of power relations in our most intimate communities of character formation. He thus failed to see the ways in which larger social groups play out power patterns learned in smaller ones. Feminists have rightly lodged a sharp criticism of him and of liberalism for this. Considering how deeply the distinction of domains goes in U.S. mainstream culture, in Niebuhr's beloved Anglo-American social and political philosophy, and in the German Protestantism of his own influential household, his retention of it is readily understandable, even if not acceptable.

Feminists also criticize his core doctrine of sin. It fails to distinguish clearly enough the two types of sin: the sin of pride, with its refusal to relinquish power, and the sin of sensuality, with its refusal to claim power. Niebuhr's understanding of sin as sensuality is especially underdeveloped, probably because he himself was far better equipped to fathom the sins of the powerful than those of the powerless. He was utterly clear-eyed about the sins of those who, holding power, extend and abuse it, rather than surrender or share it. He was less clear about the social-psychological dynamics of relatively powerless people who must proudly claim power in order to experience pride in a strongly self-affirming, constructive, freeing, life-giving and self-empowering sense.

It is certainly the case that Niebuhr's experience and perspectives, and the circles in which he came to move with real influence, were the circles of North Atlantic, largely white and male, shakers and movers in the worlds of academy, religion, culture and public policy. He was also a piercing critic of these, an unmasker without peer of any reigning ideology of power and the power of any reigning ideology. Though he was always a little surprised to be in the king's chapel and the king's court, he was there as the prophet. The point, however, is that even though he invariably took the side of the less advantaged, he did not always understand their worlds. So it is not coincidental that the article which helped launch the feminist movement, Valerie Saiving's "The Human Situation: A Feminine View," included major criticisms of Niebuhr. What Niebuhr called human nature did not include much of women's experience, their nature, their sin, or their experience of power. Nor is it coincidental that sharp criticism has come from Black and Two-third's World theologians. To be sure, it is the criticism of those close to him, those who pay him the utmost respect of taking him very seriously just because he *is* so relevant to them in positive ways, the criticism of those who recognize in him a friend and ally. It is significant criticism, nonetheless, and it punches precisely at his sweeping claims about human nature and power.

There may be a highly personal factor at work here, buried in those universal judgments about human behavior. Roger Shinn has written that Niebuhr was himself so incapable of apathy that he probably could not give the traditional sins of sloth and indifference their proper place, or — more importantly — truly understand the state of mind and soul of people buried in the struggle who have given up altogether. He had boundless energy for championing their cause, even when it seemed a hopeless one. He frequently asserted that the marginalized and powerless had knowledge and insight the powerful were overlooking, ignoring, or denying. He even acknowledged, in a sermon rewritten for the volume *Beyond Tragedy* (*BT*), that most people died "in weakness, frustration and confusion," with lives "determined by circumstances" [beyond their control] (*BT* 156). Nevertheless, Shinn says, Niebuhr had relatively little to say about the common and terrible places where

> frustration is so oppressive that it is hard to awaken people to action; where the development of some pride, or at least self-respect, is painfully difficult; where apathy day in and day out is a greater enemy than the fanaticism that occasionally breaks outs; where progress depends less upon shattering vain ambition than upon overcoming hopelessness. [Niebuhr] has less to say about defeatism than about vanity, about indifference than fanaticism (Shinn 160).

In a word, while Niebuhr is without peer in his insights into the psyche of the powerful in society and their use and abuse of power, he is not the person who best understands or explains powerlessness as a common dynamic of human nature and experience. He is without peer as the analyst of the varied forms of sin as overweening pride. He fails to match this with a parallel analysis of the forms of sin as self-denigration, deprivation and powerlessness itself.

I have often wondered what difference Niebuhr's Christology made for his theology and ethic of power and what difference it might have made, had he not held to the Jesus of Protestant liberalism. He largely followed Troeltsch, Harnack, and other German liberals here, due in no small part to his father's strong theological influence on him. Their common picture of Jesus was Jesus as the perfectionist and heroic embodiment of a love which renounces power and thus, in Niebuhr's own words, "does not deal at all with the immediate moral problem of every human life — the problem of arranging some kind of armistice between various contending factions and forces." That citation is from *An Interpretation of Christian Ethics* (45), Niebuhr's most extended discussion of the relationship of Jesus to issues of power in Christian ethics. Niebuhr here is following Troeltsch in *The Social Teaching of the Christian Churches* and elsewhere in Troeltsch's conviction that Jesus had "no social program" but rather lived "a free personal piety" of utter trust in God to make a way where there was none. The conclusion of Troeltsch and Niebuhr is that Jesus actually "transcended" power conflicts and thus was and is not *directly* relevant to the social ethics of public life. The church thus had to work out its own social ethic as all the issues of survival and empire impinged upon it in the course of the receding return of its Lord and in the course of its own expansion as the religious bearer of civilization itself. For Niebuhr Jesus *is* deeply relevant, of course, but he is relevant as the perfect embodiment of a transcendent, non-resisting and power-denying love. He is relevant as that unstained, "disinterested" agape which stands as the undefiled and purging norm for the rough justice which power must seek to establish as best it can in society. Power, which is invariably "interested," is also invariably corrupted and thus at a great moral and human distance from the Christian's Savior and Lord, who is pure self-sacrificial and self-denying love.

Like Shinn, John Bennett notes a personality trait which may well stamp this Christology. Bennett says that

> the vigor of Niebuhr's attacks on perfectionism comes partly from the fact he has always been much tempted by it. He preserves the perfectionist element in Christianity in his own statement of the nature of Christian love, in his way of interpreting the relation of Christ to historical forms of power, and in the tribute that he pays to the perfectionist forms of pacifism which makes no claims for the applicability of pacifism to political life (Bennett 104f.).

Still, the query is less about Niebuhr's personality and more about the difference his understanding of Jesus might make for his perspectives on "the historical forms of power." If Niebuhr had read the Jesus of the Gospels as deeply involved in power conflicts and choices, deeply immersed in struggles "between various contending factions and forces," and as having an explicit social program — namely, fashioning a community reflective of the nature of the God he utterly trusted — might Niebuhr have struck different emphases in his ethic of power? Might Jesus have been not only the embodiment of the transcendent moral norm of agapaic love, but also the realistic, even tough, practitioner of that love in the midst of power conflicts and with love's own preferred forms of power? This discussion would soon lead us into a very long discussion about Niebuhr, Gandhi, King, John Yoder, Walter Wink, a number of feminist and womanist ethicists, and others. I am not going to entertain that at the moment, but simply say for the sake of later discussion that if Niebuhr had lived to benefit from the last decades of scholarship around Jesus the Jew and his movement, he might have given more time and attention and development to those remarkable lines from *MMIS* I cited in the second lecture, that "non-violent coercion...is a type of coercion which offers the largest opportunities for a harmonious relationship with the moral and rational factors in social life" (251) and that "there is no problem of political life to which religious imagination can make a larger contribution than this problem of developing non-violent resistance" (254). And if Niebuhr had had another rendering of Jesus, one not insistent upon the disavowal of power, he might have avoided some of the conclusions — wretched conclusions, in my judgment — that obstructed the pursuit of these claims of his own I just read; he might have avoided conclusions like this one: "Nothing is clearer than that a pure religious idealism must issue in a policy of non-resistance which makes no claims to be socially efficacious. It submits to any demands, however unjust, and yields to any claims, however inordinate, rather than assert self-interest against another" (*MMIS* 264). Or like this one:

> the religious ideal in its purest form has nothing to do with the problem of social justice. It makes disinterestness an absolute ideal without reference to social consequences. It justifies the ideal in terms of the integrity and beauty of the human spirit...Pure religious idealism does not concern itself with the social problem...It may believe, as Jesus did, that self-realisation is the inevitable consequence of self-abnegation. But this self-realisation is not attained on the level of physical life or mundane advantages. It is achieved in spiritual terms, such as the martyr's immortality and the Savior's exaltation in the hearts of his disciples. Jesus did not counsel his disciples to forgive seventy times seven in order that they might convert their enemies or make them more favorably disposed. He counselled it as an effort to approximate complete moral perfection, the perfection of God...He did not say that the enemy ought to be loved so that he would cease to be an enemy. He did not dwell upon the social consequences of these moral actions, because he viewed them from an inner and a transcendent perspective (*MMIS* 263f.).

This entire rendition of Jesus, the moral and religious ideal, and Jesus' relation to power is, in my judgment, problematic in the extreme, as is Niebuhr's contention in *NDM* that "perfect goodness in history can be symbolized only by the disavowal of power. But this did not become clear until the One appeared who rejected all concepts of Messianic dominion and became a 'suffering servant'" (II: 22). We must take this very seriously not only because Niebuhr says it both early on and in the midst of his mature work, but because it is at the very heart of the way Niebuhr buttons his Christology and ethic to power. Thus I raise the intriguing query as to what difference a different Jesus might have made for him. It has to be a different Jesus, since what Niebuhr has done, finally, as Cornel West suggests, is give up the illusions of liberalism for society and history — perfection, kingdom of God on earth, ultimate harmony — *while yet retaining those illusions* as the mythical ideals which supply *the* reigning moral norms for human action and the inspiration for heroic energies in a tragic, often very harsh, world (West 155). Niebuhr is a serious Christian and it is his Jesus above all who gathers up these ideals into the normative substance of a Christian ethic. I have more to say by way of criticism but none is more important and far-reaching that this contention that Niebuhr has, in effect, undermined and shortcut his own greatest contribution — his ethic of power — by holding to a Christological base and norm which denigrates many of the positive forms of that very power.

My remaining remarks drift from the pages of his published critics to come at an assessment quite differently. I am not starting from the impressive Niebuhr corpus and taking the measure of his theory of power from within its framework and on its own premises. That we have now done. I begin with a notion of power which I bring to Niebuhr and ask how the Niebuhrian melodies then sound.

My notion of power does have a bias and a polemical edge. That you should know up front, just as you should know that Niebuhr would have known and spotted the fact of bias and polemics immediately. I think our dominant understanding of power, in reigning Protestant theology and ethics as well as in reigning social theory and practice, has been skewed by understanding it primarily under the rubric of the doctrine of sin rather than the doctrine of creation, and this is the case for Niebuhr.

When power is understood with a view primarily to humans as sinners, the forms it is presumed to take and usually does take, are two: power as power-over and power as power-on-behalf-of; differently said, power as control (including counter control) and power as benevolence. Usually power is also viewed with an eye to the socially powerful and/or those aspiring to be that. The issues for power then are such issues as: how to gain ruling power and rule well, how to seize a patrimony, how to secure and defend rights, how to make, justify, or defend a revolution, or some other order of governance. This is also power generally viewed from above, from the high places from which power presumably flows. Power is regarded as flowing from sources who have it to recipients who don't. Power then is also regarded as a kind of commodity or possession governed by the dynamics of a zero-sum game: i.e., more power for one party translates as less for another. Likewise, in the view of power as a possession, power is an entity to be retained or lost, or redistributed.

It is important to say that power in this perspective can be used in ways both just and unjust. It can serve good ends and destructive ones, it can be repressive or creative. It can hold on to unjust privileges or take the side of those opposing them. It can work on behalf of the powerless, i.e., it can be power as benevolence, or work against them, i.e., it can be power as dominating control.

Usually under the rubric of the doctrine of sin, power has all these characteristics. And when our sinfulness in the employ of power is emphasized, as it is with Niebuhr, the necessity of using power is often closely tied to the dangers of its use and a warning about its own corrupting powers, indeed its idolatrous propensities. In the Augustinian and Reformation tradition, extended to Niebuhr, a true son, a tragic perspective on history is wed to a sensitive account of the inordinate reach of overweening pride in all domains of our existence. Fortunately, Niebuhr brilliantly turned this basically Augustinian and conservative perspective into a force for progressive justice. That is, he took the characteristics of power as power-to-order-and-control, and put them in the service of power as power-on-behalf-of the relatively disadvantaged in any given social struggle. Yet, and this is my point, Niebuhr's notion of power remains within the paradigm of power as a domination dynamic in a fallen order. It remains primarily coercion as exercised by and among intrepid, skilled sinners.

Power under the rubric of the doctrine of creation does not deny sin, of course, or foolishly set aside Niebuhr's massive contributions to theological and social anthropology. But it does insist that there is something even more basic about power than the characteristic forms of domination and benevolence. More basic is simply power as power-to, power as the energy inherent in "being," power as the agency of creation itself, the dimension of vitality pervasive of all existence as such. In this perspective, no one and no thing is utterly without some essential power, even though they (if we are speaking of humans) may be without organized social power. Basic power, the power pervasive of creation, is what lets us stand out from sheer nothingness. What we call "powerlessness" is not the utter absence of power. It is misdirected, frustrated, bottled up, or untapped energy. In short, power is the flow of energy in the universe, apart from which nothing that is, exists. Incidentally, this is an ancient claim made not only by science but by philosophers and theologians from Plato to Tillich. In this perspective we rightly say that while nothing evil happens apart from power, nothing good ever happens apart from power, either. And for the same simple reason: *nothing* happens apart from power. Nothing can.

Theologically put, the claim of faith is that in and through creation, God has become in the first instance a power-sharing God. God is, as the Eastern Orthodox have said for nearly two millennia, the uncreated energy of the created universe. This is the day-to-day, breath-to-breath, cell-to-cell, atom-to-atom meaning of the claim that "all power is from God." Power at its most elemental, most vital, is simply "power-to," the power of agency, human and non-human agency alike, in the vast web of this miracle called life and the cosmos itself, every particle and wave of it an expression of God's own life. "Power-over" and "power-on-behalf-of" are but two common human social forms of "power-to."

Incidentally — or rather, not so incidentally — these two — power-over and power-on-behalf-of — are the two forms which do *not* tend to generate other social forms of power such as "power-with" and "power-within," forms we now frequently designate with the term "empowerment." Rather, they tend to suppress empowerment, usually in the name of necessary order and/or benevolence and well-being, and not infrequently in the name of justice itself. Let me only add, in a passing reference to a Jesus very different from Niebuhr's, that the kind of power seen in Jesus is actually less a "representational" and "benevolent" power in the sense of power as power-in-place-of or on-behalf-of, and more the power of agency, release, engagement, yes, empowerment. Jesus, ministering amid the supposedly marginal and powerless parties, evokes a power among them they hardly knew they had. Yet they soon claim it as their own God-shared power, against which the very gates of hell will not prevail. Jesus' kind of power-to as "power-with and power-within" (the power of the Spirit) is nicely captured in the discovery of the Filipino farmers: "We're the people we've been waiting for!"

I do not wish to draft a typology of power viewed under the rubrics of sin and creation and then set one type against the other. Nor am I arguing that you should make exclusive choices among discrete types of power. Creation exists and manifests its sinfulness, and I assume both are relevant to our understanding and exercise of power. But I do want to say that power-to, power as the energy of creation, is more basic than the forms power often takes as power-over and power-on-behalf-of. And I want to go on to say that while Niebuhr knows plenty about power as power-to, his theory and strategies of power tilt again and again to the grammar of a too-limited-notion of the forms of power. In his treatment of power, he often makes the doctrine of sin more basic than the doctrine of creation. This is the reason he is vulnerable not only to accusations of a certain profound pessimism, but to the criticism of feminists, African-Americans and other minorities in the U.S., as well as "Two-thirds" World peoples who detect in him a subtle cultural imperialism of power-as-controlling-order and power-on-behalf-of. These groups know the colonized mind needs a separatist movement of self-discovered empowerment at least as strong as any integrationist alliance with the already established powers and way of life. Niebuhr understood and appreciated Martin Luther King and he also knew about social dynamics that made for alienation and rage. But I doubt he truly understood the psychic appeal and power of Malcolm X, which was not, in the first instance, an appeal to make effective, socially transforming alliances or even to organize for the purpose of wresting or sharing power. It was first of all an appeal to social nobodies to discover in their own bones their own power to be somebodies on their own terms; in other words, to be a people, indeed a people of God, rather than, say, a "minority," "Blacks" or some "interest group" seeking to share the mainstream.

You understand that my criticism, which must now come to a close, is not intended at all to put Niebuhr to the side as a "dead white Eurocentric male!" I am fully convinced that he remains *the* theologian, social critic, and ethicist to contend with on the ever-critical subject of power. Indeed, I do not want to draw a strong line between Niebuhr and the causes of minorities he championed or between Niebuhr and liberation theologies, since he stands almost alone among white male U. S. theologians who, fully *against* the culture's grain, understands both suffering and tragedy, understands them theologically and in terms of the morality of power. He knew what to do theologically with historical pain, sorrow and even Sisyphaen struggle. So let me close with appreciation, set against the backdrop of my criticism that he has nonetheless undercut theologically and in practice his own very best contribution — a sophisticated theory of power.

He teaches us to be well-attuned to the reality of evil, surprised by nothing, and to expect ambiguity in most uses of power. He would have shared his wry smile or laughed aloud at Richard Rorty's comment about Heidegger: Heidegger was a Nazi, "a coward, a liar, and the greatest philosopher of the 20th century" (*New York Times Magazine* (December 2, 1990), 57).

Niebuhr teaches us neither to forget the tragic character of existence nor to be paralyzed by it, just as he teaches us to face both the beauty and the terror of life squarely and to live in gratitude for the former while not denying the latter or being overwhelmed by it. He knows that power is not only given to corruption; sometimes things just go awry and power wreaks havoc when the motives are laudatory rather than venial.

Niebuhr himself had, and he teaches, a profound spirituality for risky and ambiguous but justice-directed uses of power in a season when the reigning paradigm of growth and social progress is itself on the rocks. His utter honesty about both the beauty and terror of life, not least in changing and convulsive times, an honesty grounded in his theology of the cross and suffering divine love, is at the heart of this spirituality of boldly exercising precarious power.

Niebuhr also knows that the many forms of power — power over, power on behalf of, power with — can all serve both justice and injustice. Yet that does not translate as moral equivalence for all forms of power. Kinds and degrees matter immensely. There is often daunting moral complexity in our choices and in the exercise of power in arenas large and small. This is one reason why grace and forgiveness and mercy are such important entries in Niebuhr's life vocabulary and in his theology.

I do think, as mentioned above, that his preoccupation with human sinfulness sometimes obscures the fact that power is the only possible vehicle for good itself, just as I think that because Niebuhr was an utter master at the "hermeneutic of suspicion," on the basis of his doctrine of humans as sinners, that sometimes his power analysis is so well-wired for suspicion, corruption and idolatry that he does not regularly uncover the routine goodness of ordinary human and non-human achievements. His treatment of power sometimes fails to name *as* expressions of *power* all those wondrous workings of common grace that Niebuhr appreciated deep down, like arriving alive in Victoria Station when alive was what you wanted to be and Victoria Station was exactly where you wanted to be that way!

I end on the important reiteration that while Niebuhr treated power chiefly within the doctrine of sin and overlooked some of the insights of power and empowerment as a subject of the doctrine of creation, he never let that be interpreted in such a way as to bolster the ranks of the complacent or give comfort to the holders of dominating power, just as he never let the moral agony which power choices sometimes create slide into the moral relativism or indifference of crude *realpolitik*. He consistently did power analysis and made his own commitments so as to nurture in whatever way he might justice-making power. In that way he in fact put whatever grams he could — and they were many — on the scales favoring creation's own fulfilment. He did all this, finally, with a genuine humility that flowed from his recognition of human limits as well as possibilities and with genuine trust in the power of God's power to bring all things to their promised end.

GENERAL BIBLIOGRAPHY

Arendt, Hannah. 1958. *The Human Condition*. Chicago: Chicago University Press.

Bennett, John C. 1984. "Reinhold Niebuhr's Social Ethics." In *Reinhold Niebuhr: His Religious, Social and Political Thought*. Ed. Charles W. Kegley. N.Y.: The Pilgrim Press. Reprint of the 1956 edition, edited by Charles W. Kegley and Robert W. Bretall.

Brown, Charles C. 1992. *Niebuhr and His Age*. Philadelphia: Trinity Press International.

Harrison, Beverly Wildung. 1985. *Making the Connections: Essays in Feminist Social Ethics*. Ed. Carol S. Robb. Boston: The Beacon Press.

Lasch, Christopher. 1991. *The True and Only Heaven: Progress and Its Critics*. N.Y.: Norton.

Niebuhr, Ursula M. (ed.). 1974. *Justice and Mercy*. N.Y.: Harper & Row.

Niebuhr, Reinhold. 1928. *Does Civilization Need Religion?* N.Y.: Macmillan.
———. 1929. *Leaves from the Notebook of a Tamed Cynic*. Chicago: Willet, Clark & Colby.
———. 1932. *Moral Man and Immoral Society*. N.Y.: Scribner's.
———. 1932. *Reflections on the End of an Era*. N.Y.: Scribner's.
———. 1935. *An Interpretation of Christian Ethics*. N.Y.: Harper and Brothers.
———. 1937. *Beyond Tragedy*. N.Y.: Scribner's.
———. 1940. *Christianity and Power Politics*. N.Y.: Scribner's.
———. 1941. *The Nature and Destiny of Man*, Volume I. N.Y.: Scribner's.
———. 1943. *The Nature and Destiny of Man*, Volume II. N.Y.: Scribner's.
———. 1945. *The Children of Light and the Children of Darkness*. N.Y.: Scribner's.
———. 1952. *The Irony of American History*. N.Y.: Scribner's.
———. 1953. *Christian Realism and Political Problems*. N.Y.: Scribner's.
———. 1959. *Faith and History*. N.Y.: Scribner's.
———. 1965. *Man's Nature and His Communities*. N.Y.: Scribner's.

Rasmussen, Larry L. 1991. *Reinhold Niebuhr: Theologian of Public Life*. Minneapolis: Fortress Press.

Saiving, Valerie. 1960. "The Human Situation: A Feminine View." *The Journal of Religion* (April). Reprinted in *WomanSpirit Rising: A Feminist Reader in Religion*, ed. Carol P. Christ and Judith Plaskow. San Francisco: Harper, 1979.

Shinn, Roger L. 1968. *Man: The New Humanism*. Philadelphia: Westminster Press.

Stone, Ronald H. 1992. *Professor Reinhold Niebuhr*. Louisville, KY: Westminster/John Knox Press.

West, Charles. 1992. "Christianity in Eastern Europe." *Christianity and Crisis* 52: 278–280.

West, Cornel. 1989. *The American Evasion of Philosophy*. Madison, WI: University of Wisconsin Press.

List of Contributors

Terence R. Anderson is Professor of Christian Social Ethics at the Vancouver School of Theology, Vancouver, British Columbia

Oscar Cole Arnal is Associate Professor of Church History at Waterloo Lutheran Seminary, Waterloo, Ontario

Alan T. Davies is Professor in the Religion Department of Victoria University, Toronto, Ontario

Aurelia Takacs Fule is an Associate (Faith and Order) within the Theology and Worship Unit of the Presbyterian Church (U.S.A.), Louisville, Kentucky

Gary A. Gaudin is a Ph.D. candidate in Theology at the Faculty of Religious Studies, McGill University, Montréal, Québec

Douglas John Hall is Professor of Christian Theology in the Faculty of Religious Studies, McGill University, Montréal, Québec

Gordon Harland is Professor Emeritus of Theology at the University of Manitoba, Winnipeg, Manitoba

Friedrich Hufendiek is Professor of Old Testament at Bethel Theologische Schule, Bielefeld, Germany

Dietz Lange is Professor of Theology and Ethics and Vice-Rector of the University, University of Göttingen, Germany

Larry L. Rasmussen is the Reinhold Niebuhr Professor of Social Ethics at Union Theological Seminary, New York City, U.S.A.